QUEENS OF THE STONE AGE

No One Knows

QUEENS OF THE STONE AGE

No One Knows

Joel McIver   Updated Edition

OMNIBUS PRESS

London / New York / Paris / Sydney / Copenhagen / Berlin / Madrid / Tokyo

ISBN: 978.1.78305.700.9
Order No: OP56034

Exclusive Distributors
Music Sales Limited,
14/15 Berners Street,
London, W1T 3LJ.

Music Sales Corporation
180 Madison Avenue, 24th Floor,
New York,
NY 10016,
USA.

Macmillan Distribution Services
56 Parkwest Drive
Derrimut, Vic 3030,
Australia.

Printed in the EU

A catalogue record for this book is available from the British Library.

Visit Omnibus Press on the web at www.omnibuspress.com

Contents

This book is dedicated to 'Dimebag' Darrell Abbott.

He told me, "When people try to tell you what to do —
tell 'em 'Fuck you!'"

Foreword

When I was asked to write this foreword, my first reaction was that of inherent but mostly 'been-through-it' horror. Not another writer trying to vicariously 'rock' by frotting with the 'pill-iratti' of rock'n' roll's new white dope, that title belonging to rock's new figureheads, old vanguards of the new melodious heavy scree-rock sonata, Queens Of The Stone Age – in futile hope that some of the toxic sweat emanating from the pores of their double-coil AA anti-average charged battery-acid attitude will rub off on them and their calloused elbows.

The horror was ephemeral. While the author's elbows remain intact, the band's fingers drip a blistering concoction of astro-arcane, acid-rain strain of music that seethes with the feeling that we aren't the only ones around that feel the world is but a stage and we are all (guitar) players. I was lucky enough to hold court while touring with Kyuss, now the present members of Queens . . . it was a royal gas. Literally. Your Highness got lit, pilot-light sky-stylie freak-kite-flying nightly. Hardly anything done light or quietly. Extremely fun-duh-mental. Visceral and true.

The exceptional excel, and the Queens are no exception to the powers of high-frequency reception innovation. They are fresh yet hauntingly familiar, like a black cat straight from the muse-magician's hat. True, they play crop circles around the field of electricity that surrounds and grounds them. Electro-magnetic hyperkinetic-phrenetic. They are monster musicians.

The feeling I get when treating my earholes to Queens Of The Stone Age is like finding a perfectly preserved ancient buttercup stem, made from the heaviest gauge of steel, hiding behind the mouldiest of old cuneiform-encrusted sarcophagi, filled with myriad virtual musical notes shimmering inside, and in that high C moment I remember what it is that I had forgotten about . . . anyway. A dose will do ya. It's the good shit. Not for the vacuous among us. Their music spirals, ascends into 'ether world' and curls back down, only to collect the remaining sound left resounding under troglodyte ground where we mere mortals await to hear the seers lift us into their rarified-air, sans-silence, add-loudness atmosphere. May we hear their ringing ears clear from over here, have nothing to fear my dears, because as long as the day is stoned, they will continue to manipulate their hedonistic-headphone-phoenix sound, for out of the ashes of those that are Long-Gone stoned, rises a monolithic spectacle to behold (they're really tall dudes).

Here's to the rulers and perpetual reign of . . . the masters of overground. Their Sky Pilots' crown finally stripped from that Grate-fully Dead old head.

Them Kings is dead. Long live the Queens.

Kat Bjelland, 2005
Babes In Toyland, Katastrophy Wife

Acknowledgements

Emma, Alice, Tom, Robin and Kate, Dad, John and Jen, Carlos Anaia, David Barraclough, Scott Bartlett, Jacqui Black, Max and Gloria Cavalera, Chris Charlesworth, Dave Clarke, Ben Cooper, Joe Daly, Chris Dixon, Helen Donlon, John Doran, Jason Draper, Mark Eglinton, David Ellefson, Ciaran Fahy, Marty Friedman, Lisa Gallagher, Matthew Hamilton, Gemma Hill, Bill Irwin, Michelle Kerr, Tina Korhonen, Borivoj Krgin, Guy Little, Rachel Mann, Patrizia Mazzuocolo, Alex Milas, Eugenio Monti, Bob Nalbandian, Martin Popoff, Scott Reeder, Ralph Santolla, Jonathan Selzer, Kirsten Sprinks, Wes Stanton, Dan Travis, Mick Wall, Alex Webster, Chris Williams, the staff of *Bass Guitar Magazine* and the families Alderman, Arnold, Bhardwaj, Bowles, Cadette, Edwards, Fraser, Freed, Harrington, Herbert Jones, Hogben, Jolliffe, Knight, Lamond, Lamont Skeens, Legerton, Leim, Mathieson Spires, Mendonça, Metcalfe, Miles, Parr, Storey and Woollard, the many journalists in the UK and abroad who interview me and review my books, and of course the visitors to www.joelmciver.co.uk and www.facebook.com/joelmciver and followers at @joelmciver.

Introduction to the 2015 edition

THE first edition of this book was published in 2005, at least 10 years ago as you read this, which is an eon in 'rock time'. Nowadays, bands come and go with ever-increasing frequency, at least partly because the music business has been starved of cash for a decade or so and there's not enough money to go round. Fortunately, Queens Of The Stone Age, now almost 20 years in business, got in before the cash dried up and, although times are hard for them as there are for everyone in this strangest of industries, built a foundation of solid albums before iTunes and CD burners were widely available. They're still touring the globe and playing the world's biggest festivals, shedding a member here and there as they go, but managing to outface more or less all of the problems that have beset them along the way.

These have on occasion been serious: founder Josh Homme, the Queens' leader, came close to death after a botched knee operation in 2011, and a band comprising members of Homme's former band Kyuss led him to take legal action. And yet the musicians bounced back to new heights, with the creation of the supergroup Them Crooked Vultures one of their recent achievements. How and why QOTSA have so far failed to succumb to the pitfalls which have taken down so many of their contemporaries is one of the major themes explored in this book. This is a band of fighters. Enjoy their story.

Joel McIver, 2014
www.joelmciver.co.uk

CHAPTER 1

The Eighties: Desert Rats

PALM Desert is where wealthy, sun-worshipping Californians go to die.

A two-hour drive from Los Angeles, the Coachella Valley town (population circa 42,000) is surrounded by desert and started life as a community of Agua Caliente native Americans, who had been living there for over 2,000 years before the US government arrived in 1853. The authorities brought with them law, order, civic amenities and also smallpox, which wiped out most of the Agua Calientes a decade later. Generously, the officials handed out parcels of land as a consolation prize of sorts, although the recipients weren't permitted to sell the land they were given. By 1890 a few white people were living in Palm Desert, with hotels, railroads and a business infrastructure springing up in their wake. The fearsome heat that envelops the town didn't put anyone off for long.

A century later Palm Desert had seen a fair bit of life come and go: President Eisenhower's Equalization Law of 1959 enabled the Agua Calientes to make money out of their land – thus shifting economic power more squarely across the community – and more than a few Hollywood legends and visiting royalty from Europe had made homes there. A stint as a training ground for troops in World War II led to the construction of an airfield in nearby Palm Springs, which a couple of decades later had become Palm Springs International Airport. With the lush environment of the desert and the nearby Joshua Tree National Park, which offers visitors the chance to see some of the most awe-inspiring natural beauty in America, tourism boomed and the area is now a popular retirement destination for ageing Los Angelenos who want to spend their autumn years in the countryside. There are casinos, convention centres, celebrity tennis tournaments and plenty to do if you're of a certain age and disposition.

But Palm Desert has an underbelly, of course, and it's this dark, amorphous but vivid zone that we want to explore in this book. Unimpressed by the locale's cheery tourist face – the *Fabulous Palm Springs Follies* musical revue, musicals at The Annenberg Theater in the Palm Springs Desert Museum and the McCallum Theatre for the Performing Arts – a generation of bored teenagers grew up with nothing to do in the Sixties and Seventies. Just as they do in every hick-town on earth, the kids turned to music as a means of escape and self-expression – but in the case of Palm Desert, the disaffected youth had a major advantage: they could escape to some of the most spectacular open spaces the planet has to offer.

By the mid-Eighties, there was a flourishing 'generator-party' scene, where groups of teenagers would drive out of town to a secluded spot where only the moon and the sand could be seen, fire up diesel-powered generators, play music and settle in for a night of drugs – mostly home-made speed (or 'meth'/methamphetamine) – booze and sex. Local bands would bring amplification and lights, and play unhindered by restrictions of volume or curfew. Just as for Jim Morrison two decades earlier, the desert became a playground for experimentation of all kinds, where miracles could occur and the universe would give up its secrets if the music and the hallucinogens did their job properly.

The band that had kick-started the generator-party phenomenon was Across The River, a local punk trio who enjoyed a cult following in the area. The band – made up of singer and guitarist Mario 'Boomer' Lalli, bassist Scott Reeder and drummer Alfredo Hernandez – had enjoyed some Californian success, residing in LA for a while, playing the occasional major festival and travelling the scene in their van, nicknamed 'The Provolone'. The band organised and played at many desert parties, but split up, with Reeder going on to join the soon-to-be-legendary stoner metal band The Obsessed. Lalli and Hernandez recruited the former's cousin Larry on bass and a second guitarist, Gary Arce, and renamed themselves Yawning Man. The music Yawning Man would make would be a revelation.

Joshua Michael Homme was born in Palm Springs in May 1972 and attended Palm Desert High School, where he met Nick Oliveri – who, a year older than Josh, was born in LA and whose family moved to the desert in 1982 – and John Garcia, who was a year older still. Homme (pronounced 'hom-ee') was given his first guitar, a $50 acoustic Seville, by his father at the age of 10. Remarkably, his earliest musical training was a long way from rock. "I started out taking polka lessons," he said later. "It went from that to hardcore punk in about two weeks. My earliest influences were Jock from GBH and Bones from Discharge. When I first heard punk music it was so fucking bad ass. It got you completely pumped. When I hear that, I feel like I can jump off a 30-storey building and live. They never played solos that you could really hear, but they had this real straight up-and-down style of strumming chords. I still play that way.

"Originally, I wanted to play drums," he added. "When I was a kid I made a deal with my dad and he said I had to play a real instrument. Because of that, I got locked into guitar and I've played it ever since. The only thing that has helped me has been constantly playing. I don't really practise. I'm comfortable with the guitar and I know where my good spots are. I don't feel the need to become like Steve Vai. I don't feel that sort of pressure to take it to the ultimate level and become a guitar master. I'd rather sit out on the porch and strum the thing."

Of his early heroes, he said: "I've always been a huge fan of Black Flag guitarist Greg Ginn. Plus a number of other early punk rock stuff and Can had an impact. I'm influenced by different instruments and trying to translate that to the guitar. Anything that makes a noise, I try to translate that back to guitar. I play the guitar, but I'll play anything that's around."

Homme grew up surrounded by influential music, as he recalled, "My parents would only buy one record from any artist. When I was in my single digits, I remember hearing Kenny Rogers. I find it interesting that 'Coward Of The County' is about gang rape and 'Ruby' is about a crippled guy watching his wife go to town to sleep with some other guy . . ." The first record he bought was a punk classic: "It was a live compilation on Alternative Tentacles called *Eastern Front*, with DOA and Flipper. Vinyl. It had a cool cover. There were these soldiers shoving a Japanese flag into the ground. I liked it so much I bought it twice, and the first one wasn't even worn out. I haven't done that since."

The first generator party that Homme and his drummer friend Brant Bjork – 16 and 18 years old at the time – attended featured Yawning Man. As Bjork later recalled: "Yawning Man was the greatest band I've ever seen. We saw them many times at their generator parties. We had been trying to get into the punk scene that didn't even exist any more. We were into Black Flag, Minor Threat, Misfits. But when we finally tapped into the local scene, it's Yawning Man, and they're playing this really stone-y music. It wasn't militant like Black Flag. It was very drugged, very mystical. But we got into it."

He explained: "You'd get to the location, be up there partying, and then the Lallis would show up in their van, all mellow, drag out their shit and set up. It was more like something in the Sixties than some gnarly punk scene. Everyone's just tripping, and they're just playing away for hours."

Bjork and a bass-playing friend named Chris Cockrell were inspired by the Yawning Man shows to form a band, with the drummer roping in Homme on guitar, who he knew from the occasional previous jam session. John Garcia was also persuaded to become the band's singer, and they named themselves Katzenjammer.

Despite their love of extreme music, none of the musicians were particularly extreme people. As Bjork recalled, "School was fine. Sure, I got bored there like everyone does, but I didn't have any terrible experiences like some people do." The drummer, who had known Josh since childhood, described him as "one of the funniest guys I've ever known. He was a tall guy, and he had red hair, so he stood out, and he kinda had to live up to that. Clever dude, great musician, had his shit together." Garcia explained, "I was a normal kid in high school, smoking pot behind the bleachers, doing that type of shit. We all played football. We weren't jocks." But when it came to music, he added, "We just wanted to get in there and fuck people up!"

"People say, I got into music for the girls," said Josh. "But I didn't realise that until later. I got into music because I loved it, and it was like chasing shit in your head, and everyone else in our scene was the same way. Once it was like, let's be different, it became, well, how can we be different, really? You hear your favourite song and you say, that makes me feel so good. Now what if no one else played it, so I had to? In the desert, it was about having to make your own thing, and being isolated enough to do it without anyone fucking with you."

This mission was made much easier by the recruitment of Nick Oliveri on rhythm guitar, who was drafted into the band a while after Katzenjammer had first formed. Homme was responsible for bringing him in, having got to know him in 1984, two years after Nick had arrived from LA. At this stage, as Oliveri later recalled, Katzenjammer were truly forgettable, attempting to emulate the music they liked best – American punk bands like Black Flag and The Descendents, as well as others signed to the cult punk label SST – with little or no success. "We were literally in like eighth and ninth grade, and Josh was in seventh or something," sighed Nick much later. However, Oliveri's arrival did consolidate the band to a degree – he was 'a legend at school', explained Bjork: a guy with long hair who fought and drank and smoked weed – which gave the band a touch of cool. As Homme put it: "Nick played guitar and when John left after a rehearsal one day, he sang. He sang better than John, but we didn't have the balls to kick him out . . . But we did have the balls to keep Nick in."

Although Oliveri was decidedly a metal kid, Josh explained later that he himself avoided the scene like the plague as a kid: "Punk rock kicked me in the balls. I've never been into metal. I've never felt a part of it. I always get dragged in – we want you to be in the metal scene! And I'm always like, 'I don't wanna be in the metal scene!' "

Bjork recalled of Oliveri: "Nick was the guy wearing Vans, jeans, Ozzy shirt, flannel, hair down to the middle of his back. Smokin' cigarettes, doin' blow. Just partying. He's been going like that since the early Eighties! He's a radical. Josh and Nick couldn't have been more opposite, really. But equally interesting . . . Growing up, Nick was definitely the free spirit, he came from the tough side of the tracks, and we were all buddies and he was always just a couple of steps ahead of us . . . I mean Nick, he just can't be stopped!"

Homme added: "Nick was the guy in high school that I drank with in the parking lot before school. We used to play for hours and hours. SST bands like Black Flag, SWA and The Minutemen were the only bands that would play in my home town. So that shoved the do-it-yourself thing in our faces." Oliveri was the most metal-aware member of their circle, as he recalled: "When I was a kid, I really liked Ozzy Osbourne's music a lot and I still do. I like some early Judas Priest. I love Slayer: to this day, I think they're awesome, man. That band never, ever change what their vision was musically. And consistently they've sold records and they're not concerned about getting on the radio. They have very dedicated fans and they don't have to, you know what I mean?"

Katzenjammer rehearsed for a while and then set up a first gig. It sucked. Arriving at a party in a friend's back yard, the band were mortified to see that the audience were all much older than they were and in a mood to party. Unfortunately, singer Garcia wasn't there: he was parked in his car across the street, running through the song lyrics in a last-minute crisis of confidence. "There were these guys yelling at us," says Homme. "They were screaming, 'You better fuckin' play right now!' So we did – without a singer." The band had almost completed their six-song set when Garcia arrived. "After the set finished," Oliveri sniggered, "they made us play the entire thing again." Nick didn't remain a guitarist for long: Cockrell soon left the band – going on to other notable bands such as Solar Feast – and Oliveri switched to bass, where he remained for many years.

Despite the dismal start, the members of Katzenjammer persevered: Oliveri spent his free time at home trying to figure out punk songs by ear, while Homme practised during the day in garages which – he pointed out years later – would be converted by their owners into meth labs at night.

"Brant and Josh had this band," said Nick later, "and I played in my room to Ramones records trying to teach myself guitar, so it was fun to go and play with the guys that were in my grade at school. It was a very small area, and fortunately for us everyone who lived there played music, or was trying to."

Usually, however, the intense heat meant that rehearsals had to be held in houses, not garages – the band would find a room with an air-conditioning unit and attempt to refine their own musical approach. If the room was a bedroom, the musicians would push the beds and wardrobes towards the wall to make space. "In hindsight," recalled Homme, "that shows me how truly committed we really were . . . because if you have to completely dismantle a full bedroom set every time you play and put it back together just to go to bed, that means you love music."

Both Homme and Bjork came from relatively affluent backgrounds – as the latter put it, "My dad is a judge in Indio, my mom is a teacher. Josh came from a real well-to-do family" – and could see both sides of life in the desert towns. Homme in particular was keenly aware of the dead-end nature of both the rich and poor faces of his home town, recalling: "There's a bunch of small towns in the desert that are connected. At the start is Palm Springs, where retirees and Hollywood types like to have nice places. And then it ends at the Salton Sea, where it's speed freaks and ranches and farms and Social Security folks and RV campsites. It's like an onion: there's that rich retiree layer, and then the people that work for them, and then the people that steal from them . . . and they're all locked together."

Bjork later drew a distinction between the high and low desert – that is, areas of land divided by the nearby mountain range: "The high desert is probably closer to what people imagine the desert to be like. It's less populated. Less mountains. It's more vast. Little houses. Real, real small towns." Josh – who explained, "I was born and raised in the low desert: I lived in Palm Desert, Rancho Mirage, Cathedral City, Palm Springs" – described the high desert with subtle rancour: "You don't want to run out of gas out in the high desert. The people that live out there? You go to breakfast at the Country Kitchen, you'll hear, 'Well, Clara was supposed to babysit little Timmy, but all she did was stay up and do speed and never even saw the kid, and he was eatin' paste in the back' . . . It's very much like getting caught in a David Lynch movie. But wherever you are, whether it's the low or the high, you'll be driving through the desert, and it's hot as shit, and you'll see a guy just walking on the side of the road in the middle of nowhere. That's Walking Guy. There's one in every desert town."

As the band slowly evolved from unlistenable to tolerable, they began to play gigs at generator parties around Palm Desert and in Joshua Tree with other similarly minded local bands. A common venue was a disused nudist colony, where a drained swimming pool – nick-named the 'Nudebowl' – filled with skateboarders and party-goers. As Homme recalled with nostalgia: "When we went to throw a party at the nudist colony, guys were getting photographed for the skate magazine *Thrasher* while the sun was going down. They're like, 'Fuck yeah!' They already have a generator, so do we, and the party starts . . . It's too bad, I heard they filled it with sand. People are digging it out already, though – they'll do it. I've had a lot of good and bad times there, played a lot there. I had friends die up there, people stabbed, and also had some of the most amazing parties. When all the walls were up, it was brilliant.

People would sit on walls and in the windows, there would be a fire behind the drummer, and we'd play as loud as the generator would let us go. One time this guy was running around stabbing everyone with a penknife. Our last show on tour with [legendary punk band] The Dwarves was at the nudist colony on Halloween. They borrowed all this equipment from another band and then destroyed it all after 10 minutes!"

Although the parties were sometimes busted by prowling police officers, the kids knew how to minimise the risk: "We'd drive four-wheel-drive trucks up there because the cops would get stuck in the sand," remembered Oliveri. "There would be three or four bands, a keg of beer, and a raging bonfire. We were all under age. People would run around naked and there was sand everywhere. In your amps, in your ass, what you coughed up the next day. But it was worth it."

Josh explained the attractions of the generator scene with the words, "It had moments of true beauty where it was, [we said] this is amazing. There was one time in Indio Hills. There's a bonfire in front of us, so no one's standing directly in front of you. But they're on the edge of the fire. The canyon was tight, and there's little fires in the walls of the canyon, in these perches, where people were standing around these little fires. And you could see the shadows on the canyon walls. And you'd look up and see girls on top of the hill, dancing. And I remember playing, in that moment, going, this is definitely it." He added that playing in the desert "was the shaping factor. There's no clubs here, so you can only play for free. If people don't like you, they'll tell you. You can't suck."

Sometimes, however, the parties turned sour, when gang members would arrive, with violent consequences: "There were plenty of moments when I was like, 'Everybody's dancing and drinking and having a good time,' and then there were other times where I was like, 'Look at the Mexican with the shotgun' . . . the problem with anarchy is that anyone can do whatever they want. Whether it was the wind telling us what to do, or Mehi [Mexican] gang guys coming in and stabbing someone in the ass with a penknife, or someone [with a gun] and they're freaking on acid, that kind of shit can stop a party fast. I remember when they lit a car on fire. And it was like, this is definitely not it."

Mostly, however, the scene functioned as it was supposed to, with the bands who played either improving their act or being booed off. With no conventional restrictions on what they played and for how long they played – apart from the notoriously unreliable generators, which would sometimes go into meltdown without warning – Katzenjammer could extend their songs into long, psychedelic jams that twisted and turned according to the players' whims. After all, the crowd were happy as long as the noise the band made was loud, heavy and didn't stop.

After a few months of playing desert parties, the members of Katzenjammer changed their band's name to Sons Of Kyuss, the meaning of which was much debated in ensuing years. The word 'Kyuss' rhymes with 'pious' and comes from the Dungeons & Dragons role-playing game so beloved of American youth since the Sixties. Kyuss was the name of an evil high priest created by the D&D authors in 1981 who created 'Sons Of Kyuss' – revolting undead corpses with green worms oozing from their skulls. Not that the band were particularly interested in the word's derivation, simply adopting the moniker as a suitably obscure name "that no one else had," as Garcia later explained.

The band had also evolved its own musical direction, focusing on down-tuned, super-heavy jams which combined the crushing, ominous guitar riffs of Black Sabbath with the trance-like extended repetition of Hawkwind and other space-rock giants. It took some time for them to hit the right approach, as Garcia later reported. An early rehearsal saw a complete musical about-turn: "They were playing this mean, heavy, fast punk rock music. Wow! I started singing this really fast punk rock style, blah balalalahhha! And Brant stopped right after the first verse and he goes, 'No, John. Try singing it like this.' And he started singing me this really beautiful melody. I said, 'Well, fuck, you want me to really sing!'" As for the heaviness of the guitar sound, Homme – the man most responsible for this aspect of Sons Of Kyuss' sound, now that Oliveri was on bass – explained that this was accidental rather than intentional: "We didn't have enough money to buy tuners! And so we kept tuning down and down and down, until the strings were flopping, and then you'd just bring it barely up. Then we would all tune to each other, and the gig would start."

The initial problem faced by Sons Of Kyuss was trying to avoid sounding like their influences – an obvious mistake to make in front of the desert audiences. As Homme said: "That was the main thing in the desert: you had to sound like yourself, or else people would talk shit about you. The toughest thing for me was trying not to copy Mario Lalli of Yawning Man. He's my favourite guitar player in the world, because he's so original. Like I have a certain lead flick that I do all the time, and it's from him. I can't help it, it's so bad ass." This was made all the harder by the fact that Sons were playing some of their own material by this stage – a brave, some might say suicidal, move. "We played original songs, which is pretty shocking to think about today," as Oliveri explained. "Normally, you go and play Ramones covers or something. We did some covers – 'New Rose' by The Damned and 'Blitzkrieg Bop' by The Ramones. But we also had four originals. And to us, that meant we had a band."

But the musicians had found something – a sound and a style all their own. Drummer Bjork and Homme had a mutual spark that made their band something special, even at this early stage. Garcia explained in awe: "The majority of our material was written by Josh and Brant. That was the best chemistry between two people I will ever, ever, ever see in my entire life." Oliveri pointed the finger at Brant's diverse influences: "Brant would make the beat roll. It did something to the music. We loved our music so much, we would play and pay no attention to the audience. Never wrote a set-list. We could jam any of our songs at a moment's notice."

Bjork had a punk background like the rest of his bandmates. He explained: "I started as a drummer and then I got an acoustic guitar not long after that, so I've been noodling on both instruments for quite a while. I came from the school where you try to play to Ramones records, drums and guitars, and after you learn the whole Ramones catalogue, you move onto your own. And for me, I learned a lot of guitar from listening to Jimi Hendrix . . . obviously I'm not even in the same universe as him as a musician, but just his basic curiosity and being unafraid to do anything with rhythm [was] what inspired me and got me to try things on the guitar. And it doesn't have to be radical. I don't know anything about the guitar, scales, notes, I've never taken a lesson on either instrument, any instrument. But just by ear, I like to listen to guitar players who freestyle."

He added: "I was just a kid who loved music. I mean, I went through my stages when I was into punk rock, and then heavy rock and acid rock, and I did a lot of my homework and connected the dots with different artists and listened to all kinds of music, and I've always had an open mind. I just wanted to be a musician and make a living creating music, and I've done that. And that's what I'm most proud of, just the whole thing . . . Of course I'm not rich or anything, but that was never my goal anyway."

In 1987, as the Sons Of Kyuss roll-call of original songs approached a professional level, the band booked studio time and cut a demo tape. Still only in their mid-to-late teens, the musicians managed to nail a level of musical authority helped along by Homme's hugely bottom-heavy guitar sound, which he had honed by running his signal through both guitar and bass amp cabinets at gigs. This was the element of the Sons Of Kyuss sound which would be the passport to their future – as was noted with great enjoyment by the musician, producer and all-round music scene legend Chris Goss, who received a copy of the demo from his wife, who worked at the music publishing organisation BMI at the time. Goss, who has built a successful career as the frontman of the alternative rock band Masters Of Reality (who also hosted the occasional generator party), later said: "I think it was the low end that did it." Attending a generator party at which SOK played, Goss was blown away: "I have enchanting memories," he recalled later, "where you're driving toward where they're playing in the middle of the desert, and you're totally lost, but you see some car parked by the side of the road lookin' like it's been abandoned by some drunken kid. And you see someone else stumbling out in the darkness. So you know you're getting close. And then seeing a little glow, a single halogen light on a pole – just one light, so the generator wouldn't blow out. And then actually getting there, and seeing [the band] playing, sur-rounded by a few hundred kids slamming in the sand in the middle of the night, with the wind whipping sand around everywhere. And then the sound of it, like you're listening to them in a tornado, and you could only see this cacophony of bodies, of fucked-up kids, slamming into each other. It was like stumbling on the Plains Indians doing a war dance."

"Those were pretty wild times," said Nick Oliveri, pretty wild himself, later. "We were kids and they were anything-goes kind of parties. Nobody was there to stop it. These things would go on for days sometimes. It was really something special. It was a great time of my life. I wouldn't change a thing. Good bands, under-age drinking – all that kind of shit. It was cool."

The desert shows were no easy ride, as Homme recalled: "If people see you for free, if they don't like you at all, they tell you now, not tomorrow, and not behind your back. They don't even leave, they stay there and fuck with you. I just remember people saying we sounded like this or that, and Nick and Brant came over and said we need to change all our sounds . . .

"We hung around some crazy motherfuckers," related Josh fondly. "You're *surrounded* by a whole bunch of wacky motherfuckers. It's a small town: you either drink, fight or fuck. Someone's always proving something there all the time . . . it's anarchy. If it decides to be peaceful then it will, but if it's rough there's no one there to stop it. The best is when you walk past the bonfires and see people making out and drinking, but the worst is when Mexican gangbangers are firing shotguns into the air and walking around starting shit with anyone who will match their gaze . . . We played one party where I thought I was going to the bathroom, so I walked into this garage and it was a huge meth lab. Everyone looked at me like, 'You're a dead man!' I was 15 years old with no ride, no way to get out, going, 'OK, I'm not gonna piss in here.' That's a real slice of life."

"We had a big punk-rock influence," explained Nick Oliveri, when asked later on if, in fact, it had been grunge which was the biggest influence on his band's music. "We started pretty early, probably around the same time when all those grunge bands started. But we were just in a different location and didn't really know anything about them. We were just doing what we did – Black Flag meets Black Sabbath, that kind of attitude. And yeah, we finally heard all the bands, Nirvana and Mudhoney and all that stuff, and we liked it, [but] we didn't really feel part of it, because we weren't from Seattle. We were very proud that we were from the desert and not from LA!"

Their roots were important to them. He added: "We made it very clear that we're from the desert! We were from Palm Desert. It's just triple digits all the time, 118 degrees dry heat. You can't even go outside, so what you do is stay in beside the air conditioning and write songs and play and jam with your friends. So that helped us along because there was nothing else to do. But that was one of the things we always set ourselves aside from. We're not grunge, we're not from

Seattle, we're not an LA metal band. We're dirt rock from the desert. That was the little trip we were on."

Goss was one of the first to witness the band's initial gigs outside the desert environment. By 1988 Sons Of Kyuss were making the 117-mile drive to Los Angeles to play live dates in the completely incongruous environment of the hair-metal scene, then at its commercial peak. As Josh remarked, "It was weird because there were still a lot of hair bands around . . . Actually, a lot of people hated us . . . I think we got into fights at like 13 or 14 straight shows." Goss was at their very first LA show – played in front of five people at the now-closed Hollywood club, The Gaslight. He later marvelled, "I went apeshit. I hadn't felt heavy music like that since I'd seen Black Sabbath in the early Seventies. There's a thing that happens when guitar and bass play a slow riff and the drums are swinging under it – it's a body thing, your spine almost turns to jelly. The drums were swinging under these really low riffs, and there was a great singer. I'd been a fan of heavy music all my life, and here were some kids doing it as good as, or better than, I'd ever heard. So I walked up to Josh afterwards and I said, 'Are you a Sabbath fan?' And he said, 'No, I've never really listened to Sabbath.' And then I knew we were on to something. This was coming from *them*."

As the band admitted, some of the fights were – if not actually started – then certainly provoked by them. Bjork remembered: "We would go into LA and see these bands that would go on before us take shit from club owners and stuff. We weren't having that. One night we upstaged [punk act] Jack Grisham, whose band we were opening for. The club soundman shut off the PA in the middle of our set and got on stage and started taking the mikes down. We hurt the dude pretty bad. I'm not proud of this era, I've since mellowed out, but I mean, that's how we were. We were young, we were pissed, we were punks."

Interestingly, it emerged much later that Homme also had a hand in the then-new techno scene, helping out at the impromptu raves which were briefly the order of the day. As he recalled several years later, "I used to work at raves in 1991 to '93, set up lights for free X [ecstasy] and dance. You'd have to get five or six phone numbers and find the guy with Mickey Mouse hands and a glowstick around his neck and shit."

But in spite of all the teenage aggression, Sons Of Kyuss were at heart an intelligent band who were growing up rapidly. Veterans of the punk scene – to which SOK belonged, in spirit if not exactly in musical terms – admired their style in the face of the vapid glam-metal scene and were moved to help them out. As Bjork added, "We were very lucky. We had an innocence to us. There was so much conviction in what we were doing that people couldn't deny that. So these older guys would protect us, and help us do what we wanted to do. Like, eventually we got [experienced punk sound engineer] Hutch as a soundman. He knew how to take [us] and make it sound proper and rad in a club."

Although their first demo had been something of an achievement for such a young band, Homme & co. had further ambitions and decided to record an entire album. Lacking the contacts and, frankly, the interest from the industry to attract a record deal, Sons Of Kyuss resolved to release the album on their own Black Highway label. In true indie style, and flying directly in the face of the then relatively new CD generation, an LP-only, clear vinyl pressing of 500 copies appeared.

Sons Of Kyuss opened with a bold statement for such an inexperienced band. 'Deadly Kiss' starts with a slow, sludgy riff and soon expands into a mid-tempo, almost jaunty song over the vocals of Garcia – who sounds unbelievably youthful to the listener of today – and is full of stock, metal-of-the-day tricks such as bass guitar and kick-drums punctuating simultaneously. 'Window Of Souls' pulls off an unexpected tempo change – a trademark of Homme's writing to this day. A slippery, snake-hips song, it suffers from a very Eighties noise-gated snare drum (where the sound is cut off artificially before it can decay fully, leading to a tacky, almost drum-machine effect), but is basically a slow blues jam, similar to The Doors' 'Roadhouse Blues'.

'King' is stripped down, with a fat, finger-style bass and understated guitar allowing Garcia to explore a little more with his voice: "I'll never say it to you!" he warns, before a warm, bluesy guitar solo cuts in. A trancey jam laid on top of a blues riff rather like that of 'Window', it doesn't really depart from standard bar-room cabaret. 'Isolation Desolation' begins as a simple acoustic song, backed up with reverbed guitar wails, but evolves into a much more sophisticated, darker anthem than the previous songs: it's flashes of inspiration such as this which make it clear that Sons Of Kyuss had learned much from the endless desert jams that had shaped them.

'Love Has Passed Me By' begins with a snatch of ambient noise that recalls the grim tolling of the intro of Black Sabbath's 'Black Sabbath', but lifts into a droned, almost punky slice of unremarkable rock. 'Black Widow' is the first song to hint at the heaviness for which the band would later become famous, and the lyrical venom which Garcia would often introduce into their work, with a double guitar solo on each side of the mix wailing in pure Tony Iommi homage. The ironically titled 'Happy Birthday' takes a while to bring the listener in, stamping away in a drone that is one of the high points of the album, and then flowering into a slab of Ramones-style sneers. Homme's soloing is noticeable for the sheer volume of space it takes up and, while on previous songs he has displayed some touches of youthful virtuosity, here he keeps it raw and almost amateurish. The album closes with 'Katzenjammer', an atmospheric, wailing attempt at a punk song with a big chorus.

Is *Sons Of Kyuss* a good album? Considering how young the band were, it's certainly a decent debut record and it has plenty of punk aggression which fans of US hardcore would relish. But the production (in particular those vile snare-drum noise gates) lets it down. Unsurprisingly, it made no impact on the music scene on the West Coast and is almost impossible to find today. Little wonder that Josh said some years later that, "We made 500 copies . . . I still have about 150 of them in the house here."

In years to come, the value of those albums would equal a large percentage of the house in which they were stored. Momentum was building.

CHAPTER 2

1990–1993: The Million Year Trip Begins

AFTER the *Sons Of Kyuss* album vanished without trace and it seemed that only the desert would be their permanent friend, Garcia, Homme, Oliveri and Bjork continued to seek more exposure on the Hollywood rock club circuit. By 1990 they had managed to attract more attention, with LA journalist and promoter, Chris 'Hot Rod' Long, prominent among them. Long, who reported on the local music scene for the *Hollywood Rocks* fanzine and also worked as an A&R man for the small Chameleon label, was an early fan: "I did tons of stuff on them," he said. "I wrote about them in every issue for two months."

Long spoke enthusiastically about his new find to his colleagues at Chameleon, and Sons Of Kyuss were invited to play a showcase concert in early 1991 at the Raji's club in Hollywood. The label president Bob Buziak had heard Long's recommendation and was blown away by the band's performance, offering them a record deal with the Chameleon subsidiary label Dali. The band were ecstatic, but knew that some changes needed to be made. One of these was a name change, which was necessary if their presence was to be felt more fully: Sons Of Kyuss was just too long and too meaningless to be effective and, after some discussion, they shortened it to Kyuss.

Rather than write, record and release an entirely new collection of songs for the new Chameleon/Dali album, Kyuss made the decision to re-record some tunes from *Sons Of Kyuss* and add them to the handful of new songs they had. The result was the *Wretch* album, released later in 1991 and taking 'Love Has Passed Me By', 'Black Widow', 'Katzenjammer', 'Deadly Kiss' and 'Isolation Desolation' (reduced to 'Isolation' here) and adding new songs '(Beginning Of What's About To Happen) Hwy 74', 'Son Of A Bitch', 'The Law', 'I'm Not', 'Big Bikes' and 'Stage III'. Although the old songs' re-recordings were both cleaner and rounder than the originals, and the new tracks – 'Son Of A Bitch' and 'The Law' especially – showcased a darker, heavier side to the band, *Wretch* suffered from the same slightly weak sound as its predecessor and is evidently the work of a band still in development.

However, before long – like the many other bands before them who could tear it up on stage but for whom the studio was hostile territory – Kyuss steadily gained a reputation for the fierce, unending jams which they had honed at the generator parties. The aggression of the musicians – all brought up on the second wave of punk – came through in both their performance energy and their music and crowds began to be drawn to Kyuss shows. Chris Goss, now a friend who wanted to help Kyuss as much as he could, saw them play and knew that only an album that captured the band's phenomenal live sound would be truly representative.

Goss was a powerful ally on the desert scene and maintained a relationship with the band from then on. He saw them play on October 11, 1991 at the Off Ramp Music Café in Seattle, with The Dwarves headlining. As Garcia later recalled, "The Dwarves were the first band that ever took us out on the road, and they're fuckin' nuts . . . You ever seen the cover of their album, *Blood, Guts And Pussy*? It's two naked chicks and a naked midget holding a dead rabbit with blood all over them. And it's real rabbit blood." Homme added: "Their songs are like, 'Fuck You Up And Get High', shit like that. 'Back Seat Of My Car'. Fuckin' punk rock shit . . . like, they play naked or with women's lingerie on. Fuckin' spit on people and hit people with mikes. [Guitarist] He-Who-Cannot-Be-Named wore a mask, and he never took the mask off. He'd be naked with shoes and the mask on . . . You know, it's like, if there's a chick up front, the lead singer will be singing, he'll have his pants down around his knees, he'll be bleeding, he'll have the microphone in his mouth all the way, and with both hands grab her by the hair . . ."

With this kind of live experience freshly in mind, Chris Goss approached Chameleon head Buziak and explained his case. He wanted to produce the next Kyuss album himself, selling the label boss the idea as a fellow desert resident who 'knew' how the band could and should sound, and – because he was a musician in a band of similar, if not identical, style – that he had the technical skills to perform the job. The approach which would serve the huge riffing of Kyuss, he reasoned, would be to reduce the sterile environment of the studio to the point where the band could jam with no physical or psychological limitations, and to give them what they needed for their best performance: freedom. Buziak bought the idea, and commissioned Goss to produce the next Kyuss album. His decision was timely and insightful, and perhaps explains that after various manoeuvres Buziak would find himself president of the mighty RCA label over a decade later.

Released at the end of June 1992, *Blues For The Red Sun* was a revelation. The previous year had been pivotal for American rock music, with three key albums transforming the musical landscape – Nirvana's *Nevermind*, Metallica's *Metallica* and the Red Hot Chili Peppers' *Blood Sugar Sex Magik* (the bands' second, fifth and fifth studio albums, respectively). While Kyuss didn't have the experience, the finance, the backup or the influence to reshape the world of music to anything like that degree, the similarity between all four bands is that their new album drastically changed their fortunes, gained them a new fanbase and changed the public perception of their music to an unthought-of degree. *Blues For The Red Sun* isn't as heavy as Metallica's album, as politically ground breaking as Nirvana's, or as funky as the Chili Peppers'; but it is as radical a departure from the sound of its predecessors as any of them. Goss' warm, organic production lies squarely on the vast riffs of Josh Homme, themselves underpinned by a huge bass sound, surprisingly tender drums (no rock-giant percussive fireworks here) and Garcia's distant, emotional vocals tying up the whole. "Chris was a godsend," Homme said of Goss. "When we hit Chris, he knew exactly how we wanted to sound, and how to get it out of the board."

Working with Chris Goss was also a high point for Oliveri, as he recalled later on: "It was great, you know? He was like the fifth member with *Blues For The Red Sun*. He knew the band's vision and he also helped us find a lot of our vision at that point, because we were pretty young at the time. We kind of came up together, because I believe that it was the first album he ever produced. It was our first big record to record and his first big record to produce, or first record to produce on his own. So we both came up and had to trust each other to work well together."

On *Blues* Homme takes his previous multi-layered guitar approach and evolves it to the next logical level, tracking epic, galaxy-wide sheets of sound and interspersing them with his trademark Hendrix-influenced fusillades of lead guitar and some unexpected funk stabs. There are lashings of Deep Purple and Black Sabbath all over the album, but it's far from a simple homage to these pioneers: there's far too much subtle emotion at play for that. How had they gone about constructing such a mammoth sound? Nick: "We wanted to make an album that had more bass – and basically make it heavier than anything that was out there at the time just by having such a rumble that like, 'Holy shit, what the fuck was that?' Know what I mean? It's really one of those records that if you put it on, and you had been listening to something else, you're definitely going to have to fuck with your EQ. If you just put it on and have it turned up full blast, never hearing it before, there's a good possibility that you'll blow your woofers. That was one of our things, let's blow people's speakers! You know, when you're kids, you want to do fun, silly shit like that. It was like, what if we had something that was so heavy, if people just left their shit turned up and they'd never heard it before, it could possibly blow their speakers?"

'Thumb' is a key sign that things are going to be different on the new album. An ambient intro leads to a bluesy – but not awkwardly so, as on *Sons Of Kyuss* and *Wretch* – riff which settles into a mighty, strolling guitar storm. John Garcia sings in the background – maintaining a distance from the furious proceedings upfront – and the song builds and builds to epic levels completely unheard on previous Kyuss recordings.

'Green Machine' is one of the few nods that Kyuss gave to their earlier, punk roots, with a moderately speedy structure focusing on deft picking rather than all-out fuzzy sludge. The song would be released as a single, backed with a remix and another *Blues* track, 'Thong Song'. Garcia has a slight punk sneer edge to his voice, but otherwise the direction in which Kyuss appear to be heading is more about metal obliteration than punk aggression, as evidenced by the fabulous 'Molten Universe', the band's first really psychedelic composition. A deadly slow roll through the acidic territory pioneered by Sabbath in their earliest incarnation, this instrumental tune throws up tempo changes and a filthy stop-start riff that is straight from the late-Sixties sludge basket of Blue Cheer and Vanilla Fudge.

'50 Million Year Trip (Downside Up)' shows off a slightly different side to Kyuss. Homme's frantically scrubbed intro leads into a fusion of Deep Purple-style fuzz warmth and a punk energy that takes its time, like so many other Kyuss compositions, before building into a heavy-weight drama of pummelling bass and drums. Loaded with layers of guitar, the song is the first burst of genuinely passionate energy on *Blues*, anchored by Garcia's yelled promise of "I'll never forget you". 'Thong Song' is calmer but more sinister, leading the listener into blind alleys with fragmented riffs that resolve into a quiet, almost eerie background for Garcia's vocals, which are mixed higher than in most other Kyuss songs. "I hate slow songs!" he grates, with knowing irony.

'Apothecaries' Weight' starts with a clutch of bass chords from Oliveri and becomes a song which could have come straight from a Hendrix jam, so stoned and meandering are the extended solos which follow. Homme's soloing, while never approaching the technical virtuosity of the big-hair shredders of the day such as Steve Vai and Joe Satriani, is perfect for the arid, rehearsal-room vibe of the song, diving into and emerging from the dark depths of Oliveri and Bjork's interplay with alacrity. Perhaps this was the best example in Kyuss' work to date of capturing the live sound that Homme and the others wanted to hear on their records, and this is largely down to the expertise of producer Goss. As Josh explained: "Our first record, *Wretch*, doesn't sound like us at all . . . Chris showed us how to get our sound on tape. I've been trying to learn from him about how to keep that natural-sounding process without using a $100,000 rack just to get the sounds that were there in the first place. He's a smart guy and he knew that we were coming from playing outdoors, and he knew that we needed to let it all hang loose. He hit record, and here we are. It shows what a good ear Chris has. We're totally different than Masters Of Reality and yet we are the same. Like minds attract each other."

'Caterpillar March' is a short segment of riffing and ambience with little apparent direction but loaded with menace, and 'Freedom Run' is looser still, a classic Led Zeppelin-infused tight-but-loose jam that focuses on a massively distorted riff straight from the Jimmy Page canon. It extends for a trance-like seven minutes and offers the musicians plenty of time and space to stretch out and improvise without restriction. '800' takes this free experimentation and focuses it into a tighter, more confined space – only one and a half minutes of it – and is mostly a weird, drums-based mantra with echoing background moans from the musicians, before leading without pausing into 'Writhe'.

One of the darkest songs on the album, 'Writhe' leans towards what would now be recognised as the classic Nirvana quiet-loud-quiet-loud template, but without the pronounced peaks and troughs. Once again sitting atop a mighty pile of compressed riffs, the song features John Garcia singing in an understated, almost restrained style without resorting to the histrionics or sarcastic sneer of earlier songs. At one point Kyuss allow the song to decay into a simple bass and drums figure with a low-down solo circling above it, with none of the huge riffs of before: this awareness of light and dark shades is what makes *Blues For The Red Sun* – and many other seminal albums – so influential. It's one of the biggest and most memorable tunes on the record and, if you need an introduction to the early sound of Kyuss, it's a perfect song with which to start.

The overall sound, with its impenetrable density, was a crucial part of the Kyuss approach, as Homme later explained: "The parts themselves are insignificant. It's the sum of the parts that matter. It's not guitar riffs, or the bass or the drums. It's the whole picture. The point for us isn't for you to listen to Josh Homme play guitar . . . there's all kinds of filler stuff all over our music. If you had everyone really trying to show their stuff, then you wouldn't hear [the filler]. Our style is more one of individual restraint and letting the song take over."

In contrast to all this doom and heavyweight oppression, 'Capsized' is a short, presumably intentional Zeppelin-like acoustic guitar piece that comes as something of a breath of fresh air. But 'Allen's Wrench' is as close to a pure metal song as Kyuss had come to date, matching the speed and dexterous fury of early-to mid-period Sabbath, with a huge guitar sound. Homme later said: "The volume of our music keeps our ears clean because it blows the wax out . . . As long as you can feel it, you feel like you can push the sound around and it's all over you."

The six-minutes-plus of 'Mondo Generator', which would later lend its name to a band fronted by Nick Oliveri, is the most chaotic on the album, layered with distorted vocal howls from Garcia and a suitably ponderous riff at its centre. Garcia's vocals aren't decipherable, and his occasional explanations weren't much use – for example: "'Green Machine' is actually, you know when you were a kid, and they had The Big Wheel, but they also had The Green Machine? And you had the little handles on the side that actually turned you. That's what a Green Machine is." As for 'Thong Song': "That's not actually about bathing suits, it's actually about wearing thongs [flip-flops]. We were from the desert, you know? No shoes, just thongs. That's just about living in a hot shithole." Caterpillar March: "There's these big giant earth moving machines called Caterpillars. And in the desert there's a lot of building going on, especially eight or nine years ago, there was a lot of earth being moved, so Caterpillar March."

But as Josh once said: "The more you don't know what we're personally thinking, the better . . . [the lyrics are] all part of the bigger picture and it makes everything out of focus. I think people do know what our lyrics are about in a strange sort of way. I think there's a couple of keys to how you should look at them. You should know they're gonna be ironic in some way, because a sick sense of humour is what it's all about . . . [and] you should never know what our political views are through our music." At one point he became quite trenchant on the subject, explaining with some passion: "It doesn't matter what bands look like or say. Fuck all that stuff! I mean, if we're dicks, it shouldn't matter, and if you think our music's cool, it doesn't mean *we're* cool, y'know? I just want our music to be the only thing. We should be able to be total flaming assholes. Nowadays, everyone goes, 'Oh, I don't like that band, they have blue tennis shoelaces,' or something. I wanna skip all that shit. It shouldn't matter. Music is for listening. All that other stuff just fucks up the music."

The final song on *Blues For Red Sun* isn't a song, it's a four-second silence in the middle of which one of the musicians flatly says, "Yeah." Named after that staccato monosyllable, it's a suitably anticlimactic follow-up to the enormously psychedelic sounds of 'Mondo Generator'. And so Kyuss had made their definitive statement to date, with their grasp of heaviness, atmospherics and experimentation available for all to hear.

It emerged that it had taken some time before drummer Bjork – a talented songwriter who simply did not know it – began to contribute material to Kyuss, as he recalled later: "Well, in Kyuss it started out pretty much that Josh wrote most of the songs, because we were young and I didn't really know what my responsibilities were as far as songwriting goes. I was a drummer and I thought that was that. I was already a guitar player, but I didn't know I was a guitar player. I could just play a couple of things. But we would rehearse in my bedroom at my parents' house and all this shit would be set up all week, and I would noodle on Josh's stuff. And it wasn't until we got together one day to jam and I told him I had something, and I played him 'Green Machine' and he was like, cool. And that started out to be a chemistry between Josh and I writing together, which I thought was really good. Josh was probably the key core songwriter, but I could throw riffs at him, and I did from that point on, and he would definitely dig them and get into them."

Blues For The Red Sun saw Kyuss elevated to the public eye. Commercial success came slowly, but when it came it reached respectable levels. The band were interviewed on MTV shows by presenters such as *Headbanger's Ball*'s Riki Rachtman, whose programme was among the few of the day that brought heavy music to the mainstream. This was helped along by video clips made for 'Green Machine' and 'Thong Song', and also radio airplay on major stations in Los Angeles, Seattle, San Diego and Chicago. A WHMH Minneapolis employee called Bob Burt – whose title was the somewhat odd 'Metal Director' – said in an interview: "I think this band is going to be around for a while. I was pretty sold on the *Blues* album. It went three tracks deep with us. We still use it recurrent." The press also reacted well to *Blues For The Red Sun*, with *Kerrang!* awarding it a five-K review and *Spin* including it in their Top 10 Underrated Albums Of 1992 (the album wasn't released in the UK until 1993). The 'underrated' tag isn't quite as accurate, perhaps, as 'under-sold': the album only sold 39,000 copies on its original release. (It was reissued on vinyl in 1999.)

Later Kyuss albums also appeared on old-fashioned vinyl, at the band members' insistence: "You gotta have vinyl!" crowed Garcia at one point. "If fuckin' eight-track cartridges were still being made I'd be putting those motherfuckers out too. I still collect eight-tracks. I have an eight-track player in my car, a 1980 Chrysler Cordoba. Right now I have Lou Rawls in the son-of-a-bitch and it's nice to throw on an eight-track every now and then. I grew up on that shit. I always used to put in my older brother's eight-tracks . . . I'm not trying to get all

Seventies retro but I grew up on that shit and I want it released on that type of stuff . . . And coming from a collector's point of view, because I collect vinyl, if I were to get a Monster Magnet limited edition print in Italy, *only* in Italy, with lyrics included on purple vinyl – I'm all over that shit. It's only for the collectors. For people like myself that love vinyl. People that love turning on the turntable, throwing on a piece of plastic, and jamming out. You know, listening to it crackle after a hundred times you've played it."

The Kyuss message was brought forcibly home to the masses by the extended touring they carried out after the release of *Blues*. Several notable musicians had seen them live and been impressed, including Glenn Danzig, who asked them to support Danzig and White Zombie. Of the hulking Danzig, Garcia later said: "Hats off to that motherfucker because he's doing it. He's had 10 million managers, 10 million record labels, 10 million booking agents and all the past ones hate him. But yet he's still doing what he likes to do and he'll still be touring and he'll still be singing, getting it out to the old Misfits fans. Hats off to him. That's somewhat the attitude that I carry on these days. It's something that's a little frustrating sometimes to me. Life isn't easy and no one ever said it was . . . No one is going to get anything for you. Anything! You have to do it yourself. It's like that old saying, if you want something done right you have to do it yourself. That takes a lot of hard work and that's something I'm into. I'm into staying busy and making sure my shit pops off. I get really emotional about this. I get real frustrated because some-times things don't work out my way. I just got to keep pushing and keep my head straight and keep talking off the town."

A 36-date US tour supporting Danzig and White Zombie stretched from October to December, with many fans' eyes opened to the power of Kyuss for the first time. Perhaps the most influential of the friends Kyuss made among the musician community was Nirvana drummer Dave Grohl, who (along with his bandmate Krist Novoselic) saw them play in 1992, met them after the show and became friends. "There's some great bands that came out of Seattle, but it got so blown out of proportion, it became too much of a good thing," Homme later com-mented of the grunge explosion. "It's the same reason why people got sick of hair bands. When you first start out playing and writing your music, the environment that you learn to do it in becomes your roots forever. Someone planted a seed here, and this is what we sound like

26

when we grow." While Nirvana were riding high on the grunge wave after the enormous, unprecedented success of their second album *Nevermind*, with Grohl spending the next few years on a constant wave of popularity with Nirvana and his subsequent band Foo Fighters, the friendship remained strong and would yield unexpected results a decade later.

In the meantime, turmoil awaited Kyuss. Bassist Nick Oliveri had had enough of his band's ponderous, riff-heavy music and was looking for a less sophisticated, more unhinged musical outlet. In late 1992 he and Kyuss parted ways amicably and he joined none other than The Dwarves, adopting the *nom de guerre* Rex Everything. After a short period of discussion and auditions, Homme, Garcia and Bjork recruited bassist Scott Reeder, lately of the doom-metal band The Obsessed and previously one of their desert-party inspirations as a member of Across The River back in the Eighties. Reeder, a scintillating but refined player, gelled immediately with the Kyuss members and came across strongly in interviews. Asked if Kyuss attracted a lot of strange people to their shows, Reeder remarked: "I hope so! If there's gonna be five people here, I hope one of them's a crazy metalhead, one's 40 and one's a grunge dork, y'know?" On the subject of the immense volume that had characterised Kyuss shows since the desert days, he mused: "I hope it doesn't get to that point [deafness], but it's like an addiction, and the deafer you get, the louder you play. I don't want ear plugs. I've never worn 'em and I'm starting to suffer. My ears are ringing all day every day. I try to tell myself that music is such a cool thing that you have to pay the price for taking it, and the ringing is just part of the bad side. The perfect Kyuss show would be where half the people are dancing, half are slamming, and the other half are . . . wait, that's three halves! But y'know, outside the gig is like a sick carnival; there'll be fires and like 30 people playing bongo drums. Every concert should be an event."

As Kyuss gained more and more success – particularly after a short December/January tour with Faith No More and Babes In Toyland – one inevitable side effect was that musicians' magazines became interested in their sound, one which was similar to their contemporaries from the desert scene but which only Kyuss had so far managed to bring to the public's attention. Josh in particular was – and still is – often quizzed about his super-heavy guitar tone, with the instrument tuned down to C and run through bass and guitar cabinets simultaneously for a fatter sound. However he was reluctant to reveal the full details of his approach, telling one interviewer: "My sound is important to me, and I've spent a lot of years just working it over with little tricks here and there. I almost feel like if you reveal too much of that, you give away something that's near and dear to you. It's like you put it up on the altar and say, 'Here, everyone take a slice.'"

Away from the journalists, he said: "Sometimes I talk to a guitar magazine and they're like, 'What equipment do you use?'" adding with slight irritation, "Why would I tell those guys? That means any old guy that wanted to, just had to read that and get all that stuff and something I spent years figuring out . . . Taking all those ancient Chinese secrets and revealing them for the fuck of it. I just think, 'What am I – a retard?' Yeah, 'Here's a pen, write it down.'"

However, Homme did admit that his favourite guitar was a vintage Ovation: "I bought it on consignment in Northern Idaho in this really small store. It was 199 bucks. It was the only guitar that could tune down well to where we're down to. I can't play anything else. I tried to buy this gold top Les Paul and I just couldn't." He explained that he sometimes shopped for old guitars: "If you pick up a used guitar that's a piece of shit because it's been worn the wrong way, then you won't enjoy playing it. But if someone has put the right wear marks in it, then it's a beautiful guitar. That's so personal. I'm not talking about something that you can easily fix, like the neck's bent. It has to do with where all the wear marks are and where are all the switches are." As for effects, he added: "I don't like to have a lot of pedals because you think you're tap-dancing. So I try to use pickups and I change the settings on the amp during the show or recording to do the work instead of a lot of pedals.

"I go through phases. Sometimes I'll use delay and a phase shifter; other times a Rotovibe. There's no consistency. They break, so I pick something new. I like having options but I don't want to be a slave to the shit. Sometimes you've got to draw a line between having all the options and being a slave to the things, using them every time you play the guitar. I'm trying to keep a real inconsistency to the pedals so that it's something new every time. The effects are a significant part of our sound, but if you were to hear a different sound in place of the one that's on the record it wouldn't matter. The sound is always the same

28

but the texture may be different. Pedals are all about changing the mood. It's like the same room with different coloured lights. It's not necessarily about playing the song the same every single time."

By the end of 1992 Kyuss were in a strong position. *Blues For The Red Sun* had been a critical, if not particularly commercial, success and had led them to make some powerful allies and expand their fanbase through high-profile touring. With new bassist Reeder in place – a more reliable character than the mercurial Oliveri – the future seemed bright.

1993, however, would be their strangest year yet.

In the early months of the year Kyuss recorded their third album, to be titled *Welcome To Sky Valley*. All went well with the sessions, which were their most ambitious yet. Josh decided that some inventive album sequencing would take place with the songs, but details were held back from the press until the scheduled time for release, which was initially planned for late-1993. However, no sooner had the recording and mixing been completed than the shock news came that the then-biggest rock band in the world, Metallica, had invited Kyuss to support them on an Australian tour. It emerged that James Hetfield, Lars Ulrich and co. were huge fans of *Blues For The Red Sun*, although the styles of music that the two bands performed were radically different.

At this point in their career (although telling changes would occur in the band's sound within a couple of years), Metallica were coming to the end of a massive, three-year world tour, on which they blended their old, thrash-metal songs – speedy, quintessentially Eighties compositions – with their newer, more bludgeoning, chart hits. Both approaches were worlds away from the semi-controlled, sludge-laden Kyuss sound, which led the band and their associates to wonder if a tour support would be the right thing. "It was tough to say yes to a band like Metallica, because we weren't a metal band," Homme said later. "Punk Rock guilt ran rampant through our little desert scene. It stopped so many people from doing things. It was, do well, but don't do *too* well." However, the offer was one that no sane band would refuse, and when it emerged that Kyuss supporter Dave Grohl had been instrumental in securing them the gig, they accepted that offer.

The nine Australian dates – performed between March 27 and April 8, 1993 in Sydney, Brisbane, Melbourne, Adelaide and Perth – were a revelation, recalled Homme, who later said that Metallica "had no idea who they wanted" to open for them. However, "They had heard *Blues* and they were into it . . . [The tour] was quite an experience. Just being in Australia alone was amazing." Drummer Bjork remembered the concerns Kyuss felt beforehand: "We were like, 'Who's gonna know us in Australia? The first night, the soundman from Metallica came up to [Kyuss soundman] Hutch and said, 'You got full PA. You can just rock. Don't worry about it, man, everything's cool.' Hutch looked at us and went, 'All right.' And, like, the first song, the first night, we had thousands of people – fuckin' boom! With our volume getting up there, and with Josh playing out of bass cabinets, you could feel the floor shaking. People couldn't deny it." However, this didn't last, with Metallica and their sound engineers wising up a little to the enormous power of their support act: "The next night, and for the rest of the tour, we didn't have full PA," Bjork chuckled.

Once back in California, and recovering a little from the shock of 12 months in which they had gone from desert anonymity to the chosen openers for the biggest band in rock, Kyuss considered its future. All was not well with Bjork, who was feeling some dissatisfaction: "I was drinking a lot, smokin' dope, the business was startin' to get to me," he said later. "Josh and I started running at a little different pace. Our ideals started to change a little bit. Which is natural because not only was the band developing, but we were becoming adults, too." His perspective on the band was changing, and inevitably so: after all, he had been in Kyuss since his teens. "Kyuss was my life," he added. "I started to see it become a demon, and I was burning out simultaneously. So I just decided to leave when I knew I was ahead. As far as I was concerned, we'd just blown Metallica off the stage. I was like, where do you go after that?"

Although Bjork's departure, which finally took place in autumn 1993 after some extended discussions, occurred shortly after that of Nick Oliveri, Homme and Garcia were understanding. "We grew up playing together," Homme said of his departed friend, "and on this record we peaked together."

Bjork looks back fondly at his times with Kyuss: "We recorded *Blues*, and then we toured solid up until *Sky Valley*. For me personally, we were very young, we were very stupid, and we were very drunk and stoned at all times. And you know what? That was part of what made

Kyuss exciting, so I'm not down on that at all, that was great. But by the time we were finished touring and we got into the studio I was completely burned out. We weren't getting along. Artistically I was kind of nervous. I didn't know in what direction the band was going, and just for me . . . it was the exact opposite from *Blues For The Red Sun*. Nick wasn't in the picture any more, and Nick was a very important part of the Kyuss sound and vibe. And that was a total buzzkill – and I had some songs that I wanted to get on the record that for whatever reason, to this day I don't even know why, it just never really happened that way. And I was probably a little bitter about that." The recording sessions were agony too, as he explained: "On top of all that, my wisdom teeth had come in and they were crowding my mouth and I couldn't even eat because my mouth was in so much pain and my teeth were overcrowded. But I didn't have time to go get them pulled. So I recorded the whole record in this excruciating pain and I couldn't even eat any food, and I was just like smoking and drinking so I could get rid of this pain in my head. We basically just rolled tape and did it and got it over with."

Bjork's actual departure happened quickly: "I finished all the basic tracks, and I had already told the guys prior to this record that I was leaving the band. This would be my last record. So I finished the basic tracks and I just split. I said, 'I've got to go get my teeth out.' I couldn't take it any more. And that was it, I never returned to the band again. And I didn't know what was going to come of the record: I got a tape of it a couple of weeks later and Josh and I sat down and listened to it. I mean, listening back to it now, it's an amazing record. It's almost like . . . I don't know, I don't know how that happened. But the song 'Whitewater' on that record is just an amazing song to me."

The remaining members had other issues to consider at this point. While searching for a replacement for Bjork, their record label Chameleon gave them two pieces of good news: firstly that they would delay the release of *Sky Valley* by a few months in order to give them time to find a successor, and – more importantly – that the new album would be released not on Chameleon's subsidiary Dali but by the main label itself, a sign of the importance the label executives placed on it and their recognition of Kyuss' importance. The release date was now set for January 1994, and Chameleon bosses prepared to promote it by giving key industry contacts a sneak preview of the new songs, in September, at the Concrete Foundations Forum convention in Burbank, California.

Encouraged by these events, Homme, Garcia and Reeder settled in a new drummer, the jazz-trained Alfredo Hernandez, like Reeder a veteran of the Across The River days and a member of desert legends Yawning Man. Hernandez fitted the bill perfectly, listing his influences as "Minutemen, Black Flag, DC3, Meat Puppets . . . the punk-rock way is still our way of looking at the music industry. I remember when one of my brothers brought home The Germs' first album. That's when I started getting into punk." Homme explained: "Fredo's a tight drummer. He can hold it all in and let it all go when it needs to be let go. He's the only one who played where Brant played, because Brant was the king of drumming to me."

Of the recent ups and downs in personnel that had occurred in the last few months, Josh later mused: "I was very grateful to do those Metallica shows in Australia, but it was the most confusing thing we've ever done. It was such a strange situation, it was Brant's last tour and we all pretty much knew it. We tried to grit our teeth, grin and enjoy it, and we did have a good time. But it was almost in reverse of what we were trying to do. Us trying to pull Brant back in, Australia just rattling our heads, playing with Metallica in front of 15,000 people. I mean, that many people is not really where we wanted to go with our music, just because it seemed so much less effective. And even playing with Metallica . . . mind-blowing, like playing with the President. So the whole thing for us was insane. And right after the tour finished, Brant left."

The chase for the right drummer had exhausted Homme to the point of almost no return, as he revealed: "You think you're the only one going, 'What's going on, what are we doing, what are we thinking, what are we expecting?' . . . trying to find a drummer and thinking, 'Fuck it, no band is worth this shit.'" Hernandez, who had arrived almost by chance (Homme: "This was after giving up and getting a call from Alfredo saying, 'Hey guys, do you wanna play?'"), had been a valuable boost to the band: "It was like the perfect move . . . finding Alfredo, someone who plays like he does, who we've all known for a long time, who Scott Reeder played with, and after looking so hard before him. He's changed the way we play."

With Hernandez and Reeder bringing their original sound to the by-now finely honed melodic and vocal abilities of Garcia and Homme, on the musical side Kyuss seemed to be ready to take the next step. However, the music industry – which the band had always professed to hate – was about to show its true colours. It turned out that the Chameleon label was having financial problems, and that it had been hoped that Kyuss could solve those problems, but by the close of 1993 the end of the road had been reached. On November 11, the company officially ceased trading. "It was a pretty big shock," said Homme, admitting, "I kinda think that I knew it was going to happen someday, but that we could be the label's saviour band . . . The morning before the closure, I'd had great conversations with people at the label."

Fortunately, all was not lost: based on its own successful joint venture experience with Chameleon in the past, the major label Elektra – then and previously home to Metallica, Mötley Crüe and AC/DC – stepped in and purchased the label and its artist roster. Kyuss were informed that *Sky Valley* would be delayed, but that it would certainly get a release, probably in March 1994, and all parties breathed a sigh of relief – tempered with the ironic air of the new situation of their being affiliated with a major record company. "We're just excited to get something out so we can start work on the next thing," Homme said at the time. "I'm in no rush, but at the same time, I don't want to wait around either."

On that score, the situation would get weirder before long. Steve Ralbovsky, then the senior vice-president of Elektra's A&R department – who would later find acclaim as the man who signed acts such as The Kings Of Leon to RCA – heard the still-unreleased *Sky Valley* and told the press, "By the time I sat down and listened to the album, I said, 'Where the fuck have I been?'" He also asked members of Nirvana and Metallica, as well as agents and managers, what they thought of Kyuss' potential, and was surprised by how effusive those polled were. After meeting the band in December 1993 in their Coachella Valley rehearsal studio, Ralbovsky offered to sign them directly to Elektra. The band agreed, with the only fly in the ointment being their search for management: Kyuss' old manager had left or been fired just previously (details of this development remain elusive). Ralbovsky, elated by his new signing, explained, "I think alternative and metal have to be approached simultaneously . . . I don't want the fans at metal radio to feel slighted, but there's also a similar free-spirited feel to Kyuss that some of the 'new hippie' bands have. And the guys in Kyuss are punk-rock kids beneath it all." Homme agreed with this approach, adding that the band's unusual sound "is our curse and our blessing. I don't know where we are yet, and I love that most of the time. Other times I go, 'What the fuck – can't we get it right?'"

But they *had* got it right. In just over a year Kyuss had replaced half their personnel, and signed a major record deal. Could the future repay the expectations that now surrounded them?

CHAPTER 3

1994–1995: The Spaceship Crashes

"1993 was a fucked-up year," said John Garcia in early 1994. "With the record already being recorded, then the company going under, us canning our manager and losing our drummer – yep, it was a pretty fucked-up year." The singer was optimistic, however, adding: "Now we got a kick-ass manager, a kick-ass drummer and a new label, so things are starting to roll again. We're glad that everything happened when it did instead of five years down the line . . . It was early enough for us to keep our heads together, still respect each other. In fact, we've convinced ourselves that Kyuss never existed before this line-up!" The more sanguine Scott Reeder reasoned: "Everything that's happened has brought us together and made us stronger. Good things come to those who wait – and we waited this long . . ."

What the good things were was obvious. Kyuss were now that rare thing: a cult musical act whose name was mentioned in the highest circles (witness the endorsement of Nirvana and Metallica, the two biggest rock bands of the era – discounting the contextually *very* discountable Guns N'Roses) but were not yet subjected to the rigours of personal fame, as most of the public hadn't yet heard of them. The delayed release of *Sky Valley* on February 27, 1994 had been repaid with much critical respect: the band were delighted with the album and didn't hold back from praising its many qualities. It emerged that the departed Bjork (whose drumming on *Sky Valley* had been his last recorded work with Kyuss) had suggested that the production be transferred from Chris Goss, whose approach had made *Blues For The Red Sun* so scintillating, to the stoner-rock man of the moment, Monster Magnet frontman Dave Wyndorf. However, as Homme explained: "I like working with Chris Goss a lot. And I don't wanna break that off just yet."

Goss himself explained of *Sky Valley* that, "It's an open horizon, and nothing sounds closed in," while John Garcia added: "Black Sabbath was heavy, but it sounded indoors. Kyuss sounds like it's outdoors."

"I think stylistically everyone [in the band] has tried to carve his own niche," Homme said. "I think there's a definite, audible difference to all three of our albums. On the first one a lot of the stuff was recorded when I was 16 years old, so I was just finding my way on the guitar. The way I'm tilting now is that I'd like to be able to sing a lot of the leads I play. I want to get to the point where I'm looking over at the rest of the band members and my guitar is just singing. I'm not talking about solos. I just want everything to flow and be kind of groovy and heavy; in between chords and bridges when you throw in a little line that just sings.

"I tried to take it to the next level without reinventing the wheel. We tried to stay the same sonically. We went to the same studio, we used the same equipment. It's the same band playing some new songs. I'm not in a race with anyone. For the most part, the more I try to work out songs, the more I paint myself into a corner. Songs will either finish themselves, or they won't get played – and that's OK too. I think you can feel the difference between something that came out real smooth and something that I worked on. When I bring in the song, I can already hear the whole thing in my head. If someone has other parts in the same key or in the same groove, we kind of set up this frame-work and then we fill it in."

Josh was later asked what Sky Valley actually was: "It's a big area, with no one living there," he said. "It's like a house, two miles of desert, then another house, a gas station. But the area is huge. That's where all the Hell's Angels used to live, where all the meth labs still are. There's a midget colony out there. There's spas and retreats, like the Heaven's Gate bullshit. And we used to throw parties out there because it was such a shitty place, nobody would ever fuck with us up there. It's the ass end of our town." As Scott Reeder put it, "Where we live is considered the boonies, but that town is *really* out in the boonies."

The album hadn't suffered from spending a year in the vaults at Elektra since its recording. The bassist explained, "It still sounds fresh after a year. It's everything we are. The way we've been brought up, the way we live, what we listened to when we were kids: Bob Dylan, The Beatles, King Crimson, Pink Floyd, Jethro Tull."

Grand names to drop, indeed. But not without reason: *Sky Valley* contains elements of all those bands' work, starting with the progressive approach of Floyd and Crimson. The album is laid out in three suites of songs, which a CD player can't subdivide – thus forcing the listener to absorb the whole album in three large bites. Part I contains three songs, 'Gardenia', 'Asteroid' and 'Supa Scoopa And Mighty Scoop'. The first of these is a dark, atmospheric song built on a deep riff with more top end than previous albums, thanks to Goss' improved production. It's Homme's song and is the sound of Kyuss evolving. 'Gardenia' sounds like an adult way of making music, even though those concerned were only in their early twenties. Almost seven minutes in length, the song's highlight comes when it breaks down to a semi-solo, semi-rhythm approach loaded with plenty of wah pedal. 'Asteroid' is quieter and more sinister, full of dark, decaying chords with feedback-heavy tones. There's a dash of screeching fret-buzz and total unstructured anarchy for some seconds near the beginning, before the musicians drop into virtual silence and a horror-movie motif appears. The fast, snaky riff at the song's close is as fast as anything Kyuss had done to date, and ends suddenly. 'Supa Scoopa And Mighty Scoop' boasts a jerky, one-note riff intro before billowing into the classic Kyuss sound. There's a tempo change and some counterpointed guitar parts, along with some very Hendrix-like solos. At its finish, there's an extended stop-start section full of ever-lengthening silences.

Part II begins with '100°', which is a change in pace and direction, with its live-sounding, chicken-scratch, almost funk guitar and extended wah wah-laden solo. At one point Reeder seems to have roused from his deep, deep groove to almost funky levels of activity. "One hundred!" screams Garcia, before another sudden ending. 'Space Cadet' leads in with some expert bass chords, which provide an Eastern, sitar-like tone. Seven minutes of trippy, ambient guitars sit on top of that bass riff: the song is an excellent, total departure from the aggression of before. There are some almost folky elements and a slight indication that the song could build to power-ballad size, but of course Kyuss avoid that particular mistake and the song remains a thing of understated beauty. 'Demon Cleaner' is again more mellow, making this section the relaxed central core of the album: Garcia's singing is calm, and Goss lays off the big production techniques, allowing space for the instruments to breathe. However, this feels a bit weird at first: we're so used to huge, soft guitars that when there's a space, it feels a little as if there's a hole in the sound.

The four-song Part III combines the bigness of I with the atmospherics of II. 'Odyssey' has a relaxed guitar intro with a bass swamped in studio effects, before a big riff comes firing back in. Later, the drums and bass relax to a Grateful Dead-like improvised middle section, and there are more Eastern sounds. 'Conan Troutman' is more punkish and less disciplined, with a thrash-metal drumbeat from Hernandez. So far, it seems that every album had to have a punk song – and this is it, with the drummer giving it all he's got. The ending is violent, with deep, string-bend riffs. 'N.O.' – a cover of an old Yawning Man song – is similarly aggressive, although it has a warm Deep Purple-esque sound that becomes a classic desert drone. Finally, 'Whitewater' – nine minutes of solid riffage – fluctuates between angry and mellow sections and winds up with a spinning drone, rather like The Doors' 'Riders On The Storm'. There's also a comedy fragment of a song at the album's end – simply a joke fairground organ with someone proudly repeating "You can and will lick my doodle" or words to that effect.

Brant Bjork remembered that the sessions had not gone well initially: "I remember the first night recording *Sky Valley*, the first track we were recording was 'Odyssey', which we had been playing for quite a while. We kind of knew what was going on with that song . . . with Kyuss, we would usually go to tape within the first, maybe second take. [But] with that one it was the third take, and we just weren't gelling. And I remember Josh was about ready to put his guitar through the wall because the sound wasn't what he was going for. I just remember it being very frustrating . . . You see, the thing with *Blues*, we had everything pretty much down. We knew what we were going to do. *Sky Valley*, we had no idea. We had like three songs that were solid, and the rest we improvised. The three that were solid were 'Odyssey', '100°', and . . . shit, that might have been it. 'Demon Cleaner' was just totally off the cuff, I remember we just went for that. That was a first take. 'Gardenia' was pretty solid, although we would jam that live so much. It never really had a beginning or end, so we finally just sorted that out and went to tape with that. 'Whitewater' was kind of the same deal."

So does *Sky Valley* stand up to *Blues For The Red Sun*? Well, it's a more introspective album, on which Homme and Garcia have refined their expression for the sake of subtlety and on which Reeder and Bjork stretch out more than Oliveri did on the two previous records. All this makes for an intriguing listen, but it doesn't quite have the luxurious, curled-up vibe of *Blues For The Red Sun*, nor that album's horizon-straddling jams. But it remains a must-listen.

Either way, the band didn't care for this kind of analysis. "There really isn't anything to say about it," Garcia said in an interview at the time. "Just don't try to figure it out. You can't. I can't. If you try to, you'll wind up going fuckin' nuts . . . It's 99.9% emotion. There's not much intellect involved in what we do." Reeder, asked if Black Sabbath were a major influence – and there's elements of Iommi and co. all over Kyuss' vast sound – replied: "The Sabbath comparison doesn't bother me, really. I'd rather that than many other things." Garcia added: "I had heard Black Sabbath as a kid growing up. Never into them, as I said. I was listening to Earth, Wind And Fire when Black Sabbath was doing their thing. And it wasn't till we started playing, and it wasn't till people started saying we sounded like Sabbath, that Josh finally put on a Black Sabbath record and was like, 'Yeah, I can see the similarities.'" Homme: "Like, the first seven albums with Ozzy, I know all those songs. I've heard 'em a bunch of times, but I don't buy 'em 'cause I don't want them to be in my head."

An aspect of Kyuss' working methods that lent their music a degree of mystique was the fact that they usually declined to print their lyrics. Garcia later explained that the point was to accept the music wholesale: "Don't try to sit there and try to decipher my poetry . . . All of my lyrics, they're pretty much along the same lines . . . whatever they mean to you, they mean to you. If you were to listen to 'Green Machine' or 'Odyssey' or even 'Thong Song', some songs you can actually figure out the lyrics and you can write them down. Some of them make sense and some of them don't – the majority of them don't make any sense, at least to the average listener – whether it be a 14-year-old kid that listens to a Kyuss tape in mom's BMW on the way to school, or whether it's the 45-year-old speed freak who cooks speed out in Sky Valley. In that sense it's like, 'Whatever, you have the lyrics.'"

One thing that many reporters focused on, now that Kyuss had been prominent for a couple of years, was the desert origins of the band members. In a vain attempt to convince the city slicker writers that the desert's influence was too huge to encapsulate in words and too nebulous to fit into a soundbite, Garcia tied himself into knots of protest, saying: "We were really stoned . . . We went into the studio and did what we fucking wanted to do. It's everyone doing their own fuckin' thing all at once. We don't have a concept of anything here. To me, Kyuss is four guys from the fuckin' desert playing in a band together, and that's all it is. Everybody gets their own feeling out of it. That's the way it should be . . . If you go out to the middle of the desert and sit there, you can see every colour in the world. And when you sit there for a while, baking under the sun, dust in your face, that's Kyuss in a fuckin' nutshell."

It did no good. Everyone wanted to know what Kyuss were about. Asked about politics and whether, like the newly successful rap-metal band Rage Against The Machine, Kyuss had fixed views, Homme laconically batted the issue aside: "Well, they do that and that's cool, whatever . . . but I'm not into that. Not for us. We're the non-preachers, we speak for the non-preaching." As for the suddenly cool desert-rock scene, Josh explained: "It's what the bands in this scene *won't* do that will make it the cool scene. Hopefully not a lot of people will come here. Instead, the bands will travel. Desert bands will leave, go on tour, make their records, and come back, and it will remain low-key." It emerged that MTV had placed a request to send a camera crew to a desert party, no doubt hoping to unearth a cache of sand-dune-riding hippies and punks living it up. Kyuss had declined the offer, with Garcia explaining: "I could sit here and try to explain it all day. But you have to be there, really, even grow up there to truly understand everything that goes on in the desert. Full-on dust in your face! When you take a drink of your beer and there's fuckin' mud in your cup, you laugh and go, 'This is great!' "

Scott Reeder: "It's the clearest place in the world, too: I played a party that had to be at least four miles from anything or anyone and somebody fucking complained. The police came and broke it up. Guess it must have been the animals." "These parties played a huge part in our development," Garcia added. "Because we all come from the same area, we all have that same background, the peace, the desert, the generator parties, the mountains, the canyons. And that's a huge part of

Kyuss, where we're from." New recruit Hernandez (of whom John had said, "He's great, man. He's an amazing drummer, you know, and he's also from the desert, born and raised. We're really lucky to have him") wasn't slow to offer an opinion: after all, of all the musicians, he had been a desert musician the longest. "Playing outside anywhere is very inspiring. It's like playing the best club in the world. It's unreal. Non-stop partying, hangin' out all day, foolin' around, chasing geckos, havin' frog fights, dust in your face . . ."

After four March dates with Fishbone and Biohazard, Kyuss made their second trip overseas, playing to a larger-than-expected crowd at London's Borderline venue. They would return to the UK for a set at the Underworld in September in advance of a 10-date US tour with bands such as Dinosaur Jr. and Ween. The band was beginning to gain a name for itself, with Garcia's emotional, versatile vocals a major discussion point. At one stage the rock band Karma To Burn, an established act signed to Roadrunner, made overtures to the singer, hinting that he might like to jump ship, as Garcia recalled: "Karma To Burn asked me to come out and sing on one song of theirs. I wound up doing it. Elektra let me do it and Roadrunner let me do it. I went out there and did one song for them. As time went on, they wanted me full-time. They pretty much wanted me to quit Kyuss and come to sing for them full-time. That was something that at the time I couldn't do. I was singing in Kyuss and that's my main love and that will always be my one true love: Kyuss, and Josh and Scott and Alfredo and Brant and Nick and Chris Cockrell. Those guys . . . they devirginised me . . . I love them, all of them, like my brothers. I couldn't leave."

Despite his loyalty, Garcia apparently gave the matter some serious thought, even performing live with KTB at one point: "They called me and said they wanted me. I said there's no reason I can't be in two bands, it's been done before. I went out there and sang on eight of their songs. We never recorded anything. We went on a short tour down south and played Kentucky, West Virginia and all these states down south. They wanted 12 songs and Elektra would only let me do eight. So I told them, let's do eight. There's no rule that says there has to be vocals on every song. You know, there could be three instrumental songs. Look at Kyuss, it's a prime example of having something instrumental. [But] after they found that I couldn't do the 12 songs that they wanted, we parted and went our separate ways and it just didn't happen."

1994 passed in a flurry of tour dates, press interviews and more contact with new bands. Kyuss, now secure in their place in the middle of the alternative rock scene, played a memorable date at the Nassau Coliseum in Long Island on July 13 with the Reverend Horton Heat, Babes In Toyland and White Zombie. Lead Babe In Toyland, Kat Bjelland remembers: "Alfredo used to call me the White Mexican! They travelled in a trailer and in style. They had it down. Margaritas made fresh in the blender, good drugs . . . even a light show with fog inside the trailer once! The people they chose to surround themselves with also made a big difference. They were just a really solid group of 'dedicated to rock' people. Not an attitude among them. Good people – smart and funny!"

By the end of the year, plans were even being laid for the recording of another album to follow up *Sky Valley*. Asked why the band were in such a hurry to do even more recording, Josh laughed and said, "We just stay in our space, doing our own thing, and when the record company tell us that it's time to start working on a new album, we have enough stuff jammed so we can just go in and make one. They don't come in here and they don't say things about what we do!" Spring 1995 was taken up with recording (sessions stretched from March 1–20, longer than usual for Kyuss) and the new album, titled . . . *And The Circus Leaves Town* was released on July 11.

Once again Goss was the man chosen to produce the album, and once again Homme paid him the compliments he was due: "I love working with Chris, he's the shit," he said. "Christopher living and being down here has made it so we all feel, when we go in, that it's all right. That recording's going to be the one place where everything will be OK, and that makes you wanna be there, it makes you feel that you will be able to pull off anything that you wanna try in the studio." It seemed that *Circus* had been no easy ride: "This new recording was the toughest," Homme continued. "We look at this like a project. We wanted to see if we could consistently, without changing too much, change all the time. It was obvious what we had to do: doing it is not easy all the time, but we learnt an awful lot about ourselves with this record."

What *had* they learned? "We stick together more than ever now, we communicate a lot more and the four of us try and put that stuff aside, just take care of what needs to be taken care of and learn that this is just all a part of it. The perspective change is kind of like this: you don't have to say you love it, but you do have to do it. The quicker you can take care of it and cut other stuff off at the path, you actually see there's so much you can do." This had translated into an independent spirit of activity for Kyuss, even in day-to-day business: "Instead of having to do so many stupid photo shoots, we went and took our own pictures. There's so much you can do in eliminating aggravation from your lives and distancing yourselves from it. So we're actually more 'do-it-yourself' than ever before." It seemed even record-company issues weren't dampening Kyuss' spirits: "One thing I'm happy about is that through our relationship with Chameleon and Elektra we can turn around and say, 'OK then, what do we need to get done?' They say, we need a record and so boom! We go in, do one and send it to them with the cover already done. We do our own T-shirts, we're directing our own videos and all with our own cash. We save money and then buy a good mike here or a good piece of equipment there to the point where we're an island unto ourselves."

Asked if the album title had something to do with escaping the big city, Josh explained: "It means many things, and that's perhaps the least of them. In many ways things have increased for us, but we've been able to leave town and shed the shit. It's more about where we're headed, what we're trying to put together ourselves, in terms of what the band is and what we're meant to be. Europe's been great because we've been able to develop a style of touring for ourselves, where we've really started to almost enjoy touring, where you almost make it like a little travelling carnival. We try to bring that same sort of thing to someone's head, the rock'n'roll version of 'come in and make everyone forget' and leave town. I like the connections of mystery with the circus, that whole idea."

But there was only so far Josh would go with discussion of the new album: "I get reluctant to answer all those questions like, 'What does this song mean?', because to me it means one thing but to you, and you, and you, it could mean something totally different. Which would mean it's achieved its goal, to mean as many things to as many people as possible."

So how had the new album turned out, recorded so soon after the release (if not the actual studio sessions) of its predecessor? Well, for many Kyuss observers it was a case of the band making the same record as before, but it still being a damn good record. . . . *And The Circus Leaves Town* was loaded with the steaming heaviness of both *Blues For The Red Sun* and *Sky Valley*, with its first three songs, 'Hurricane', 'One Inch Man' (released as a single) and 'Thee Ol' Boozeroony', the expected gritty riff-heavy workouts. While these were atmospheric and thoughtful – 'One Inch Man' even had Garcia wistfully keening a repeated mantra of "Ever so lonely . . ." – there wasn't much in them that even the most devoted Kyuss fan couldn't find in their earlier albums.

It doesn't really change radically from this point on, although it's all good music if the generic Kyuss sound is to your taste. 'Gloria Lewis' is a slow, dark, trance-like burn through the vintage desert sound, as is 'Phototropic', a laid-back, sensitive doom anthem. 'El Rodeo' is a little more anarchic, with its knowingly sideways lead-guitar intro and crashing, descending chords, and 'Jumbo Blimp Jumbo' disguises itself in a fractured funk workout, but 'Tangy Zizzle' is back to the oceanic riff-mountain that anchors all of Kyuss' albums, distant vocals and all. 'Size Queen' is an overlong, bluesy song based on a strolling bass and Garcia's oddly processed vocals, and 'Catamaran' is another sweet, space-cadet trip of the kind that Homme and his band could knock out in their sleep. Perhaps the closer, 'Spaceship Landing', provides the album's only real new direction, stretching over 11 minutes in a seemingly never-ending jam. After 20 minutes of silence comes a hidden track, the superbly relaxed 'Day One', which features excellent, Beatles-like acid vocals and surely deserves better than to be tacked onto the album's end so carelessly.

Time has not been kind to . . . *And The Circus Leaves Town*, with Kyuss' critics usually referring to it as weak or uninspired. But perhaps the truth is that the band had run out of new ideas after four albums: at the time Homme spoke, unusually, of some difficulties when it came to managing the band's career. "Sometimes I feel like some of the stuff we're doing is pretty hard," he said. "Finding the right tour, because pretty soon you'll run out of Faith No Mores or other bands where you just think, 'Wow, we should play with them, it'd be a great show!' But I'd rather have it that way . . . We never felt in control of everything. It's such a circus, man . . . there's so much to it. You're constantly having to learn from your mistakes. Now we've become more self-sufficient. If we're gonna be a band then we want to present what our band is, and we're able to do that now more than ever before. We finally don't feel like we're anyone else's experiment. We're doing the experimenting! So it's been good to wait for things, like waiting to do the desert recording, because it'd just be us and no one else interfering."

As before, Kyuss' love affair with the Coachella desert was in full flame. Asked what Palm Desert was like, Homme remarked, "It's the type of place you move to only when you're ready. You can't just move from a big city and immediately expect to like this place. You've gotta know what it is, what you're getting into, to pull it off or you'll arrive, take one look around and be off very quickly." But he knew how far he could go before spiralling off into pretentious territory, adding: "It's not so much 'We are the desert' or some corny shit like that, it's more a case of we were dealt the desert because of where we grew up. We were dealt some beautiful scenery, some of the best places to try and cultivate ideas, it's so easy to access. We can go into the desert and take pictures of something amazing, alone, and it's free, it's just right there . . . I still go to the same places all the time and I'm continually blown away every time, it never ceases to make you feel small, make you feel in awe of things, things that aren't something that we've all done as a group of people."

Kyuss hadn't stopped recording after the *Circus* sessions: they had also laid down four extra songs to be used as B-sides for the 'One Inch Man' single and beyond. For this they located a studio out in Joshua Tree, even further out into the wilderness than their home towns. "We've talked about [actually recording in the desert]. That's definitely the next move," Homme continued. "We actually know the canyon we're going to. The heaviest thing we've done are those B-sides we just recorded in Joshua Tree. They're the most cut-loose-here-we-go, rawest form of what we're doing. We're not bummed because at first we had this idea that we were wasting all this stuff on B-sides, but then we realised it was positive in as much as 'Fuck it, carry on, who cares if that well's dry, we can always find another,' that line of thinking, y'know? We just had a really big perspective change in the Joshua Tree studios, where we don't necessarily feel invincible, but we know the only people that can throw us off track is us." One of these songs was a cover of Black Sabbath's 'Into The Void', which had been requested by their friend Frank Kozik, an artist, studio owner and indie record label proprietor. His label, Man's Ruin, was scheduled to release Kyuss' cover version at some point in the future.

In preparation for more recording, Kyuss moved their choice of studio away from the big professional facilities to a more down-home location: a venue called Rancho De La Luna, the converted Joshua Tree Park desert home of a Texan musician and producer called Fred Drake. Homme and Garcia had been introduced to Drake by an LA musician, Dave Catching, who worked at Drake's studio and played in a band called Earthlings? with Wool singer Pete Stahl. The sessions were memorable, as the band explained: "The place was covered from floor to ceiling with this amazing stuff Fred had bought at swap meets," said Homme, "and filled with old keyboards and organs and little amps. Little lights everywhere. Going to bed there was a 30-minute experience, 'cause you had to power down the building." Departed drummer Brant Bjork also recorded at Rancho De La Luna and added: "The kitchen is five feet from the mixing board, so Dave Catching would be in there cooking up an insane meal, you'd smell garlic and herbs and spices, and you're sitting there in the next room tracking drums and the bass. Fire pit out front, a hot tub up to the left, a huge view where you could see for miles. We did the [session] on mushrooms for three days straight . . . Were the drugs totally necessary? I have no fuckin' idea. There's a long list of things it takes to make music, and drugs is on there, but the list is not made in order of importance."

The meeting with Drake had been a turning point for Kyuss, as Homme recalled: "Dave Catching was friends with Fred – Fred had lived in LA, that's how Dave met Fred. Fred had moved out there, to get away. Dave turned us on to that place and Kyuss went out there and did this thing for Man's Ruin where we just basically took mushrooms for three days straight. That was probably the best Kyuss session ever, with the gnarliest Kyuss songs ever. Once we met Fred, that was it. I just started going there, all the time.

"Fred was one of the most special people I've ever run into through music. He was this tall, skinny cowboy with a hat, kinda like the Marlboro Man. He didn't look like people probably thought. They probably thought he'd be this bearded, longhair, hippie dude in the middle of the desert. But he couldn't be further from that. You're sitting up there after a long night of recording, and he's already up at 6:30 in the morning having coffee, he's got his cowboy hat, he's already fed his horse, he's got his cowboy boots on, he's already been to the swap-meet and bought four new things. He was always burning a joint, all day. Had a nice even keel. He was sophisticated, he was smart, he had a great sense of humour. Just really mellow. He was definitely the captain of that ship."

By the end of 1995 . . . *And The Circus Leaves Town* had sold well in Europe to Kyuss' ever-growing fanbase, with over 12,000 copies shifting in its first week in Germany alone. Even if the band might never break their home country, a future of overseas shows seemed viable with '95 being Kyuss' most successful touring year; a European trek in the spring took in most of the continent, a US jaunt through July with White Zombie, Babes In Toyland and the Reverend Horton Heat, a German festival slot in August and a further two-week sweep through Europe which finished in Italy on September 9. The band was on the point of a one-month US tour with their heroes Monster Magnet when, in October 1995, they suddenly parted ways for good.

Homme, Garcia, Reeder and Hernandez all had much to say on the subject in ensuing months and slowly a picture emerged of what had happened. Apparently, the band had not argued, nor run out of money, nor been stabbed in the back by the industry: with everything going for them, in true perverse desert style, they had simply got bored. "It was just the right time," said Homme soberly. "We made four records, and we just wanted to have a good solid ending with a finishing point." He stressed that mainstream success had never been Kyuss' goal: "We played for respect, mostly. We deliberately sabotaged any chance at selling records or being famous. People dug the fact that we were playing for music's sake." Some of the motivation for the split came from the old punk values that inspired, and hindered, any band which espoused them: "I came from a scene that's very similar to Seattle," Homme continued. "I'd come home after touring, and someone would say, 'What's up, rock star?' But instead of saying, 'If you don't like it, forget it,' I'd sit down for, like, two hours trying to explain what we're doing to some jerk.

"I didn't want to just play one type of music any more," mused Homme. "Kyuss was everything, too. When you're in a band since you're 15 years old, by the time you're 22 you're like, 'This is all I know, this is not a good idea.' There weren't any hard feelings at all. It was like, 'The band's breaking up, I'll see you at the barbecue on Sunday.'

"Kyuss was very deliberate in some ways. With bands we liked, we always listened to their first couple of records before they began to change. So we were very adamant about playing heavy groove music and never letting that change. By the same token, you can paint yourself into a corner. We were extremely concerned with the 'they' theory. It was like what would 'they' think? Will 'they' say we've sold out? That's not a real good cycle to get yourself into because 'they' will never be happy and you'll never know who 'they' really are."

Josh looked back with some exhaustion on the rollercoaster career of Kyuss: "Kyuss' first record was when I was 17. We did *Blues* when I was still 18; 19, *Sky Valley*; 20, *Circus*. And then we broke up when I was 21. On the last couple of tours, Kyuss was starting to eat itself anyway. I was disillusioned. Punk Rock had blown up in my face. What I thought it was, was a total lie. And then I heard Iggy Pop's *Lust For Life* and *The Idiot* for the first time. If you're a band on tour, those lyrics hit you – they were so true. And then I heard The Stooges' records. And those records said everything I wanted to say better than I could say it. It made me want to quit. So I did."

One of the more revealing and philosophical analyses of the entire Kyuss freak show came not from Homme or Oliveri, both of whom would be quizzed endlessly on the subject for years to come, but from ex-drummer Brant Bjork: "*Blues For The Red Sun* was the classic Kyuss record . . . And we just kind of imploded after that. Musically and spiritually, I think *Blues For The Red Sun* captured what we were all about. That was a tough record to follow up. Some of us thought that we had to change, some of us thought that no, we could just stay and do whatever the fuck we wanted. Some of us wanted to get more psychedelic. Some of us wanted to be more straightforward and just rock and jam.

"People come up to me – and they have for years – [saying] 'What happened to Kyuss? What happened to Kyuss? Yadda yadda.' And I'm like, 'Dude, Kyuss was a fuckin' freak of nature anyway.' I mean, we were young kids, we were young. When we were doing *Blues For The Red Sun*, we were 18, 19 years old. We were just punk kids from a small desert town that didn't know anything else. We grew up and we just worshipped our records, like kids should worship their rock'n'roll records. And when you do, and you have nothing else to do, scary things happen, you know! And that's what we did. And someone, somehow gathered us up and organised us enough to put us on tape and put us in a fuckin' van to get out and play live shows. And we just went along for the ride. We had no idea what we were doing. It's amazing that band lasted as long as it did. So it was just natural that we would just fall apart."

With the dust settling over Kyuss, the ex-members returned to the desert to get their heads together. It seemed as though the story might be over.

CHAPTER 4

1996–1998: Teenage Hand Models

1996 was a strange year for American alternative rock.

Kurt Cobain had been in his grave for two years, and grunge had died with him. Punk was restricted either to the hardcore scene which had been bubbling away on the East and West coasts for almost two decades, or to gurning, semi-punk bands like Green Day, who had yet to be swamped by the tide of pop-punk acts that would plague the charts before too long. Metal was torn in two, with the newly christened nu-metal scene focused on the hip-hop angst of Korn, the ardent strife of Rage Against The Machine and the occasional bit of art freakery from dissidents such as Tool.

Kyuss had been influential during their short lifespan. A whole musical movement, variously labelled stoner rock, desert rock, fuzz rock and so on, with varying degrees of accuracy, was building momentum, with fans of the genre's tranced, super-heavy atmospheric grind looking for the next scene leader to emerge now that Garcia, Homme and co. were out of the picture. But if fans were expecting the members to bounce back with a new collaborative project, they had a long wait on their hands – at least on the surface. As Kyuss' principal songwriter, Josh Homme was offered a deal with Elektra – a deal he rejected. Tired of the endless punk-rock guilt trips and the feeling that his music had reached its logical conclusion with Kyuss, he wanted out. But one last recording remained before he abandoned the desert: a session under the name Gamma Ray, a short-lived project that produced a seven-inch single (in a limited edition of 2,000), released by Frank Kozik's Man's Ruin label in early 1996. Laying down three songs – 'Gamma Ray', 'If Only Everything' and 'Born To Hula' – Josh handed over the tapes to Kozik and took off.

Asked why he had become so tired of music, Homme replied, "I would say I was disillusioned because the thing that I like the most – and the thing that got me into music – was the punk rock DIY mentality. Do-it-yourself is a great mentality, until everyone realises it's true. Then everyone starts doing it. I felt there were just so many bands and so many ways to skin a cat. I began to feel like it didn't make any difference whether I was here or not. I guess I stopped feeling like a snowflake.

"I quit for a year," he later mused. "It was me basically trying to . . . I needed to have a reason to put myself back in the fire. I felt like there were so many bands and, you know, in the days of, like, Hendrix and stuff that I grew up listening to, there weren't that many bands really. I felt, like, now there's thousands of bands and what does it matter what I have to say, and who cares? But then I realised after a year . . . that it was necessary for me and it didn't matter if it was necessary for anyone else. It wasn't about that, and it just took a while to figure that out – I mean, shit, I was only, like, 21 years old."

Homme's destination was Seattle, until so recently the home of a flourishing music scene but now slumped in artistic decay after the demise of grunge. "I knew the music scene was dead there," he said, "and I wanted to quit playing, and go to school." The wintry, rainy climate in Seattle was the perfect antidote to the oven-like environment of Palm Desert, and for a year – most of 1996 and into 1997 – Homme soaked it up, retreating to his Capitol Hill house when the weather got too harsh and occasionally playing music. Sometimes, however, the conditions got too bad for him, as he later related: "I lived in Seattle two separate times . . . I came from the land of sunshine, and it was always the winters that drove me out – by the end of winter, I would be like, 'I can't take it here any more!'"

But his self-imposed therapy worked. "I went to the one place I knew music was dead – Seattle," he said. "Grunge was over, and if the semblance of any good band or any scene started, everyone in Seattle just killed it. They were trying to destroy everything, they hated everything. I was like – perfect. So I went there to *not* play. I was trying to get off of my record label, Elektra. I had this plan to ask for a ridiculous amount of money to do demos, thinking they would just say, 'Fuck this,' and write it off. And they didn't. Instead they gave me the money! I thought, 'Well, I'll sing – that'll get me kicked off.' And it did."

Free of industry obligations, Homme also planned to expand his mind with a few college courses after he eventually returned from Seattle, but as time passed he inevitably found himself drawn to the area's musicians, now working in subtler, more diverse directions than full-on grunge. One such contact was Mark Lanegan, frontman of the respected alternative rockers The Screaming Trees. Too melodic to have been at the forefront of grunge and too dark in theme to have made much mainstream headway, the Trees maintained a low-level, degree of success, touring and recording constantly. Homme's first meeting with Lanegan came about through Dinosaur Jr.'s Mike Johnson, a musician with whom he had jammed sporadically alongside other local semi-luminaries such as Soundgarden's Ben Shepherd, former Monster Magnet guitarist John McBain and sometime Pearl Jam drummer Matt Cameron. "I met Josh through Mike Johnson," recalled the lugubrious Lanegan. "I asked Mike to go on the road with the Trees and he said, 'Absolutely not. You're insane. But my friend will do it.'"

After his break from the music scene, Homme agreed to join The Screaming Trees as a touring guitarist, on the 1996 Lollapalooza tour among other jaunts. He would spend almost two years with the band, an experience he later described with nostalgic pleasure as "Two years where all I did was smoke pot, play music and read books . . . It was great to be with the Trees and not have any responsibility. I was just there to add more sound to their live show. I played with them 'cause I don't like to be caged in as a musician and have people expect me to play a certain way or certain style. For me it was a great experience to be out with them. It was perfect 'cause it had nothing to do with Kyuss. It was about the subtle art of playing rhythm guitar and enjoying it."

"I was only gonna go for one tour," he explained. "I told them that I'll do Lollapalooza, and then I'm goin' home to go back to school. But then when I was driving [the] truck on Lollapalooza, somewhere in New Mexico, I had an epiphany. I was like, 'What am I doing, going to school? Who cares if there's too many bands? Who cares if no one else likes my music?' That's what I hated about punk rock, trying to anticipate what someone you don't know might think. The 'they' theory . . . I dropped all that shit, left that attitude behind.

"It was a desert epiphany. The desert is a place where you see forever, and you feel small. It makes everything that really is important stick out, and everything else is gone. Mountains in your life get shrunk back down to molehills."

Homme wasn't the only ex-Kyuss musician planning a musical change of pace. Singer John Garcia found himself still wanting to perform, and looked around for an outlet. "After Kyuss broke up, I was looking around for just anybody to play with, just to fuck around," he later recalled. Fortuitously, Garcia had met three musicians: guitarist Chris Hale, bassist Damon Garrison and drummer Brady Houghton. The four agreed to form a band, and chose a suitably desert-oriented name: "Slo-Burn was formed by pretty much all four of us . . . Almost this weird type of magic happened. We kept on playing together and things progressed and progressed, and we just kept fucking around and went in the studio and kept fucking around, then we sent around a few tapes, just to see what would happen. And a lot of things came out of it. I'm just kind of fucking around with them now and trying to get things up and off."

John had considered working once again with his old collaborators Karma To Burn, once Kyuss were out of the way. "After Kyuss split," he explained, "they came out to San Francisco and I hooked up with them up there, [but] they were on a different level than I was. They had just moved out from West Virginia and were, like, let's just see what happens. I needed more than that, I needed more of a commitment. I'm not talking bad about those guys, I love 'em.

"Kyuss was such a great band and we didn't get the recognition in my eyes that we deserved. Whether we sold five records or five million, I didn't care, but it wasn't there . . . it wasn't properly pushed, it wasn't available to all ears. It frustrated me that I was signed with the major label and nothing happened. It was one of the reasons why Kyuss broke up – pure frustration. Me and Josh were trying so hard. That guy, that guy . . . he taught me everything I know. Everything I know. Everything that I learned, knew, that I sung, sang, everything. He's my teacher. Hats off to him. He's got me on the right track.

"I talk to [Homme] pretty much every chance I get. We're still very close. I still talk to Scott Reeder almost every day. He's up in the studio now doing work with a lot of movies and stuff. Josh just got off the road with The Screaming Trees and he's trying to do a lot of producing right now. I was in the studio at Chris Goss', this studio called Monkey.

And Josh came over and we hung out and drank a couple of beers and smoked a joint, like we do. Like you know, Kyuss wasn't a drug band. We liked having an occasional beer or an occasional joint when we got off stage but it wasn't a major thing for us. We hung out again, and I go over there or he comes over here and we eat lunch or whatever."

The two also worked professionally on the little-heard Gamma Ray tracks: "He [Homme] flew me and Chris Goss up, he was living up in Seattle . . . I sang background vocals on 'Born To Hula'. But he did all the singing. Throughout all the Kyuss sessions he was on the other side of the glass when I was in the studio singing. This time I was at the board and he was on the other side of the glass. I laughed my ass off because I gave him such a hard time like he gave me . . . I was like, 'See what it's like, see what you put me through!' " Garcia mused on the quality of Homme's singing voice: "It was cool to hear him sing, he has a great voice. A lot of people trip out on his vocals because they're like, 'Wow, that's Josh.' As you know, Josh wrote most of the Kyuss songs, and he used to sing to me how the songs should be and some of the melodies, and I'd come in and put in my two cents. So it's weird because people hear Gamma Ray and they go, 'It's a trip hearing him sing,' but I've heard him sing all along since he was, like, 14. And it's kind of refreshing to hear him sing. I actually think he has a great voice. I always wondered throughout the entire Kyuss years why he even needed me.

"Josh just flew me up there to hang out, you know, hang out with an old friend – and I just wound up putting some vocals down for him. Those songs were, from what I understand, he told me in a strange sort of way . . . the next group of Kyuss songs before I got to them or Scott got to them, Brant or Alfredo got to them. It was pretty much Josh, and he popped it off himself and those were going to be the next group of Kyuss songs just without the original boys. It's all good.

"Some [of the] songs are a lot like Kyuss songs, they make you want to go out and kill somebody, and other times they make you want to go out and cry to an old girlfriend or cry to an old dog you had. It's all pretty emotional."

Garcia revealed that he had spent the time since the demise of Kyuss training and working as a veterinary surgeon, something he had wanted to do all his life. This ideally would run in tandem with his career as a musician: "I'd like to be able to make a living doing my music," he said. "I had a new car, a new house and everything – and I lost it all and I don't have anything. I'm not trying to make some kind of sob story, but sometimes you lose track and you lose it all. Once again I would like to have, for lack of better words, the American Dream. I would like to have my beautiful wife, five Great Danes, my cats, a truck, a bass boat in my garage and be able to restore a '56 Chevy from scratch. That's something that all comes along with money and if I can make a living like that from doing music, I'll do my best. But it's not something that's going to stop me from working with my animals. I'm in surgery five hours a day at a vet clinic and I make a pretty good living, I still have a few things. I'd just like to have that again."

The industry, it emerged, had been responsible for some of the issues that split Kyuss – even though, on the face of it, the band's tenure with Elektra seemed to have been both fortuitous and beneficial: "I'm 26," the singer remarked in evident annoyance, "and I'm not going to do this one more time and get fucked around like I have in the past – release something and after one month be put on a back burner and have Keith Sweat take the place of me. I don't want to talk bad about Keith Sweat, but I think the music I play deserves to be heard. I don't mean 'deserves to be heard' like it's the most fucking awesome music in the world. But for those who wanna feel what I'm feeling when I'm singing and playing and listening to it, it's there. And I want to make sure it's there for those people . . . Sometimes I go, 'Fuck it, no one needs to hear my shit, I'm fine doing what I want to do,' and I really am . . . but if I'm going to sign with a label, their job is to push the fuck out of it, down everybody's throat whether they like it or not. To have somebody kiss my ass and tell me, 'We got you on the Ozzfest,' to shut me up . . . that's not what I want. I want commitment. I want to know they're going to do their job right because I know I'm doing my job right, at least the way I want it to be done. Nothing or nobody is going to get in my way. If they do so, they pay the consequences, whatever that may be."

While Garcia tried several bands and studied his navel in the desert, Josh Homme returned to his own music. It emerged later that on his return to California from Seattle he had recorded enough material for an entire album – music which would be simpler and more direct than – but just as gripping as – the canon of Kyuss. His musical collaborators in those early days included much-admired contemporaries such as the aforementioned Mike Johnson, Matt Cameron, John McBain, and Victor Indrizzo of Redd Kross. His longest-standing colleague, however, was ex-Kyuss drummer Alfredo Hernandez.

By early 1997 Homme was also jamming regularly with his old friend Chris Goss. "Josh and I became fast musical friends," said Goss. "He'd come over and we'd pull out a couple of acoustic guitars and just go at it for hours and hours, usually outdoors. Jamming, talking, listening to music and smoking weed. He was trying to figure out what he wanted to do."

The issue of what to do next was made easier by the arrival of an unexpected musical accomplice. In the second week of March, Homme was playing a low-key slot at the South By Southwest Music Festival, an annual music and film event in Austin, Texas. In the next room was a chaotic gig from a band named Mondo Generator, which was the project of sometime Dwarf Nick Oliveri, now an ex-Kyuss alumnus of five years and counting. Homme was delighted to hear that his friend was nearby: "I said to some friends, 'Let's go see my friend Nick's band,'" Homme recalled. "We walk in, and Nick is completely naked except for a pair of black Converse [sneakers] and black socks. I'm exchanging glances with Fredo [Alfredo Hernandez]. Then Nick lights this piece of paper on fire, puts something in his mouth and turns around and blows fire right into the audience, right through all of these record people, and they're like, 'Ahhhh!' Then he throws the piece of paper that's on fire, and it bounces off this guy's chest, and he's like, 'Ahhhh!' I looked over at Fredo, and I'm like, 'Dude – I'm calling in Nick right now!'"

Always up for a challenge, Oliveri agreed to join forces with Josh once more on his as-yet untitled project. Asked what the hell he had been doing since leaving Kyuss in 1992, he sniggered: "I joined The Dwarves, and played guitar for one tour, but then everyone realised, 'God, you suck at guitar.' I just faked it, man. So I moved back to bass. I played on two Dwarves records, then came back to the desert from San Francisco 'cause I got thrown out of The Dwarves. Then I got rehired. Then I quit in '96. I went on tour with Slo-Burn, with John Garcia, and I stopped in Austin. I had a friend there I'd jammed with before in Baltimore, so I ended up staying with him and playing, and that's the beginning of my band Mondo Generator." Nick's need for off-the-wall zaniness hadn't abated since those early desert days of being the school 'living legend'. "I had two bands," he added. "I joined a band my friends already had called The River City Rapists that only did, like, four shows. We'd get boycotted. We'd call the news on ourselves . . ." Asked if he recalled the Kyuss records fondly, he laughed, accurately: "Shit, man, the Kyuss records after [I left] are cooler, anyway . . . Most of the time, I was just drunk. I just really wasn't vibing when I was younger."

Homme's earlier choice of band name – Gamma Ray – had come to nothing after another outfit (probably the German power metal band of the same name, but this has not been confirmed) asked him to drop it or face legal action. It was time for the new band, with all its enthusiasm and experience, to christen itself. The source of the new name ironically came from the man most responsible for Kyuss' success.

Chris Goss: "Josh called me from Europe in the middle of the night. He goes, 'Guess what I'm gonna call my new band? It's something you used to call Kyuss in the studio.' I couldn't remember. He says, 'Queens Of The Stone Age . . .'"

In summer 1997 the Dutch division of the rock and metal label Roadrunner assembled and released a compilation of new and forthcoming bands, calling it – somewhat naively – *Burn One Up: Music For Stoners*. It featured songs by established Kyuss-style drone-rock bands such as Karma To Burn, Fu Manchu (where Brant Bjork had laboured since his old band's split two years previously), Spiritual Beggars, Sleep, Cathedral and lesser-knowns such as Floodgate, Slaprocket and Blind Dog. The CD case bore a large sticker with the words, 'Featuring Josh Homme's (Kyuss) new band, Queens Of The Stoneage [*sic*]'.

While it afforded a platform for a debut release, *Burn One Up* also landed Homme's band with the dreaded 'stoner-rock' label, a tag which would weigh heavily on him in years to come. But this innocent, modest-selling album was responsible for much more: the impetus to make the new outfit a bona fide band. As Josh recalled, "I'd done a couple of songs to get kicked off Elektra. It was mostly by myself, that's where the idea started. Then I started hooking up with [Earthlings?'s] Dave Catching and we just started writing some songs. We happened to be in Amsterdam at the end of The Screaming Trees tour and this *Burn One Up* compilation came up. So we grabbed a couple of friends from this band, Beaver [also on the album], and recorded a song. That was so easy and casual that we were, like, well, maybe we should play these songs that I recorded before and turn it into a band."

Asked endlessly about the name, Homme said: "We had this other name, Gamma Ray, and someone threatened to sue me over the name. Chris used to call Kyuss 'the Queens Of The Stone Age', and it worked on so many levels. We thought people driving by a marquee and seeing Queens Of The Stone Age would make them giggle."

Chris Goss: "I had called them that a lot. You know, word playing. It actually got to the point where someone had even designed a figure that they thought was a 'queen of the stone age': a cement skeleton with a limp wrist!"

Alfredo Hernandez: "When Kyuss were recording their albums, Chris Goss would jump around and tell the guys that we all sounded like a bunch of queens of the Stone Age – and it just kept coming out, and every time it would be a laugh and a joke. He's a funny guy and so it kinda just became the name. I like it, it sounds good and it's catchy and it has something to do with the past – it's great."

However, once the words 'stone' and 'stoner' had become disseminated and conflated, the more the media assumed that Homme et al were just another bunch of bong-loving desert freaks (perhaps justifiably, given their past work in Kyuss). "If I had a choice, I would take that away," Homme responded. "Stoner rock, to me, is like saying the crucial element is drugs. And I don't believe that that's the case. I'm not an AA guy or anything, but at the same time I don't need any of that to make music . . . Hopefully you can listen to the Queens when you're angry, mellow, happy, sad, running around town. It's user-friendly. That was my one thing with Kyuss as well, that I felt like we had to play heavy and that was it. With this, we should be able to play what we think is good."

At one point Homme and the founder of the respected website Stonerrock.com got into a heated dialogue, sparked by an interview the singer had given in which he discussed the stoner-rock tag. As Homme explained: "He sent me a direct message to my girlfriend about one of my responses in an interview with *Kerrang!* magazine. Which was taken out of context in the *Kerrang!* interview but basically it was close enough to be correct. Because he was comparing punk rock to stoner rock. And I said that punk rock was this movement

[from] The Cramps, to Motörhead, to X-Ray Spex, to The Subhumans, to Black Flag, [who] were all liked by punks. It was this vague, huge thing with all these styles of music. But stoner rock is way more finite . . . but unfortunately it came out as if I was saying that stoner rock was insignificant as a whole.

"I have nothing against stoner rock, but in comparison to punk rock, there really is no comparison. But I think the stoner rock lists and stoner rock sites are really cool. It's about people loving music and it's a labour of love. But if anyone thinks that they're going to build a box around me, try to shut the lid, expect me to get in, crawl in there, get in the foetal position, and lock the lid – then you're out of your mind. Kyuss never did that, Queens has never done that. You expect me to do it now because you want me to. Then you must be crazy. You must not have heard anything I've ever played. Or you must never have understood any of it. I would never put down the sites or the bands. But I don't think that it's good enough for the sites or the bands. It just doesn't do them justice."

Revealingly, it seems that the term itself was invented by record company executives, allegedly at Roadrunner, as Homme explained, "Just that you know, I was at this meeting where they were throwing around this term. They asked me what do I think and I just said, 'I think it's fucked.'"

The key attribute of Homme's new band was that the songs were different from those of Kyuss. Where the older, Garcia-led band had been a crushing behemoth with weighty riffs straight from the Sabbath stable, the new outfit was sharper, cleaner, more focused and much less conservative, as Josh put it: "I'm still into heavy rock music, but it's going to be way more diverse, I think. I want to fill the gaps – whatever isn't going on in music, I want to go over there . . . I think the only way to make something truly heavy is if not every other song is heavy, too. It's like vanilla, man, and I just think we'd be better off skipping vanilla." Of the stoner-rock tag, Homme again bluntly stated: "We hate it. That phrase took off in Europe, but I mean we're not a stoner-rock band. What is that? If anything, it's something we were doing four years ago before they called it stoner-rock. What am I gonna do? Call everybody and say, stop the madness? I just show up and play, you know."

'Show up and play' could have been the motto of Homme's next project, a loose collective recording project comprising songs created by a bunch of disparate musicians and lumped under the term 'Desert Sessions'. These sessions – which first came together in August 1997 and form a significant part of the Queens' recording activities to this day – covered a wide musical base and were evidently a refreshing change for the musicians involved – as a change from the restrictions which inevitably shackled their main bands. "Desert Sessions is good for musicians," reported Homme, "because you get with a bunch of people you do and don't know, but these are amazingly talented people, and hear things done in a way you never would have thought of, and now you have a chance to. And you play for the sake of music."

Those first sessions are now the stuff of Queens-related legend. Alongside Homme, Oliveri and Hernandez, the recordings were attended by Chris Goss, the ever-reliant Brant Bjork (now a full member of South Californian rock band Fu Manchu), the Lallis from Across The River and Yawning Man and various members of Monster Magnet, Soundgarden, Eleven and Hole. Long-time associate, Dave Catching of Earthlings? was also on hand for recordings such as a cover of The Groundhogs' 'Eccentric Man'.

"Desert Sessions is just a musical experiment," Josh explained. "Some musicians know each other, others don't. You sterilise them and mentally test them and then ship them out to the desert in wood crates and get them to play together and switch instruments and write songs on the spot. They don't have to go on tour and there are no obligations. It's really cool. When I see reviews of the CDs that we've released from these sessions I laugh, because it's not meant for any of that. It's purely for listening. It's also kind of like a recording school for me. I don't see why it should stop. There's an endless supply of cool musicians out there. If someone came up to me and said, 'Do you want to show up for a weekend and play whatever instrument you want and whatever you want?' I would like that."

Once sessions had come unsteadily to a halt, with the musicians recording and jamming as long as they fancied before wandering off again, Homme turned his attentions to his new band. A Queens show (or, in reality, an impromptu jam) had taken place in the summer at a Palm Desert restaurant on Highway 111 called El Café de Mexico, with about 25 friends in attendance. But the band's first real gig was scheduled for November 20, 1997 at Seattle's OK Hotel, where several friends and acquaintances were eager to hear Homme's latest work. The set-list consisted of new songs-in-progress – 'These Aren't The Droids You're Looking For' (a line from *Star Wars* character Obi-Wan Kenobi, as geeks everywhere will know), 'The Bronze', 'How To Handle A Rope', 'Walkin' On The Sidewalks', 'Teen Lambchop', 'Avon' and 'Mexicola' – many of which would emerge in fuller form the following year.

1997 finished with the release on Man's Ruin of a now difficult-to-find split EP containing three Kyuss songs and three Queens Of The Stone Age tracks – the first since the appearance of the *Burn One Up* compilation. The Kyuss tracks had been recorded two years earlier and began with a near-psychedelic version of Black Sabbath's 'Into The Void', along with two apparent tributes to Mario Lalli's new band Fatso Jetson, 'Fatso Forgotso' and 'Fatso Forgotso Phase II'. The second of these is a heavy, more classically Kyuss song than the others, as Garcia's vocals on the Sabbath song aren't quite as successful as the original Ozzy version, despite being allegedly recorded on 'musharitas' (tequila margaritas with magic mushrooms). However, the three Queens songs were promising, if less than consistent: 'If Only Everything' would later resurface as 'If Only' and, while it isn't as developed as that particular standout track, it shows how far the band had come since the unilateral, crushing approach of Kyuss. The arrangement is based on a stop-start rock riff with a busy, semi-funk bass-line that is light years away from the deft but straitjacketed playing of Scott Reeder, for example. 'Born To Hula', a slight song featuring a looped siren sample that becomes irksome after a few plays, benefits from the backing vocals of Garcia, and 'Spiders And Vinegaroons' is a trance-like drone without much to offer after the first couple of minutes.*

The split EP was, in retrospect, an interim stage between the last vestiges of Homme's songwriting in Kyuss and the newer, tighter, more melodic approach he was to employ with Queens Of The Stone Age. The same could be said of the first two volumes of the Desert Sessions, released in February 1998. Perhaps this is why both releases

---

* Homme: "A vinegaroon is like a scorpion-like, spider-like thing, and if it bites you, you get that vinegar flavour [in your mouth]." The intimidating vinegaroon, or giant whip scorpion, must have been one of the more unusual features of growing up in the Coachella desert: under the right chemical influence, these almost extraterrestrial-looking creatures would scare the hell out of anyone.

are interesting rather than essential. What is clear is how much Homme had tired of the unfocused, wilfully 'desert' approach of Kyuss, wanting to hone his songwriting down to a tighter, more poppy style, as he commented at this time, "After jamming so much, you just want to hear yourself play something succinct and to the point. Step in, take a punch and step out."

The new material, as yet unheard (apart from the early version of 'If Only') was going down well in a live situation: after another show at the OK Hotel in February 1998, Josh remarked with what might have been deliberately masked insouciance: "We're expecting nothing, really. It's good to see that there are a couple of hundred people at the shows. We've tried to prepare ourselves for five people." Although such an indifferent result would have been unlikely – bearing in mind the *Burn One Up* compilation and its proud cover proclamation naming 'ex-Kyuss member Josh Homme' – the band were clearly ready to fall by the wayside in the wake of the stoner-rock boom.

However, the industry thought differently. Support came, not from a major label, but from indie territory. After seeing QOTSA at a local gig, Pearl Jam guitarist Stone Gossard (no stranger to new band start-ups, with his cult side project Brad) offered Homme a deal with his small label Loosegroove. The Queens were delighted and relieved. Josh Homme: "We weren't looking to be on a major label because we wanted it to be kind of casual and art-related. They let us do whatever we want . . . With Loosegroove, we don't have to sell a million records or have that weird pressure. [The majors] play games, and we play music. It feels better to be a big fish in a small pond. We're not in a rush, we just want to do some cool stuff and not get fucked with."

Homme's decision was to release the material he had recorded the previous year with Hernandez and Goss as a QOTSA debut album, followed by touring. At about the same time as the release of the album, Frank Kozik's Man's Ruin label released an EP, this time a split with the band Beaver* (yes – 'split Beaver'). The Queens contribution was 'The Bronze' and 'These Aren't The Droids You're Looking For', neither of which would appear on the album (a sign of the collector's mentality that Homme still retained). The EP appeared on CD and pale blue vinyl 10″ and was available in the US only, although expensive

---

* Beaver contributed 'Absence Without Leave' and 'Morocco'.

import issues were snapped up worldwide. Of the project, Alfredo Hernandez explained: "It was thought up way back when we were getting the band together – Beaver are really good friends of ours from a little section of Amsterdam, and we got them to open some shows for us when we were in Kyuss, and we just kept in touch."

While excitement built among the Kyuss and related fanbases in the wake of Loosegroove's press releases, the band honed their act in June with three San Francisco dates with Mario Lalli's new band Fatso Jetson and Acid King. A trip to the UK in August included a set at the Garage in north London supported by doom-metallers Orange Goblin and Iron Monkey, giving the still-nostalgic British Kyuss fanbase much to salivate about. But it was the imminent QOTSA album which was raising the most expectation. The self-titled release produced by Josh fuelled speculation among music pundits who had heard of Kyuss and Homme – helped along by associates such as John Garcia. Homme's old cohort had some words to say on the state of rock music: "I throw on MTV every once in a while and I get sick and tired of seeing No Doubt . . . But hats off to them for cutting their hearts out and doing the best that they can to do something like this. I don't even know the music scene right now, [but] I do know one thing . . . it's lacking bands like Kyuss, Slo-Burn, Masters Of Reality, the Melvins . . . it's lacking. There's a big void that needs to be filled and it will be filled by either a band like Masters, or Kyuss or Slo-Burn or the Melvins or the Foo Fighters or something like that. It's going to be filled and it's going to be filled in a big way.

"One day, mark my fucking words," he added, "something's going to pop off with me and Josh. I can promise that. One day something will be released in the next 10 years. If he were to walk in the room right now I would give him the shirt off my back and offer him a beer. I love him like my brother. He's got something up his sleeve and when it does come out to the public it's going to be fucking major."

Josh had a few simple words to place before his public: "This is an announcement. This is gonna be heavy, but it's gonna go out there, too."

In September the truth behind his words was revealed – in abundance.

CHAPTER 5

1999–2000: Feelgood Hits

LANDING loudly on CD players (the Loosegroove issue) or turn-tables (the limited-edition black, yellow and green vinyl LP licensed to Man's Ruin) in September 1998, *Queens Of The Stone Age* made an immediate impact. It starts with 'Regular John', the most Kyuss-like song on the record. "Open up your eyes!" pleads Josh repeatedly, his vocals left low in the mix – just as John Garcia's had been on Kyuss albums – on top of a long, warm, trance guitar riff that loops and turns just as before. However it's a more condensed song than the famous space jams which had so typified the old band, making its entrance and exit with a certain dignity without falling apart at the seams.

'Avon', a more structured, droning song with a strolling riff at its core, is three minutes of a figure swelling under Homme's distant, near-falsetto keening, laden with echo, and is one of the darkest songs on the album. Its sudden ending plugs straight into the unexpectedly funky stop-start contemplation of 'If Only', brushed up from its earlier EP appearance (as 'If Only Everything') and given a subtler overall sheen than the riff-heavy depth that the earlier material offered. 'Walkin' On The Sidewalks' takes a different approach altogether, with the fat, slightly overdriven bass-line (credited to Carlo, or Carlo Von Sexron, but probably courtesy of either Josh or Chris Goss, given that Oliveri joined Queens after the sessions had been completed) pushing along an unusual, hooky guitar figure that lurches left and right for a few seconds before settling into a background, ambient drone beneath a bluesy solo.

The album changes direction again: 'You Would Know' is a para-noid, spiralling track with none of the bludgeon or bluster of Queens' heavier songs. A wailing guitar underpins an equally keening vocal and, all in all, it's one of the weirder songs in the QOTSA catalogue, missing a beat every bar for a gloomy, dark effect. 'How To Handle A Rope' is a heavily distorted song about suicide with plenty of tight percussion from Hernandez, while 'Mexicola' starts with a lumbering bass-line and riff straight out of the Sabbath drawer, with the bass counterpointing the guitar elegantly (and hinting directly at the fill technique of Sab's bassist, Geezer Butler). Homme sings in a higher range than usual, a sign of his willingness to venture into new musical territory.

Influences abound, although warped beyond easy recognition: for example, the nasty industrial glitter of 'Hispanic Impressions' is like a random noisecore song gone rancid. Then again, The Beatles-like trip of 'You Can't Quit Me Baby' is mellow, soft and sweet, with the emphasis on cymbals and the guitar drone reminiscent of a bygone era. 'Give The Mule What He Wants' is a more straightforward rock song, with more confident vocals from Homme than before, based on a twisty riff in the patented Led Zeppelin style, plus backing vocals and extended harmonies.

The closer, 'I Was A Teenage Hand Model' is grimly fascinating. A dark, Tom Waits/Nick Cave-style horror ballad of sorts, it sits on a subtle piano figure, swamp percussion and a chanted, evil-sounding mantra. It descends into a miasma of electronic, theremin-like squelches and distorted vocal radio traffic, a fitting end to this envelope-pushing album. 'I Was A Teenage Hand Model' was recorded at Rancho De La Luna (Fred Drake and Dave Catching's studio in Joshua Tree), unlike the rest of the album, which was laid down at Monkey Studios. Wrapped up in a provocative sleeve – the bottom half of a model in a bikini – *Queens Of The Stone Age* is fully formed in every way. Asked whether the design might raise eyebrows in some quarters, Homme scoffed: "I like nudity. I don't get why it's such a big deal . . . I don't understand why so many eyebrows go up and so many cheeks get red. It was a postcard I bought in Amsterdam six years ago and it always fascinated me." Reviewers were bemused, then enthusiastic: retailers less so. "K–Mart freaked out," explained Josh, "so I got their catalogue with all the lingerie ads and I told them to look at that stuff. They carried the record."

In response to the success of the album, Homme had started to show his quirkier, less aggressive side to the press. As he once said, "I love to say clichés when the conversation gets really bizarre – like, 'Well, takes one to know one,' and 'A penny saved is a penny earned' – I'm fascinated with them. Actually, I have a book of 10,000 clichés. That's how I avoid them when I'm writing and how I know what they all are. They don't come out of thin air, though . . . I just read my clichés book on the plane and memorise them because I don't have a computer." Asked about the polka lessons that were his first musical training, he said, smiling: "I think the rock world needs polka and they don't even know it. We have a couple of polka-style songs on the new album, but see, they're masked properly. I don't think we would bust an accordion or any shit like that. Some of the coolest stuff I've witnessed is people using instruments incorrectly."

Musically, the man behind the heaviest riffs the Californian desert had ever produced stored some surprises up his sleeve when it came to likes and dislikes: "The Stooges were the best band in the world and it could never happen again. In the time frame – the peace and love generation – they were these thugs from Detroit, or Ann Arbor to be more exact. Everyone hated them when they were around and they played less than 20 shows.* I didn't even know that and I love The Stooges! They were dropped from every label they were ever on, and they degenerated production-wise on every album – that never happens. *Funhouse* is the shit, and I say that 'cause I'm supposed to, 'cause I'm a purist. But *Raw Power* is so gnarly. Take the craziest album from the craziest band in the world and play them back to back – *Raw Power* first and then the craziest band after – and they'll sound like a bunch of pussies. And the later demos are cool too. Songs like 'Shake Appeal' make you want to fuck. It's tough enough for the guys and sweet enough for the gals, which is the ultimate goal of all music – to straddle that line . . .

"I love old garage rock. And I'm an even bigger fan of Sun Records, Roy Orbison in particular, and that era of Elvis. This was definitely a record where we felt we could incorporate our influences without aping them. And so it became, we've got to go all-out on this record. Orbison is one of the vocalists I'm most amazed by and maybe because that's where my voice naturally sits, in that [register]. I can't scream, so I don't get to choose where my range is. For me, I'm glad, because it's where my favourite singers are."

---

* This is untrue as The Stooges certainly played upwards of 100 gigs!

A UK and European tour followed (Dave Catching of Earthlings? accompanied the band on lap steel guitar and electric piano), with the band taking advantage of the accompanying interview schedule. Of the album's recording, drummer Hernandez explained that the record was financed by Homme and had included the work of more than one bass player. "We actually started in August 1997," he pointed out, "and by January or February we were in the studio and it took us about two weeks to do the final tapes and everything. It went pretty much to schedule." Label interest had been fierce at one point. He added: "There were a few labels interested – like Interscope – and there was a lot of small labels that were really interested, and once we decided that we were going to go with Loosegroove, even more labels came . . . We just tried to make it more like our project and keep it that way, you know? It's the only way."

The line-up had come together with a degree of serendipity, it seemed: "Josh and I actually talked prior to getting together to practise – we just talked about getting a band together. It was about last summer, just over a year ago, just the two of us. Nick and I had talked prior to that about playing together, so it kinda like all came together as a whole. The final picture it was like, you know, we were looking for each other. At the time we were living in Seattle and Mike Johnson of Dinosaur Jr., who had broken up, was out doing a solo thing and he is a good friend of ours, so basically we asked friends of ours who can meet what we need, and we asked him: Johnson is a great guy and a great player. It was good enough just to be with him at that period of time."

Interviewers often wanted to know what Kyuss fans attending the shows thought of the Queens. Something of a hot potato, this subject gave the band cause for thought. Hernandez: "I think the response so far has been a bit of a mixture: there were a lot of unhappy people that were expecting more Kyuss, but there were a lot of people that did like it and just fell into it, and then there's people who never heard Kyuss who are now listening to this and liking it – but generally the response was positive. We wanted to stay away from Kyuss but keep the same energy. It's a bit like starting a new book – we kept it away from what we were doing before. We're all older, and as you get older you get more able to absorb more."

"There's a lot of curiosity from Kyuss people, and some of them aren't going to dig it, which is good," Josh added, labelling the experience a 'trial by fire'. "I've always been into frustrating some percentage of the audience, and I think Queens tries to frustrate a large percentage while trying to make a larger percentage happy.

"I'm sure some Kyuss fans were disappointed, but it seems most are not," Homme continued. "In a way, I want some to be disappointed a little. We can't be the same band forever. There were a lot of things I couldn't do with Kyuss because of expectations people had of that band. We were really into Kyuss, so I don't want to sound like we're throwing it all away. It'd just be nice to be able to play whatever you hear in your head."

Nick Oliveri was less diplomatic, reasoning that: "There's a lot going on in Europe that we don't have a grasp on over here. [In Europe] when they like something, they're not afraid to show it, you know what I mean? It seems like here [in the US], a lot of people are scared to, like, be into something, or let themselves be loose at a show or something, you know."

The album "was recorded in, like, 20 days," he added. "It's real focused compared to what we were like in Kyuss, where we'd go off on these spacey jams for, like, 20 minutes, you know? The songs are more structured and have more focus where we have background vocals and actual choruses and stuff like that – which we never would have thought of doing with Kyuss! So it's a little more focused, and a lot more, like, robotic." This word would come up time and time again in the early days of Queens Of The Stone Age, perhaps because interviewers and reviewers were so interested in pigeonholing the band into a category that Homme et al were obliged to invent a genre label – 'robot rock'. This didn't last long, of course, but did seem to have some relevance in the light of the trance-like, repetitive riffs that Queens (and to a much lesser degree, Kyuss) incorporated into their sound.

More knowledgeable writers also pointed to the famous 'motorik' beats of the early Seventies Krautrock movement, although this usually served to muddy the issue rather than offer any clarification. "We try to take a riff and, uh, pound it into people's heads by doing it over and over again," Oliveri reasoned. "But we're trying to do stuff where we don't have to stick to doing one thing . . . every song kinda has its own little theme. We're sticking to not having any limits or any boundaries. If we like it and it sounds good and it works, then we're gonna play, you know? Instead of, 'Well, I have to sound like this.' So it's something

Desert rock's Lennon & McCartney? The original creative core of Queens Of The Stone Age (from left): Nick Oliveri (bass, vocals) and Josh Homme (guitar, vocals). ANDY FALLON/CAMERA PRESS

Kyuss at their Sky Valley-era commercial peak (from left): bassist Scott Reeder (who replaced Nick Oliveri after *Blues For The Red Sun*), singer John Garcia, drummer Brant Bjork and guitarist Josh Homme. LFI

The young Josh Homme. Note skater-boy gear and natty dreads – a far cry from the 'rock accountant' look he would later adopt with Queens Of The Stone Age. MARTY TEMME/WIREIMAGE

Screaming Trees singer (and later Queens member) Mark Lanegan, pictured at the height of grunge in 1992. STEVE EICHNER/WIREIMAGE

Kyuss in Chicago, 1992: self-funded photo shoots such as this saved the band from being puppets at the hands of their record company, they believed. PAUL NATKIN/WIREIMAGE

John Garcia and Josh Homme in full flow at the London Underworld in September 1994. UK rock fans embraced Kyuss far more quickly than their American counterparts. GEORGE CHIN

Josh during the Screaming Trees' set on the 1996 Lollapalooza tour: he joined Mark Lanegan's band as backup guitarist after splitting Kyuss and moving to Seattle.
PATTI OUDERKIRK/PHOTOWEB/WIREIMAGE

Nick Oliveri: never afraid to let it all hang out on stage. At early gigs such as this he occasionally played naked in response to the heat – or at least that was his explanation in 2001 to the Brazilian cops who arrested him for indecent exposure.

Oliveri (centre, with uncharacteristic long hair and short beard) relaxing with the 'extreme punk band' of which he was sporadically a member, The Dwarves. Singer Blag Dahlia is pictured right. BLAG DAHLIA

Nick Oliveri onstage with the Dwarves at a typically frantic gig. "I sucked at guitar," he said later. BLAG DAHLIA

Nick after a brief encounter with some friends. Would you ask this man to join your band? Josh Homme did… BLAG DAHLIA

The Dwarves: an old line-up – what, no He-Who-Cannot-Be-Named? – with Blag Dahlia (aka Blag Jesus, second from top) and Nick Oliveri (third from top). BLAG DAHLIA

The Screaming Trees, with Mark Lanegan (third right) and bassist Van Conner (far right), both of whom worked with Homme in his two-year stay in Seattle alongside other ex-grunge illuminati. KAREN MASON BLAIR/CORBIS

QOTSA at the Garage again: note lap-steel player and long-time Queens collaborator Dave Catching on left. GEORGE CHIN

The newly-formed Queens Of The Stone Age at the Garage in London, August 1998. Note Homme's rare electric Ovation. LFI

Queens Of The Stone Age drummer Gene Trautman at the Garage, London, in August 2000. Trautman took over from desert legend Alfredo Hernandez after QOTSA signed with Interscope. GEORGE CHIN

Nick Oliveri and Josh Homme in an early Queens press shoot from November 2000. PETER PAKVIS/REDFERNS

A band apart: Nick Oliveri, Josh Homme and Gene Trautman in typically confrontational pose. MICK HUTSON/REDFERNS

that we strayed away from a little bit with the Kyuss thing, by not having to do the same things, but still having that element there. So it's cool . . . We're having a lot of fun doing it."

Nick also recalled his old Kyuss bandmates with fondness, as well as emphasising that his time away from Homme was all to the good (a theme which would be repeated in different circumstances a few years down the line). "We all went out and did different bands and all came back to the same place," he said, smiling. "Which is kinda cool, you know? Josh went to Screaming Trees, and I played with The Dwarves for a while, so I mean we all were doing different things, and we all ended up wanting to do the same thing, so we ended up back at the same place. I've always wanted to play with Alfredo. In fact, we had talked before about jammin' together, [but] I moved to Texas, and so it never happened, and it's great to be playing with these guys. It's great to be back playing with Josh too, y'know? I'm not on the record – I was in Texas, playing in some other band, and I'm kinda bummed out that I'm not on it, because it's that good to me."

As for his own band Mondo Generator, Nick was initially optimistic: "Mondo Generator went great, we had a really good drummer, and a guitar player, and we did a tour, and put out a single, and it was cool, and I got a full-length record that I haven't released that I'd like to . . . y'know, it's a pretty cool tape, and uh, but we're doing those couple of tunes now, and so it's better, and it's gonna be re-recorded and done right, y'know?" Later he was more dismissive, remarking: "We had a good time for a while there, and then I changed some members in the band, and it just turned into shit, so I said, 'Fuck it,' and broke it up!"

When it came to the non-QOTSA Kyuss members, Oliveri revealed that the old desert friendships stayed strong. "Me and Josh went over to Scott Reeder's, he has a pet store here in Palm Springs – and John was in there today, so we stopped in to say hi to the guys." The now-vet Garcia had moved on from Slo-Burn to Unida. Oliveri explained that Reeder, who had worked with Tool and Nebula since the split of Kyuss as well as contributing to movie soundtracks and TV commercials, owned a particularly well-stocked pet shop. ("He owns over, like, I don't know, 50 different kinds of animals and fish, and shit!")

From the off, the band were plagued with questions about a Kyuss re-formation, and the issue usually came up when Josh or Nick revealed that they were still friends with John Garcia. However,

Oliveri dodged the issue: "Right now that's something that none of us are even thinking about. I mean, as far as this band is concerned there's three members from Kyuss from different times – so I mean, it's as close as you're gonna get right now! But uh, I'm sure we'll do something with Johnny [Garcia] in the future . . . we'll definitely do some work with him, doing something else, you know. I can't rule anything out for sure, but right now this is what we're doing. We're pretty happy with what we're doing right now, and I know John's happy with what he's doing with his band so . . . I wouldn't count on anything like that."

However, Nick did reveal that there was a fair amount of previously unheard Kyuss material under lock and key. "Unreleased Kyuss stuff?" he mused. "There's a lot of it – I don't think it's gonna be released. There's a lot of stuff that didn't make it to *Blues For The Red Sun* that were good songs – you know, like '800' was a full-length song that had different parts and layers and stuff, but it got cut down."

With QOTSA awareness boosted by the release of *Desert Sessions 3 & 4* on Man's Ruin (the pattern of releasing two sessions on each package would remain a constant) in October 1998, the trio-plus-Catching played in Holland, Germany and the UK before returning to the States for a 20-date jaunt. The year finished with 23 more European shows, this time including five dates in the UK (London, Nottingham, Manchester, Wolverhampton and Bristol) and re-treads through the previous European territories as well as Austria, Italy, Spain, France and Belgium.

As the band's following grew – largely based, it seemed, on a not entirely undeserved (but still inflated) reputation that they were drug-hoovering party animals – the need for more QOTSA product intensified and a one-off split CD with Roadrunner was issued in 1999. Two Queens songs, 'Mexicola' and a live take of 'If Only' were paired with 'Hey Hey Beotch' and 'Motown' from The Workhorse Movement, an unremarkable hardcore band from the Roadrunner stable. Roadrunner were refocusing on their latest signings, Slipknot, and dispensing with heavier earlier acts (such as the death metal band Deicide) in favour of a more nu-metal slant. Strange, then, that the label should sign a resolutely non-rapping act such as QOTSA for their European releases, although the Queens' fanbase lapped up the single. The band also released a US-only single, entitled 'I Ain't Worth A Dollar, But I Feel Like A Millionaire' – lifted from the forthcoming *Desert Sessions 5 & 6*, which they had found time to record while off the road.

1999 was set to be a year of touring for Queens Of The Stone Age, with a Smashing Pumpkins support slot on an April club tour scheduled to precede a month opening for Ween in the US and solo dates in September. "What I love about Ween is that they never fall out of character," Homme said. "They never say, 'Just kidding.' That's why they're not a joke band. And even if you do characterise what they do as a joke, the level of craftsmanship on those records – to take a joke to that degree is like Andy Kaufman . . . There's no length to which they won't go for a song. They're total slaves to the music. And it all makes sense. For us, that's inspiring."

More dates equalled more press, and more press equalled more probing about Kyuss, stoner rock, and the desert. "In one way, 'stoner rock' elevated some awareness of Kyuss, but it also gave rise to some really stupid shit!" railed Homme. "I'm no guitar virtuoso or hero; I just write music. I don't carry the flag for anything, and I don't want to be the king of some clique.

"I want to get away from stoner rock because I don't want to exclude people," he added. "I want an equal amount of boys and girls to come and dance and get their heads right. You can't pick your audience, but if I could I'd pick people who are into everything. Music is part of the cool stuff that we get to do while we're walking around the Earth, and it would be stupid to assume there is only one good style and most everything else sucks. I would rather assume there's a ton of great music out there, and I want to find where it is."

"We're a little uncomfortable with that stoner-rock tag," Hernandez confirmed. "There's more to us than that. There's a lot of open space and heat to the music. When we first started this band, Josh and I were living in Seattle, and it felt like such a different environment. The surroundings in the desert are sharper. You don't see no concrete. You don't see no buildings. Your thoughts tend to flow better."

"It makes me annoyed a bit to just have people labelling us that," explained Josh, "because there is a lot of work going into what we are doing here. I would hate to have people assume that it is just pot that is the magic key to the music we are making. It's not. We're actually enjoying this and I think it comes out quite noticeably in the music.

"I saw some old Kyuss videos about a year ago. The only thing I didn't like is that we played so long! We were just there for two-

and-a-half, three hours, and I would like to stop doing that. We jam, but we don't turn songs into wanky 30-minute opuses. I think the economy is better. The idea is to take stock of what's going on in music and do exactly what's *not* going on in music. It seemed like there was a push for techno or robotic stuff, but none of it is stripped-down, played with guitars and drums with no help and ZZ Top *Tejas*-era production."

Asked about QOTSA's future sound, Josh mused: "I think it's going to expand, and modify, and change, and have new calculations. I think because of that it doesn't matter what you call it any more. Just say what you want, because it's still going to be exactly the same."

Homme also hinted that he might not always take lead vocals: "I just sang on the first record. We'll probably each sing half, or whatever songs sound good, for the next record. We'll even do a duet with Donna Summer. We'll go in and shoot everybody. So, I feel it's going to move around, it's not going to be just me or him or instrumentals. We'll just keep it moving . . . keep it interesting."

Nick was even more specific: "I think on the next record we're definitely going to share lead vocals. We're going to do a lot of different things and add some different players for live stuff. Right now we have Dave from Earthlings? playing electric piano and lap steel. We're going to do different things live, stuff we want to do. We want to do things that are unexpected but are cool and stuff we like."

Asked incessantly how QOTSA differed from Kyuss, Josh offered a variety of answers including: "We're a little more stripped down and tighter than we were with Kyuss and I think that makes it a bit more transient and robotic . . . We wanted to get away from Kyuss and not be Kyuss II. We'll let someone else do that.

"I'm unable to scream, so I don't attempt to do it. That's probably one of the top two biggest differences – that and the recording style. Where one is roomy and large, the other one is tight and dry, but with the same basic tones. It's one of those things where we wanted to bring the coolest parts of Kyuss and then add more to it so it's a little bit more diverse, so we can play a wider variety of music, because we listen to a lot of different music."

It seemed the various members didn't particularly mind being compared to Kyuss. "It's natural," said Homme, "and that's why we don't bum on it. It's like, we have one record out – and what are you going to compare it to? Kyuss. I think that's why even though it's a heavy rock record it doesn't sound like a Kyuss record. There's an easy split. You can see they are different. We knew it would come up . . . I think this record is a good first start for us and shows people where we are heading. This album has a wider spectrum of music for us. I'm proud of this. I'm very happy with the production and, to be honest, I don't think there are many bands out there nowadays that are doing such a tight and dry recording. I also feel that this record is a good representation of where we are headed and there is an arrow sending us off in the right direction."

That direction would seem to include more extended touring, as he explained: "I have learned how to tour a bit better now. It's a bit more enjoyable now. We are playing more areas now with this band, like Spain and Austria where we've never been before, and that *is* a good thing. It takes a lot to tour. It's tough. They should offer a training course to musicians. But you learn from your mistakes. I have. Now I understand touring and it's great to be on the road."

Nick added: "It's going really good and we've been having some really good shows. A lot of people are coming out and there's an even mix of guys and girls. It's nice to see some girls out there and we're having a lot of fun. Kyuss was a guy band, you know. It's not that we didn't want that, and after I left it's not that they didn't want that either. The music is appealing more to women now, which I think is cool. We're not intentionally trying to do that, but I think it's cool that it's happening because it's nice to see some pretty faces and some smiles."

Josh: "It's good to be the foreigner. That's even why we like going to Canada. We're obsessed with being foreigners. It's fun to go there and play and hang out and see architecture and listen to people speak the different language in your face."

Not that touring was always simple, as Oliveri recounted a near-death experience: "We spun out in Saskatchewan. We had our U-Haul on the back of our van – all of our gear was in it – and we spun out on two inches of black ice, fuckin' did a 360 down this embankment." The band now knew how to have fun on the road at least: "We grew up playing at parties, so that's what I like doing – playing a show that acts like a party. Not trying to, like, change the world, you know what I mean? Try to change it for, like, the next two hours . . . I don't think it's rocket science. I trip out on rock, you know? I don't think you're supposed to talk about it, you're supposed to do it. When you talk about it, it almost nullifies it."

Nick: "When I go see other bands, I wear earplugs, unless it's Motörhead, and it's so loud that I know it's gonna hurt me, so I just take them out. I only wear earplugs when there is like a shitty band. I would never be in a place where there was, like, Sugar Ray playing. But if I was, I'd have my earplugs in. I would only be there to get the 16-year-old girls, or try. Or 15 . . . OK, I'll go for 14, I'll be honest."

A major breakthrough came in the form of a record deal offer with Interscope, a powerful division of Universal. On signing the deal, the Queens announced that their album would be reissued and that a remix of 'Regular John' would also appear. On the downside of this, drummer Alfredo Hernandez announced that he was leaving the band, for reasons which have never been fully revealed but which seem to have been amicable. Perhaps Hernandez – the oldest Queen by some years and a desert veteran – didn't feel that the imminent wave of inter-national touring and major-label pressure was for him. Either way, he departed at the end of the tour. Within a few weeks Homme and Oliveri were searching for a replacement, and it wasn't long before his successor, Gene Trautmann, was installed.

In October the Ween tour kicked off, with QOTSA delighted to be sharing a stage alongside a band they had always admired. "People that are into Ween are into everything," said Josh. "They play anything, so you have to be cool." He added that audiences were still shouting at his band to play Kyuss songs – the original desert quartet was proving to be quite a difficult ghost to exorcise: "We hear it a ton. In Europe we were playing 'Supa Scoopa And Mighty Scoop' from *Sky Valley*. We played it a few times, but we try not to do it too much, because it's done. We're doing new stuff now . . . now that Nick is here it's kind of split up. We've got two different ways of delivery. He's more aggres-sive vocally. I just can't scream, but it's all going to be really cool. He adds a really cool element that wasn't there before." The fluid line-up was all part of the Queens method, as Josh explained: "Queens is kind of like, well, it's becoming the Desert Sessions in a lot of ways. Nick and I write a bunch of tunes and Dave Catching, the lap guy, he'll put something in. We like to change the line-up, keep it moving. We've toured as a three-piece; our next one will be with two drummers. It pulls me away from being the traditional frontman. We've got other people in the band who sing as well. I like that ever-changing feeling. We've set it up so we can get away with murder!"

A year had passed since the release of *Queens Of The Stone Age* and, like any complex item, myths had sprung up around it. Homme was quizzed about the inner booklet photo ("It's at the Man's Ruin office, late night. Frank is smoking Camel non-filters and I'm smoking joints. We were going in different directions, but it was cool"), the spaceship and crucifix-like telegraph pole which formed part of the artwork ("That's actually a Frank Kozik embellishment. He said, 'We gotta fuck with people.' I had said, 'Let's make that telephone pole a cross, so it's got the biblical overtones.' So he's like, 'If you're gonna do *that*, then you gotta do this!'") and the phone number that appears in 'Regular John' ("I was thinking I can't put a real number in the song. I don't want someone calling it . . . so it's a whole phone number, with one extra digit stashed in there"). The song 'Teenage Hand Model' also invited scrutiny. Josh recalled its inspiration: "I moved to Seattle before the whole Screaming Trees thing and I just wanted to move somewhere where I didn't know anybody and where the whole music scene was just dead. Everyone I knew in San Francisco was on drugs, and everyone in San Diego and LA just wasn't doing it. So I went to Seattle, because I still wanted to be on the West Coast. So I was in this bar, there's a lot of bitter people there, especially music types. Anyway, I'm in this bar and there's this guy saying the stupidest bitter drunk rant about how he was a model when he was young. He was just a toothless bum screaming about being a child actor, model and shit."

On the band's label Interscope, Homme explained: "They're all right. I think we came to the label because of their ability to push bands like Primus, which isn't a band I necessarily like, but they're really bizarre. All we're really trying to do is reach people who really dig our shit, and the hard part is finding those people. It just seems like Interscope used to be really good at pushing bands that were bizarre or weren't following this fake rulebook. And now they're not as good at it any more, but that's cool . . . Interscope merged with A&M and Geffen and cut all the bands except the ones that sold over a million copies, you know? So all they have are these monoliths like Smashmouth and U2 and whatever – Limp Bizkit. Holy shit, man."

Homme had evidently launched Queens with no grandiose game

plan, or indeed much of a plan at all: "We didn't really have any expectations [for the album]. We just wanted to put something out on an indie, just keep low for a while. We thought a lot of people would want us to be Kyuss Part II, but we can't just do that stoner-rock thing anymore. A lot of bands are headed down that road, which is still very cool, but we just can't do it any more. It's going to be that and more. The heavy shit is heavy, and some of the lazy shit is just spaced out. Sometimes we just try to give you the spins. It's wider in every aspect." On whether he thought he had made an impact on the music scene, he shrugged and responded: "I really don't know. I get so focused on what we're doing; I don't care what the impact is. When we're done with something, I want to start something else. I like to be real busy. I love not to pick my head up, just keep it down and fucking go. Because I think if you keep stopping to look around you get stuck watching instead of doing shit.

"With Kyuss, we had a desire not to be on the radio. We enjoyed saying no more than we did yes. So if there was something that seemed too much like a chorus, I would just cut it out in Kyuss. Queens is about censoring ourselves less. Just letting it be based on the song instead of making deliberate moves to manipulate things so it won't get on the radio. We wanted to set it up in this band so we could play anything. We don't want to get roped in by our own music. If anyone has a good song, regardless of style, we should be able to play it.

"There's a robotic element to our albums, like the repetition of riffs. We also wanted to do a record that had a lot of dynamic range. That element of staccato playing is roughly like saying, do it exactly the same and very rigid so that each stroke is identical. It's got that robotic element to it. Music is all based on delivery and it certainly changes the delivery of the song when I play that way. If it would be strummed a different way it would just be different."

Around this time the band also contributed a song, 'Infinity', to the *Heavy Metal* movie sequel, *Heavy Metal 2000*, which was released on the accompanying CD in April 2000. The film failed to do well commercially but the album was a useful piece of exposure for the band. Oliveri enthused: "The original soundtrack with Black Sabbath and Cheap Trick [was] killer, and we were stoked to be on the second one, but apparently the movie never really came out. It was a shame, too, but at least the soundtrack made it out! [The original] was an incredible thing for a lot of people because it was before music video, when hard rock wasn't all that present in movies . . . When I was a kid it really fuelled everything that I did, and it kind of leads up to what's happening today, at least musically for me. A lot of that stuff changed my life for sure – I wouldn't be playing right now if all that didn't go down. A lot of the stuff that is going down now, I don't know how I feel about [it], but if it's cool and the kids are pissed and they need something really heavy to get it out, then it's all good, I guess."

And so the millennium ended, and with it the first phase of Queens Of The Stone Age's collective career. They were finally shaking off the shadow of Kyuss. They had refined a unique style. And they had carved themselves critical and commercial respect in the wake of extensive touring.

The real fun was about to begin, with a whole new level of awareness beckoning.

CHAPTER 6

2000: R-Rated

WHEN Nirvana released *Nevermind* in the summer of 1991, the sudden wave of success that engulfed them was so all-encompassing and so unprecedented for their genre of music (alternative rock, for want of a better term) and locale (Seattle, Washington) that they were faced with all kinds of incongruous situations, such as Kurt Cobain collapsing in tears by the side of the stage after yet another stadium show before a baying crowd of football jocks and middle-aged accountants.

In microcosm, Queens Of The Stone Age endured a similar trajectory in the years 2000 and 2001. 2000 was the year that nu-metal really took hold, with Slipknot, Limp Bizkit, Papa Roach, Linkin Park, Deftones and others taking the formula of two guitarists (preferably playing downtuned seven-string guitars), a shouty singer (often in baseball cap and generous shorts), rhythm section and DJ (always an avowed hip-hop fan, and usually a short-haired, punkish type) to its logical conclusion. The kids loved it, making all these acts (who would, to a man, desert the style and the sound when it became terminally unfashionable a couple of years later) and their record company shareholders millionaires. The whole nu-metal wave,* which started life with Korn's debut album in 1994, may now seem passé but at the time the festivals showcasing the best and the worst of the movement grossed enormous profits and became a bona fide modern phenomenon

---

* There's a valid argument pointing out how the nu-metal scene was usurped by bands like Queens Of The Stone Age, and the rapid rise of garage-rock bands such as The White Stripes, The Hives, The Datsuns and so on, that lies beyond this book's scope and because insufficient time has elapsed for a true perspective to form (E-mail me in 2010 and I'll have an answer for you!)

– acceptable Woodstocks for a world that wouldn't tolerate a real Woodstock without burning it to the ground.

Of the nu-metal that surrounded them, Oliveri pontificated: "I think that a lot of acts jumped on the bandwagon from some of the earlier bands that had already set up and were doing this rap-rock thing. There is a lot of new stuff that I'm just, like, I don't get it. It's not all bad, but there's a lot of it that is – it's like any other music. It's tough for me to listen to it, so I don't. Some of it I can go see live and go, like, 'Fuck, this is powerful shit! You look at the crowd and they're going fucking mental, so it's cool . . . I got no beefs with the stuff. It's not my cup of tea for what I want to play, so I don't. I'm more along the lines of playing rock'n'roll, man. That's what's fun to me. It's supposed to be a good time, you're supposed to laugh and play grab-ass with some girl in the crowd if you're hot in it . . . however you want to do it, that's cool. I just prefer to play rock'n'roll, I'm not that pissed any more, you know? When I was younger I was pretty pissed off, so I can see where these kids are coming from, in the crowd, you know? They wanna hear something that's intense and like, 'Aaagh!' all the time, so I can dig that, because I was just as pissed. I was mad too."

After spending the first few months of the year recording the follow-up to their self-titled debut, QOTSA anticipated that the album would sell reasonably well and lead to more successful touring. In fact, the enormous success of *Rated R* rocketed the band up to the next level. Having survived a last-minute title change – so last-minute, in fact, that some promos went out under the original name *II* – *Rated R* was a startling leap forward to newer territories that few fans could have expected. Laden with pure pop choruses but retaining the deep rock textures that made Homme's work recognisable, *Rated R* was a fully developed canvas, taking in all areas of the popular music spectrum.

Its casual knack with a riff was encapsulated by the lead-off single, a crooned, sinister – but annoyingly catchy – song called 'The Lost Art Of Keeping A Secret'. A tense, scratchy verse, in which Josh sneeringly begins "I've got a secret / I cannot say . . .", leads into a dark tunnel of a chorus led off with the long falsetto of "Whatever you do . . . / Don't tell anyone", a melody which carves itself into the listener's head. That warm, fuzzy guitar tone that makes the Queens' sound so distinctive – and, let it not be forgotten, so suited to radio – is a slightly threatening thing of beauty.

The addictive single, released in August 2000 but released to radio a couple of months earlier in time to accompany the album, stayed on the airwaves all summer and was so ubiquitous that later pressings of *Rated R* came with a bonus 'The Lost Art Of Keeping A Secret' CD single. A video was shot, consisting mainly of the band playing to camera, deadpan of expression, interspersed with a series of images (a man's mouth; a woman's face; an ant being lowered into someone's ear) which really wasn't that exciting but which did serve to show Josh and Nick's faces – the former resembling an accountant, the latter some kind of deranged monk. The video was directed by Jon Parazzi, who – as Oliveri remarked – had "done a couple of things with the Earthlings? and we liked his stuff. It was cool because we could go in and give him our parts and he did the rest. We knew what we wanted, so we left it in his hands. He knew how to get it. He was somebody we trusted, and it turned out pretty well."

When asked if he had been surprised that it became a hit, Homme responded, "It's not a hit-type song, because it's not for kids. Our record company was like, 'This is going to be a hit,' and I'm like, 'A hit with whom?' It's about fucking. Twenty-one-year-olds and over, maybe. They were trying to shove it down the throats of 13-year-olds." Amazingly, 'The Lost Art . . .', (the second track on the album) is surpassed by the droned, rocked-out-and-having-fun mantra 'Feelgood Hit Of The Summer', which opens the record and provides a neat, spiteful, belly-laughing Queens manifesto for those new to the band to digest, and has since become infamous. "Nicotine, Valium, Vicodan, marijuana, ecstasy and alcohol!" is repeated four or more times per verse – before the 'chorus', a single stuttered yelp of "C-c-c-c-c-cocaine!" And that's the song, which builds this formula up with added venom throughout the verses, before dropping into a quiet, almost whispered recital and then accelerating up loud again for the final fling. It's a remarkable piece of songwriting that introduced more than a few non-Americans to Vicodan (also Vicodin), a powerful tranquilliser.

An unexpected guest lending some presence to the vocals on 'Feelgood Hit' was none other than Judas Priest singer Rob Halford, whose malevolent whisper and final shriek gives the song a recognisably metallic aura. As Josh recounted, "We were in Studio B at Soundcity and he was in Studio A. The hallway outside the studios is very small. It doesn't matter if you're in A or B, you're going to end up hanging out with the other band. So he was hanging out and Chris Goss, our producer, asked if he'd sing on it and he said, 'Sure!' He read the lyrics and laughed, and sang backup on it."

Nick Oliveri: "Josh wrote down what the lyrics were and [Rob] was like, 'Oh, a rock'n'roll cocktail, I think I've had this!' It was so funny and he came in and did his stuff, a really nice guy, he is a very cool dude. Being a fan as a kid, I saw Priest as a kid in like '83 and I never would have thought that in my whole life that Rob Halford would be singing on my music, never. It was actually a nice treat, we were all in the control room watching him sing in the vocal booth with head-phones on and we were all just going mental, 'Oh shit! Rob Halford!' It was so cool." Oliveri even had the pleasure of giving the Metal God some vocal direction: "He was doing some of the more sinister Rob stuff, and then when it got to the 'Cocaine!' part in the choruses I said, 'Hey man, can you do your Rob Halford thing?' And on the original version every one is, '*Cocaine!*' But we didn't want to overkill on that, so we only ended up putting the very last [chorus] of the whole song on it . . . in the rest of the song he's just doing the sinister Rob thing, but there are, like, eight different people's voices on it, so it was really tough to mix.

"You know, when I was a kid I had no idea [about Halford's homo-sexuality] and once I found out it was like, wow, it all makes sense now! He was like one of those leather-daddy type dudes and, if you think about some of the stuff that he's singing, there are all of these references to it, like 'Hell Bent For Leather' and 'Point Of Entry', and just all these things that make sense now. But you know, I don't really care what he does when he's off the stage, you know what I mean? When he's on stage and if he's throwing down, cool, I don't give a shit! His sexual preference, I couldn't give a shit because it doesn't affect me in any way. I'm not with it so how is it going to affect me? That kind of shit never bothered me."

The impact of 'Feelgood Hit Of The Summer' was subtle and insidi-ous. Firstly, the single immediately made QOTSA seem like a pro-drugs band, a far from accurate scenario. "My stance on drugs is that I'm more like a libertarian," said Josh. "I think they should all be legalised because people take them, and they hide, and they get chastised, and if you've ever known any real junkie or anything like that, you say, 'You really should quit.' Then they go, 'Yeah, I know I should.' And as soon as you're gone, they're like, 'Thank God that guy's gone.' People do what they do, and as far as their necessity for music, drugs are on a really long list of what it takes to make music, and they're no more or less important than any of them . . . I don't wave the flag for drug rock, and you know, if someone asked me drug questions, they'd go, 'What drugs do you take?' I'm like, 'What are you on, because you're out of your mind. That's none of your business.' Secondarily, I think they have their place, but not such an overwhelming importance, they're just something interesting to find out about, you know what I mean?"

Homme's stance towards stimulants was both liberal and ambiguous, as he explained, "['Feel Good Hit . . .'] lists drugs, but it doesn't say yes or no. It's almost like, what will people do if you don't swear? You say things that make them react. Some people were like, 'That song, I gotta tell you, is bad, and you guys really need help.' And other people realised that it's almost like a social experiment. It got banned in some places and went to the top of the charts in other places . . . That's what's so funny, is that the record industry and the radio refused to play the song in America and get behind it because they were afraid. But then the police took it, used it to play to schools, junior high and high schools, so you can imagine how for us, we [said], the social experiment has worked itself out!"

As for himself: "I'm an equal opportunity person. I hate junk. I like to use drugs as a means of manipulating other people. I can tell you this though, none of them are a licence to be a dumbass."

The one-two punch of 'Feel Good Hit Of The Summer' – ironically named, as it was released in the autumn – and 'Lost Art' remain unmatched for a rock album in recent years. But the rest of *Rated R* cocks a snook at the listener, sounding more obscure and nowhere near as catchy as those two unlikely radio hits. 'Leg Of Lamb' comes from the opposite end of the line, eschewing the deliberate soft-rock tones of the first two songs for a horror-movie vibe surrounding a jerky, stop-start riff. Oliveri's melodic – but not friendly – spiralling bass-line matches Homme's creepy vocal melody, with the result being one of the weirdest, most threatening songs in the QOTSA canon. 'Auto Pilot' is a shambolic affair, with a tin-pan guitar, multi-layered vocals and a certain Beatles-like querulousness that is not the album's only nod towards the vintage atmospherics of the Fab Four. 'Better Living

Through Chemistry' carries on where 'Leg Of Lamb' left off, exploring skin-crawling organ tones and trance-like atmospheres but laying on massively echoed textures and disturbing, burbling guitars. A few months down the line, the song would be used on the soundtrack of an educational film used by the San Diego County Office of Education and the San Diego Sheriff's Department to highlight the dangers of driving while drunk or drugged. Homme: "I feel like doing doughnuts [spinning car tyres hard enough to scorch the road] in San Diego County and dropping my name when the cops come . . . it's a get-out-of-jail-free card. I just want to be in league with the cops. I sort of feel like the roads should have those inflatable arm-floats [a.k.a. water-wings] along either shoulder . . . And that all cars should have 'em too so you could just bounce off everyone."

'Monsters In The Parasol' – originally a Desert Sessions tune – briefly returns to the fold of melodiousness with the 'robotic' rhythm that Homme and Oliveri had mentioned so many times before: its deadpan vocals and the twisty guitar fill that presages each line of the chorus make it a masterpiece of economy. Asked why the song had been upgraded from the third and fourth Desert release, Homme explained: "We really liked the song, and Desert Sessions is cool, but it's really limited in print. We thought the song should be more available because we really dig it."

A slice of undiluted Oliveri comes pouring out of the speakers with 'Quick And To The Pointless', a dose of punk fury with screamed vocals, aggressive riffs straight from the tradition of West Coast hard-core and plenty of nastiness – a complete change from the rest of the album. 'In The Fade', conversely, sits atop an almost reggae-fied beat which is so relaxed it's almost optimistic. Guest singer Mark Lanegan of Josh's sometime day-job band The Screaming Trees provides his standard hoarse, dark tones and in doing so keeps the song from complete incongruity. There's another gear-change with the aptly titled 'Tension Head', a fast, maddened volley of riffs, complete with layered screams and a bass part that flies all over the place in a textbook example of controlled chaos – and a further switch of pace with 'Lightning Song'. This tune places the Queens' devotion to classic, Beatles-style, quasi-psychedelic pop in context, with its deftly plucked acoustic guitar, shuffle beat and a melody unnervingly reminiscent of 'Norwegian Wood'. But the album ends with a true Queens/Kyuss-style desert riff-a-thon, 'I Think I Lost My Headache', a layer cake of fat, overdriven bass and lush atmospheres.

Rated R is quite a ride, and the most amply spread record that the band have ever produced – at least in terms of sheer diversity. Once more Chris Goss had produced the album, and once again he had made it a smooth experience, as Nick recounted: "Working with Chris is really easy. He's very laid-back, and he's a good friend of ours, and he knows the band's vision already and he runs with that. He was like the third member to me and Josh on this record. Me and Josh did all the pre-production ourselves, because Chris was doing another record, so we just had him come in when it was time to go to the studio. We pretty much knew what we wanted to do from the start anyway, and Goss, being a friend and somebody who we trust musically, threw us some ideas and we tried a lot of them. A lot of them we didn't like and a lot of them we didn't use, and the ones we liked, we used. And Josh and I had a lot of ideas and we just tried them all."

Homme: "The sound with Kyuss was identical from beginning to end, it never changed. In fact I used the same cabinet and head on every record – all Ampeg cabinets, because the goal always seemed to be bass. My perception was that to the normal guitar player they were like, 'This doesn't sound right.' But for me it was perfect. It seems using the gear incorrectly is the best way to get on. You're forced to create . . . I don't like guitars that are too light, it has to hurt after a while to hold it. I don't have many 24-fret guitars or anything like that, but it really depends. Now that I get the opportunity to play more types of music, I think things are really situational.

And the inspiration for the music? "I just think that I absorb the ideas. The reason I love being in today's music is that it comes down to your delivery. Björk plays with a 52-piece orchestra, and some guy playing champagne glasses . . . someone with fuckin' nut bells, and it works because it's in the delivery, and the delivery is correct. There is no genre for me. I don't play heavy, I don't play punk, I don't play metal, I don't play classic rock, I just play rock'n'roll and I like it vague like that, because then we can play whatever we like and not have to be like, 'No, we've got to go, chugga, chugga, chugga.' I mean, what kind of music is Björk? It's out there. And I think that's where I'd like to be. If we want to play heavy I hope the audience is like, 'Fuck yeah.' And then when it gets broken down after a while and it's quiet, I hope

record.' That's not saying yes or no, not telling somebody to do it. I don't know why cocaine has made a big comeback. I don't think it really left. It was always there, people were just more secretive about it." However often he might casually drop drug references, Josh did an about-turn in early 2003 when he told *Rolling Stone*, "I don't smoke pot, and Nick hasn't since he was, like, 12 – not that I think there's anything wrong with it. Music sounds kick-ass when you're stoned. You could get high and listen to Britney Spears and be like, whoo!"

As for any drug messages in the Queens' music, Homme said: "We don't act any different off the road than we do on the road. We're lucky to be musicians as something we do, and so I'm not gonna pretend I'm an accountant. But at the same time, even as a young boy I just was never that into peer pressure. You know, 'C'mon let's go do this!' 'I don't want to.' 'C'mon you pussy!' It's like, 'No, still not working . . . I don't want to do that, I don't want to jump off a cliff,' you know? So I think we just live how we've always lived. I think lots of the things that deal with drugs in our music are misunderstood – like we have a song called 'Better Living Through Chemistry', which is an anti-drug song. It's saying it's OK, the government says it's OK for you to take Prozac every day, every single day, to feel better and feel abso-lutely numb. Don't smoke that joint though, you! Like, the war between what some old man says is OK but doesn't know anything and what's really going on . . ."

Oliveri added: "Queens are going to make [a Mondo record] after every release/touring cycle. We're not going to take tons of time off. We're not in any situation where we can take four years off, and I think it would be bad if we did. We keep on going until it breaks up, until one of us gets tired of it."

With so much going on in the Queens camp, the other members got some interview time as well as Josh and Nick, including the new touring guitarist Troy Van Leeuwen of A Perfect Circle and Failure. After his first Queens shows, Van Leeuwen exhaled in relief: "Joining up with [Queens] was like cramming for a test. I only had 10 days from the time I was asked to do the gig to the time we left. But I like to do these things. I've been in the studio for the last year working on so many projects, looking at a computer screen and being pretty much bored, so I'm happy to be out with these guys."

Of the permanently shifting QOTSA line-up, Homme explained: "I think it's natural when something sounds great to just go with it. None of us need to be out in the front all the time. So switching hats and trying new stuff is mandatory . . . We're the first people to aggressively bridge the gap of current bands looking to jam together. Most people say, 'I would love to sit in on that band's rehearsal and see what happens,' but they don't do anything. We're like, 'Don't bullshit! Let's do it.' Some bands do work together, but we're the first to do it pretty maniacally."

Always ready with a clarification, Oliveri added: "We set Queens up to break away from how things were when we were younger with Kyuss. We didn't try anything at all back then. It was a lot of shooting yourself in the foot. And now it's just [more fun] to be able to move about the cabin freely and play with people you like. The only rules are there are no rules."

It was announced that the special guests who would appear on *Songs For The Deaf* were Ween guitarist Dean Ween, A Perfect Circle bassist Paz Lenchantin and her sister Anja on strings, as well as some guest DJs on the between-song segments. "Don't ask about the DJs," warned Homme. "I'm going to leave it ambiguous because, after all, it is a concept album . . . a mixture of our first two records. It's got the robotic feel of the first album and the groove-based song structure of the second." Whether or not Josh and Nick would be able to rope in all these guests for the live extravaganza they had promised remained to be seen, but one person dry about it all was the perennially gloomy Mark Lanegan. Asked how he was feeling about the forthcoming tour – for which QOTSA would be supported by fellow Interscope artists . . . And You Will Know Us By The Trail Of Dead – he responded, "This time around I'll be doing a lot of the dancing. I'm also trying to talk them into letting me play tambourine." Of the new album, he remarked: "I think it's a great record. To me, it's like The Ramones – it's just really distinct, and almost always really catchy. But not stupid . . . We're all in agreement that labels are stupid. The other bands that I hear mentioned under these same categories – there are elements that are similar, but Queens are really, distinctly their own thing. I hear elements of Devo and new wave and Krautrock and stuff that has nothing to do with Black Sabbath or whatever, and that's what makes it cool." Had he enjoyed working with Dave Grohl, so long Lanegan's Seattle compatriot in grunge in his old band, Nirvana? "It was cool to be on a record and to do some shows with him playing drums," Mark drawled, "because in my opinion he's one of the greatest drummers ever." Had he enjoyed his time as a musician? "Most of the earlier experiences I can't remember. But I'm pretty sure I'm enjoying this a lot more. I would say that one of them was like travelling with an unhappy family, and one of them was travelling with a happy family. Queens are a happy family."

Happy or not, a degree of disappointment was felt when, in August 2002, Dave Grohl announced that he would be returning to Foo Fighters after a year or so as a Queen. He had played some of the shows they had scheduled together, but his day-job was calling and he was obliged to depart. Although missed ("We were all disappointed, but it's nothing we weren't expecting. We just didn't think it would happen so soon," said Van Leeuwen), Grohl left behind him a more thoughtful set of musicians than he had encountered on his arrival. "I've learned a lot from Dave and now I'm like, 'That's right. I'm a fucking rock star and, while we're on the subject, you're actually not fit to talk to me – can you have him removed?'" joked Josh.

"I mean, it's OK for people not to like you," he added on a more serious note. "We were at this party and this intern from Sony was giving it to Dave and he was like, 'I don't have to listen to this. I'm going home to my mansion now . . .'"

As for finding a replacement for the frankly irreplaceable Grohl, Homme said, shrugging: "We've been jamming with some different guys. We've had drummers play on records before and then gone and toured with someone else. We look at the records as this is what they sound like here, and if you want to hear the songs just like this, you should listen to the record. The whole nature of going to see us live is that it's different every time, whether that's the set or the line-up or both. In the case of drummers, we don't want to get a Dave Grohl clone. There's people that can play what's been played there, but we want to look for a way to take it further. It's not a question of better or worse, it's like going to the side or going diagonal."

Nick Oliveri was a little more vocal about his disappointment, as he told *Entertainment Weekly*: "I was pissed for a minute. I was like, 'Motherfucker! Don't leave now!' I kept telling myself, 'Don't get spoiled. Don't get too used to this guy playing the drums.' But I couldn't help it. It was too easy. I'm still fighting it. He writes great songs and sings great and plays a good guitar – but he's a drummer. To me he's one of the top five in the world. It's like, 'Who's gonna play this shit out on the road?'"

In the end the man they chose was ex-Danzig drummer and long-time friend Joey Castillo, a man whose lengthy experience was expected to come in useful. Castillo, who had begun his drumming career with the seminal LA punks Wasted Youth, first met Homme when he played on the same bill as Kyuss. This back history was useful – as when Homme's call came, Joey had just one day to rehearse before he debuted as a Queen in the car park of a San Francisco record store. "We only jammed with four people, and we knew them all previously," said Josh. "We ended up with Joey Castillo after one day of rehearsal and then left for the biggest tour of our lives. That qualifies us for the Biggest Gamblers In Rock award."

"They threw me on the bus and I've barely been home since," said Castillo. "Everybody loves to play. The work ethic is definitely there . . . Everyone has a different personality but they mesh well together. It's never a dream but we're all pretty rational. We can tour for a long time without anyone killing a bandmate. We're what Josh calls a band of young veterans. We've all been playing for a long time but we have each other at a point where we're comparatively young and fresh.

"What appealed to me with Queens was their capability to do what-ever they wanted – be it heavy or poppy – and still have it come off as unmistakably their own. They have a certain flavour and they have a way of twisting things into their own. It's an open door. Josh is always ready to listen. There's no intimidation. No one makes anyone feel that they can't speak up. From experience I can tell you that that's special. There's no weirdness, it's just about making music and enjoying what you do. I have to hand it to the guys, because people really do think they're like that, but it's definitely not all about being one big party. The guys all mean business and they're serious about the band."

Despite all this happy talk of new personnel, Homme was getting tired of a constantly rotating line-up. Whereas once he was resolutely upbeat about new members (sample quote: "Our line-up has a way of slipping and sliding around, which is great. For me, part of the excite-ment of going on tour is that I know it's never the same. And I assume that if we're making ourselves happy, that that's what's gotten us to where we are now, and so I assume that should make everyone else happy, too"), after Grohl's exit, he clearly desired some membership longevity. "I'm starting to get sick of showing people songs," he said. "It's getting old in certain aspects. Having the same drummer, at least, seems like something we should shoot for next." A temporary drummer before the arrival of Castillo was Failure sticksman, Kelly Scott. "We played with Dave, and it was great to play with him: we've been friends for a long time," he said. "But right now Kelly is drumming. Drumming is where Dave should stay. Even if it's not with us, he's such a great drummer. And rock needs really good drummers really badly."

Expectations had never been higher among those watching developments in the Queens camp. After all, the media and the industry were now on board with each new QOTSA album: in 1999, *Rolling Stone* had labelled QOTSA one of 'The Ten Most Important Hard And Heavy Bands Right Now', while *Rated R* had been voted Album Of The Year in the *NME*. Homme wasn't falling for the hype: "It would be a bad idea to take it that seriously. Rock'n'roll's fine. It's been fine since before we were here and it's going to be fine once we're gone. We're just trying to play a good version of it while we're here."

If the last album had given itself an R rating, "This one will be rated B for bizarre," chuckled Josh. "This is the most all-over-the-place one. It's kind of like the trancey element of the first one and the musical diversity of the second one – except even further. The last record we kind of wrote about ourselves and things that we'd done, and this one, we were on tour for so long that it's not like [Bon Jovi lyrics] 'I'm a cowboy, on a steel horse I ride,' it's about what we saw – translating other people's stories from English into French and back into English. When you're just living your life and not watching anyone else's, you write about your thing and hopefully it's something people can latch onto. But when you start writing about what you see, it's certainly much more universal."

A collective sigh of relief from the Queens' fanbase came on September 2, when *Songs For The Deaf* finally appeared. It was a huge, glittering, multi-layered, expansive, all-encompassing record with a few songs that hooked themselves immediately into the listener and others which required a dozen spins before their depth was fully revealed.

Most people's experience of *Songs . . .* began with the sound of a car door closing, a radio coming on and a cheesy DJ intoning "KLON, clone radio, we play more of the songs that sound like everyone else!" – the radio inserts that Oliveri had spoken of so gleefully – but an informed few had discovered that on inserting the CD and searching backwards from zero a hidden track revealed itself. This song, entitled 'The Real Song For The Deaf', was a collage of electronic sounds, and while it was thought-provoking, it was rarely played twice.

Once the opening DJ had said his idiotic piece, the first real tune, 'You Think I Ain't Worth A Dollar, But I Feel Like A Millionaire' begins with a muted drumbeat and guitar, leading unwary listeners to turn up the volume – only for a sudden volume surge of riffs and Nick Oliveri's insanely screamed vocals to explode from the speakers. "I'll be a massive conquistador!" shrieks the bass player, in a song that manages to combine the robotic beat the Queens had been talking about for half a decade with a punk attitude. Despite the song's violence, Nick said that it had been a new benchmark in restraint for him, ". . . my first sober vocal ever," as he described it.

The remarkable 'No One Knows' is next, the first single and a career triumph to date. Easily the catchiest song Homme and friends had penned so far, it's based on a funky guitar figure anchored by a fat bass and Grohl's precision-engineered drumming, and slopes along for a couple of minutes in and out of a loud chorus and mellow verse before a back end introduced by Oliveri's simple, Lemmy-style bass solo. The accompanying video was a surreal, Kafka-esque montage of the live band – Homme and Oliveri deadpanning malevolently to camera, Grohl in power-drummer mode – interspersed with a bizarre night-time forest drive where a deer is run over by the Queens' truck. Faking death with an evil glance to the viewer, the felled animal leaps off the tarmac as the musicians approach to see if it has survived the crash, overpowers them, slings them into the truck and drives it on a mad-dened, semi-dreamlike journey into the dark. It's one of the finest artistic statements of QOTSA's career.

'First It Giveth' is a drugs song, dealing with the initial creative impact of substance use and then how those same substances remove creativity. "I think at first you can draw inspiration," said Josh when asked about the song, "and then eventually it negates any inspiration." Not that this was apparent on first hearing: initially the song seems to be one of the many tracks on the album that embrace a dark, bluesy, sold-his-soul-at-the-crossroads kind of country horror that is reminiscent of The Doors and even the more experimental work of The Beatles. The isolated, tranced atmosphere is extended on 'A Song For The Dead', with its big distorted bass, almost funky drums, the very Hendrix-like guitar wail and the disturbing, droned background vocals. Mark Lanegan takes the lead vocal, with his throaty, uncompromising rasp perfect for the lyrics ("If you're hanging around, I'm holding the noose").

Lanegan goes even further after 'The Sky Is Falling' (a mellow song with double-tracked vocals from Josh) and 'Six Shooter' (80 seconds of Oliveri's punk snarls once again) on the amazing 'Hanging Tree', a horror-movie soundtrack stuffed into a single song. With Grohl holding down a shuffling 5/4 drum pattern with machine-like ease, the Screaming Trees singer excels himself with his dank, Tom Waits-like intoned vocals against the weirdest soundscape yet heard on a Queens album. Although 'No One Knows' was an evident first single, Homme said: "I feel like there's a lot of songs that fit the singles time frame. I'd like to hear a song like 'Hanging Tree' be a single. It's a dark, beautiful song that's got a very pop sensibility, very haunting. Alain Johannes from Eleven wrote the melody and music so it's easier for me to talk about that song. I don't know any band that sounds like that song sounds like."

It's a dark, thrilling ride, and when the mood lifts on 'Go With The Flow' and 'Gonna Leave You', two much more orthodox rock songs along the lines of 'The Lost Art Of Keeping A Secret', it's like sunlight emerging from behind clouds. The latter song in particular is an almost sweet slice of pop, boasting Beach Boys-like backing vocals. Of the punk and pop balance, Homme explained: "It's supposed to be tough enough for the guys and sweet enough for the chicks. That's what The Stooges were. We've been slowly trying to weed out boys who want to bounce off each other and have their girlfriends come instead. Most of my favourite punk rock has a pop melody or pop sensibility, and since I've always been afraid of pop but liked it, I censored it from our melodies. This is the first record where I didn't do that at all. This is how I feel it and see it."

There's always a Kyuss song on Queens Of The Stone Age albums, and on *Songs For The Deaf* it's 'Do It Again', which has a stamping, semi-glam-rock drumbeat (in the sense of Slade and Bowie, that is) with the trademark drone that Homme had now refined to the level of an art form. Similar vintage influences come to the fore on 'God Is In The Radio', a slyly titled comment that is reminiscent of the loping, 'Spirit In The Sky'-level hippie optimism that had died over three decades previously. 'Another Love Song' goes back even further for the lightest, most poppy song that Queens have ever released: it's loaded with super-cheesy circus organ sounds and, despite its feather light tones, is dripping with lyrical and musical sarcasm – the polar opposite of the next song, the title track, an industrial drone, oozing sludge and decay. The album comes to an end with another hidden track, this time a beautifully crafted acoustic-guitar ballad with keening vocals from Dean Ween. Its sheer beauty is beguiling and confusing: what were the band thinking of, ending their most anticipated record to date with this slice of elegance?

The album's many styles and layers made it a feast for the ears, even if the constant DJ segments became tedious rather quickly. The six or so absolute Queens classics (headed up by 'No One Knows' and 'Hanging Tree', to these ears at least) are now as essential to any QOTSA show as 'Feelgood Hit Of The Summer'. Critics queued up to lavish praise on *Songs For The Deaf*, not least because early pressings came with a bonus DVD of live, studio, and interview footage. There was also a clean (i.e. without Oliveri's barked obscenities) version for those who required it.

Asked if he had named the album *Songs For The Deaf* because he was making fun of deaf people, Homme replied: "I think that's one of the reasons. We like to do things that are as multi-tiered as possible. There's a bunch of different interpretations. A lot of really great music has fallen on deaf ears for years so it's like, here's another one. People also get really nervous if you talk about retarded people. But it just describes a condition. It's not a bad word at all. It's only bad when a bunch of condescending fucks use it. It's like, 'Why do you feel sorry for them?' They're happy all the time. I wish I was retarded. Oh, the luxury of retardation . . ." He continued, presumably with tongue at least partly in cheek, "I've known a bunch of retarded people and they're always psyched. Unless someone is in a mental institution getting beat down, then it's great. If they don't mind, then I certainly don't mind. It looks like fun. Imagine getting all happy about balloons for 10 hours. That's awesome . . . I think we're on a search for an escape that kind of feels like that. Kind of bone-headed but uplifting and easily entertains. Music is a tribal thing and it should hit you in the crotch and the gut first. It can hit you in the head later. If not, the other two locations are just fine. So it's about grooves. It's tough enough for the dudes and sweet enough for the chicks. You don't need to be Yngwie Malmsteen to be good. Oh no, you do. Oh, wait, you don't. My notes were wrong!"

Most reviewers made mention of the album's darker, gloomier qualities. The band agreed with them. "It is darker," Homme said, "though I don't think it's depressing – because in the darkness of it, we can make it through all this. I think the real lyrical bent comes out on 'The Sky Is Falling', which is, don't spend any time on something you don't like, only give time to things that you like . . . Bad things happen, try to get past them. So I think there's light at the end of the lyrical tunnel." Both Josh and Nick made veiled comments about the depressing events that had occurred in both their lives in the interim period since *Rated R*: surely a factor in the more introspective songs on the new record. As Homme explained, "A lot of things have happened to Nick and I over the last year and a half. You lose people, or people get separated – a lot of stuff happens in a life, and what's important to me about music is that it reflects what's going on for you personally as the writer of it."

Many interviewers enquired whether the events of September 11, 2001 (less than a year previously) had influenced the lyrics. "Most of these songs, 12 out of 14, were written prior to that," said Josh, "though they certainly take on a new meaning. You almost see things in lyrics that you've written that you didn't see before, as if after they're written, you find out what they're about. [*Songs For The Deaf* is] the most deliberate record that I've ever made. I spent a lot of time planning beforehand, because of the complexity of it. My writing is getting more orchestrated – as I get older, I almost hear things in movements, and a record is a great chance to really express yourself and push it out as far as you can." The groove and feel of the songs had been crucial to him, he added: "That body groove, 'God Is In The Radio' . . . it's almost like Texas boogie. Ever since we went to Brazil and visited a samba school and really watched this kind of tribal, guttural, crotch-oriented music, it's really become more of a priority. I think we also really like the swing of 'Song For The Dead' once it gets into the verse, the almost slave-ship tempo of 'Song For The Deaf', it seems to be everywhere."

Although he was acting merely as a session musician and not as a songwriter per se, Dave Grohl's input had been noticeable. Josh explained: "The chorus of 'First It Giveth', he really improved on what was there which was already difficult enough and he made it even more difficult. There was some great spontaneous stuff. The end of 'Song For The Dead' and 'God Is In The Radio' – moments like that where it's just us playing together. It's not about did Dave Grohl make it better, or not: while he was playing, there were moments where everyone was just doing their thing, those were the moments where the best things happened."

Perhaps this was down to the Queens' methods of composing, surely rather different to his own experiences in Nirvana and Foo Fighters: "We said to Dave in the beginning, if Nick's playing a bass hook and I'm playing a guitar hook, you need to play a drum hook – because he plays all of these instruments he hears all the hooks, and is able to jump from one to the next and be really vital. You could listen to the drums on their own or the bass on its own and it sounds cool by itself. That's true for all instruments, and when they get together, it becomes gestalt. The sum of those cool parts is even bigger . . . It's the first time [Dave's] done that since Nirvana . . . it's where he fuckin' should be. He's an amazing player and he shines on the drums, and I think we were looking for everyone to stand on their own, to be an individual. You hear everyone play parts. Dave played his ass off."

Grohl himself had been thrilled by the experience, telling one interviewer before the tour: "I realise I was put on Earth to play drums . . . I just know it. I don't have to think about it. I love every minute of it, every second of it. The last time I experienced a feeling like this tour was 1991, right as *Nevermind* was coming out. Everyone felt that there was this new electricity, and other people were going to get to experience it. There was this buzz. It's really wild to experience that again 10 years later.

"This is the best album I've ever played on," said Dave, perhaps overzealously. "For the last 40 years, you've had the Fab Four and Led Zeppelin and all these bands where a specific group of people defined what the band's sound should be. The cool thing about Queens Of The Stone Age is that all the records have different combinations of musicians. This combination is fucking awesome, but the next combination could be awesome as well. And it's indefinable. It's slippery.

"We're trying to unite subcultures," he added. "Our shows are filled with Hessian [metal-loving] guys and goth chicks and punk kids, and we're trying to unite all those sub-cliques. I used to pay allegiance to punk rock – I had mohawks and all kinds of fucking shit. And then one day I realised that punk was just another clique with a bunch of rules, just like the Republicans or the Wiccans. I stopped paying allegiance to the fashion side of the rules. I think it's more punk rock to look the way I look now. I can infiltrate and be like the good cancer."

Josh: "He's one of the finest musicians you'll ever play with and he just totally transformed the band. BD – Before Dave – I was a drummer as well and on stage I really had to concentrate on the whole band. I had to cue drums and make sure everything was running right. Now, Nick and Dave are so tight together the rhythm section totally takes care of itself and it's totally freed me up to being a guitarist again, being able to concentrate on my instrument. That's changed everything – everyone now feels that they can concentrate on what they're best at, because Dave's come in and so totally taken the pressure off. You don't have to stand there saying to Dave fucking Grohl, 'Uhh, maybe things'd be better this way,' because whatever you're thinking he's already 10 steps ahead of you and thinking up some new shit that ups the ante on *you*. Playing with the best people really increases your own ability and your own openness to music. It's made, and is making us, massively better at what we do and it's given us this feel we never had before."

Nick: "Dave just instantly raised our game to a whole new level, not just musically but in the sheer energy he brings to it. A lot of musicians you see just starting try and play shit all cool, but Dave's been doing this for 20 years and he's still incredible to watch because he throws himself into it so dementedly. He lunges and he snarls and he sweats and he passes out and he drives himself so hard you fear for his safety."

Of the Queens songwriting approach, Homme said: "I think our system works best because it has no rules. Sometimes Nick or I will bring in a completed idea and then, just as much of the time, [there are] things that are unfinished or that get developed together, and we work with outside people as well. Our rule is just play the good stuff. Since we all have side projects, we kind of leave our feelings and egos at the door, like someone could go, 'What do you think of this?' And you try a few different tempos and a few different ways, and I might look over and go, 'I think this sucks.' No one goes, 'Well, I worked on it for two weeks, you know.'"

This, perhaps, is where other outlets such as Mondo Generator come in most useful, as he elaborated: "We say, well I guess this is something for my side project, because it doesn't mean it's bad, or good, it means it's not Queens for this moment. So because of that, we kind of get to skip lots of that inter-band psychology [which] is really good because we're just on a search for our best stuff now at this date."

The modus operandi of the Queens was, more and more, to do what other people didn't do. "My goal is to be a slippery fish," Homme said. "The intention is to build something unpinnable, where you have no idea where we're heading. It's a perfect situation, because it means I can do whatever I want on each album. In a way, you will shape what I do next. By saying something, you can guarantee I won't do that.

"I have pages in notebooks of what this band should be, the many layers," he added. "It works on a bonehead level. It goes all the way down, until you realise you're being made fun of at the bonehead level." The Queens' aim, Homme explained, was to "infiltrate and kill the king. And you don't do that by knocking on the fucking draw-bridge door. You become his adviser, whisper in his ear, slit his throat, blame it on the cook and run away."

The presence of the extra guests gave Homme space to breathe, as he explained: "I hate being the fucker at the front of the band directing shit. I like to be part of the mess, be pushed by other people. For too long in Queens it was like I had a million things to take care of. Now all I have to do is play guitar and occasionally sing, and it feels like way more of a band now than it ever did before. And we all kind of realised that just being unprecious about your music, allowing it to be fucked with and fucking with other people's ideas as well – often makes music that is the most precious. We're not here to dictate to anyone What This Is All About. That's for you to find out, fucker!"

CHAPTER 9

2003: No One Knew . . .

THE public reception to *Songs For The Deaf* repaid the band's collective efforts, with the album entering the US charts at number 15. Josh Homme was pleased but didn't lose his head: "We have patience with music, a year or five years down the road it may kind of rewrite itself and become what it was supposed to be. There's two songs on this record that are over five years old, you know? 'God Is In The Radio' and 'No One Knows'. I write songs around beats and bricks so there'll be four, five songs in the same kind of structure, and they can't all go on the same thing, you know, or it sounds all the same. And you can just sit by the phone, waiting for a song to call you, and when it calls you, 'You're like, thank God, where are you? I'll pick you up.' You know, you can't force it through."

Songs For The Deaf was all part of a masterplan, as Homme partly revealed: "I think I've always looked at these first three records as a set. The first one needed to distance itself from Kyuss, my previous band, without losing anybody and establishing a new sound. The second record fans out the music, so that we can play a little bit more of what we'd like to play, and I think this third record is the personification of the idea which is musical diversity, and you know, goes from garage sounds to almost like rock opera in some moments. Like 'A Song For The Deaf' is everyone singing and screaming and coming in, swirling, and I think production-wise, this is the closest to the dry old ZZ Top drum sound, dry in your face, so that anything that has any sort of effect shows depth – sonic depth.

"I've been thinking about this record since the first one," Homme went on. "But I wanted to proceed slowly or else we'd lose people."

"This record is how we are," Oliveri added. "But we had to move in

129

stages. We don't have a huge fanbase, but the fans we do have, we love them and don't want to stray too far away."

Oliveri was also eloquent about the deep elements of the new album, explaining: "It's definitely a lot darker, yeah. To be honest, it was just what was coming out, man. We tried to do other shit like that, something a little bit more in the pop vein, but I think that stuff just came out darker. What was coming out of us was what we wrote down. I don't know too much about whether *Rated R* was more poppy or not. Maybe it is, I don't know . . . we tried not to make the same record twice, obviously, so that's a hard one to answer. I'm sure there are some elements of both records in the new one, and a lot of elements and things that we're just extending on what those two are. We want to try to make records that we can't describe." Of the cause of the band's more pensive moments, he clarified: "We wanted each song to have its own feeling, and with three different singers singing . . . with 'Just Another Love Song', I don't know if it's soft, it sounds more garagey to me. I got divorced, so that was just a tune that came out. It's just one of those things about shit that's going down with you and shit like that. One of those things, man . . ."

Although Oliveri's recent divorce must have been painful, he remained upbeat about the band and the fact that there were only two principal decision-makers: "We like it that way because when it comes to making the damn decisions, there's only one other person to ask. It's just easier, man. We've been in bands where there's been five guys and you have to ask everybody and someone says no, every time . . . I can't do that. If there are people that want to play with us and they're not into it, we say we're doing this and this and if that's not good, to somebody else it will be. We just kind of set it up that way. We've got a good sound down now, so it's all cool." As for the radio commentary content between the songs, he laughed: "I think it was the only thing that could tie together the songs to seem like they belonged with each other. The thing is, we did the movie theme on the last record, with *Rated R* . . . We thought about it and we were like, 'We'll do radio this time around, because it makes sense and you can hear it.'

"I think what we've kind of done over the years is you don't write anything you can't really manhandle live. So we've kind of taken these songs and they're almost bigger now than they are on the album, and that lesson has helped us over the years. You know, you go see some people play and you're like, 'Wow, that doesn't sound very good, or it doesn't sound anything close to the record.' I think what we do is try and make it different from the record and bigger, and sort of better. We just make our favourite music, and I already think our music is pretty adventurous and our song arrangements and instruments that are used on albums – the last song on *Rated R* has a steel drum on it and it doesn't sound lame, and I think that's pretty adventurous. So I think we're searching to make the most original stuff that we can think of and try not to sound like anyone else, and I think that's what we're doing."

As Josh explained, the two writers' styles gelled well together: "Nick's style is more about not looking peripherally, just running straight at it, and mine is more scenic. That works good. I can take on that straight-ahead approach, but I don't need to, because Nick's version of it is better than mine . . . We write about what's going on, and it was kind of a rough year . . . But it's important that the music isn't negative, either, that it's almost bittersweet. That it's not being beat down on you, that it doesn't have a complaining aspect."

"We were basically just making fun of ourselves," Oliveri sniggered.

Rather than rest on their laurels after the release of *Songs For The Deaf*, at the start of 2003 the members of Queens threw themselves into more work. Lanegan had a solo album to complete and the entire cast of QOTSA lent a hand, making the record pretty much a Queens creation in all but name. Homme had been working on a project called The Eagles Of Death Metal, a band which would come to more prominence the following year, but which for now had supported the main band on a few dates. After a while this arrangement was dropped, for no particular grounds other than Homme's arcane reasoning that: "I got in an argument with myself about how much I should pay myself and then both me's realised that none of us get paid, so me, myself and I had a big meeting and a big cry and a hug."

Perhaps this off-on approach suited Josh, who told one interviewer that he lived an itinerant existence: "I don't own any houses. I rent a room at my brother's house in LA and I stay at my friend Hutch's house in [the desert in] Joshua Tree. I stay here until I get sick of it, and then I go there for a while until I get sick of it."

Around this time the author interviewed Nick Oliveri, who was still hugely enthusiastic about the new record. "We're really excited!" he burbled down the transatlantic line. "It's kind of a concept record, like all of our records are. It's all about driving from LA to the Joshua Tree in the desert and listening to the radio on the way – and as you're switching stations you hear our songs. It starts off with some of the more frantic songs and then it gets more peaceful as you get into the desert. There's some new shit on it that you will not be expecting.

"Our new record is the darkest we've made," he added, more soberly. "A lot has happened to the band in the last year – the death of Joey Ramone, for one, that was a sad day for me. He kept me playing music when I thought I couldn't. Then the terrorist shit, and relatives dying, and divorces . . . whatever, it's been a dark year. A lot of shit went down."

Asked if Mondo Generator were planning to record any more music in the near future, Nick barked: "Yes, we just did 10 new tracks with Brant Bjork. It's gonna be good, man, we're going for it. I did all the rhythm guitar and bass in one day. It's all the crazy shit and some of the more mellow shit that doesn't make it to the Queens record. It's like, you gotta put your best foot forward for Queens and use all your other shit for your solo record. I love it because it allows me to stretch out just a bit. Every time there's a new Queens record I guarantee there's gonna be another Mondo record, because I can't fit all my songs on there. With the Queens records I get a certain number of songs on there, so does Josh and so does Mark Lanegan.

"We're doing a show supporting Amen next Wednesday under the name Mondo Generator, but actually it'll be Queens Of The Stone Age. We're even gonna do a couple of Kyuss songs – nobody's gonna be expecting it. We haven't told anyone about this in the States – I'm only telling *you* because you're in England!" Of his bandmate, he said: "I was an admirer of Lanegan's voice – he gives you chills when he sings soft – so it's a real treat to play with somebody like that. I'm counting my blessings right now. I never played in a band where I felt this strongly, 'Wow, this is something good.'" The Dwarves? "Dude, The Dwarves were a nightmare and a beautiful dream at the same time. I've been kicked out of The Dwarves, I've been re-hired by The Dwarves, we've mutually decided that I should leave The Dwarves, and now we've decided that whenever I want to come in and add my two cents, I can. It's a good relationship. I still do stuff with them. Whenever I have time off from Queens I try to do as much side stuff as possible, because it allows me to get it out of my system for a couple of months. I still got a lot of that in me, so I've got to let it out."

I was intrigued to learn what it was like actually being Nick Oliveri: "You know, I was pretty wild when I was younger. I've calmed down a little bit. I was being crazy and off the hook all the time. Just everything all at once, 24/7. I was a madman. No, I've never sat down with a therapist, man – I'm afraid they'll analyse me!" How much of a drug and alcohol user was he? "It fluctuates. We don't have any habits, so one day somebody's drinking, the next day they're doing whatever. There's nothing every single day. I like my drinks. In the daytime I'm a beer guy but at night I like to drink vodka and Jack Daniel's. It's nice to have a couple of shots. I've never been a guy who sits at home in the dark with a bottle between my legs, though. I'm definitely down with a party shot with a couple of girls."

Was the seven-drug cocktail of nicotine, Valium, Vicodan, marijuana, ecstasy, alcohol and cocaine listed in 'Feelgood Hit Of The Summer' based on a real experience? "Yes. That song came about because we made that cocktail. We thought, 'Holy shit, we've done about seven different things today.' When that happens, some people get sick. Some people just keep going. On that particular day, me and Josh both kept going . . . We listed them and figured out how to say them in a row, and then it turned into a song. No, you can't get Vicodan in the UK, but you can get something similar, like a strong painkiller. If you're drinking with it, it'll really knock you on your ass. It's pretty wild. Everything's numb, you're stumbling around saying, 'I can't feel nothin' . . .'"

Would he ever settle down? "Never!" he retorted, laughing. "I'll do that when I die." And on that note – apart from one last query which, to this day, I think no one else has asked Oliveri without getting to know him well first (Q: "Why is your scrotum so asymmetrical?" A: "We call that The Kango! I'm not sure why that hangs lowers than anything else. I guess I'm just warm in that area. When it's cold it gets sucked right up, but when it's hot it just hangs right down to my knees") – he signed off.

After a while it became apparent that *Songs For The Deaf* would become a substantial hit, both with reviewers and CD buyers, though Josh and Nick knew not to take it all too seriously: "We know how temporary all that shit is," said Homme, grinning. "They've been nice to us so far just so they can say how shit we've become! Christ, I'd rather people were saying good things about our music than bad, but at the end of the day it's not gonna make any difference to what we do. Especially when you look at some of the shit that gets good reviews these days. At least we know we're getting kind words because of the music and not because of who we know. We don't know anyone, and if they really knew us and what we think of 'em, they sure as fuck won't give us a good review!"

Nick: "We haven't been propelled to a false status because of contacts or any of that shit: at the end of the day with us you have to really listen to the music and go from there, because there's very little else to go on other than some guys getting together to express whatever they've got. We're not 'trying' to do anything other than make our Queens Of The Stone Age music. Once we've done that, all the other shit is just fun and games. It's why bands get so wound up by promotion and shit – because that's what they rely on to feel like they amount to something, they're told it's crucial to the whole game and they devote far too much attention to it, more than is healthy. We always feel totally preposterous when people want to take our photo, or ask us questions, so we always do it with a healthy spirit of unseriousness and it makes it all way more tolerable. We really can't be bothered checking how bad we look in mirrors all the time. They always tell the same story. You're the ugliest one of all. Get used to it."

Was the record being bought in large quantities because the public were suddenly enjoying heavier music, as was popularly supposed? Josh shrugged this off: "The heavier the mainstream is supposedly getting, the less we give a fuck about it. We've really become better songwriters on this LP, and the lyrics really reflect us this time – we've written songs as songs and not tried to turn them into 'events'. This is the first time we've felt like printing the lyrics on the sleeve, because we're proud of them – they were honed down by each of us feeling free to chop and cut each other's thoughts. And what you get is an honest reflection of who we are right now." Nick added: "It's like the first time we've felt free to not necessarily 'rock' all the fucking time, really get beneath the bones of the songs and go where they need to go. And it all came from those sessions with Dave and the band just realising how much we could now do. The songs were mostly written before we even went in to record, but in the actual process of recording a million things happened to them so everyone contributed . . . The weird thing is with this album is that it really does seem like the time is right for it. This album's fucking needed right now. I've been waiting all my life to be in the right place at the right time!"

"It's what's best about the two previous records condensed and purified and then fucked up by all the things and people we've done and been done by in the past two years," said Josh. "There's a lot of things on it that I guess people who haven't properly listened to us won't expect. I think the fans know to expect something different from us from each album. The first album was really about moving on from Kyuss without alienating everybody, keeping the heaviness but turning it into this really trancey robot rock. The second album was about keeping part of those elements but just widening the sound so we didn't have to keep writing the same kinds of songs. This album is about, 'Right, you're with us? Let's fucking take you somewhere.' We were never like, 'cool', we made a record, let's make another one just the same, because we get bored easily. We like to keep pushing up the ante on everything we do, not because we feel like we're throwing down a challenge to anybody but just to challenge ourselves. The only people we want to better, we want to outdo, is ourselves. *Songs For The Deaf* is that next step."

Josh was keen to acknowledge that he and his band saw the bigger picture when it came to commercial success, and the position of other big bands. "It's none of my business if Creed exist or not, we're not presumptuous enough or concerned enough to really wanna 'save' rock'n'roll . . . we're not in any sense bitter about where we are. We're just eternally, totally, grateful that we're musicians and we can just about make a living from it: we've been going insane penniless, screaming off roofs and dying in basements for too long in our lives to really care about 'success' in terms of popularity. To us, success or failure is a totally musical question . . . Our attitude towards people in the industry is, you're working for me, and you're damn right we know that the only reason we're here is because other bands on your label are making you money. Go make money. We'll make music. And if you want another 'Lost Art' I'll write you one and then shove it up your ass so far you'll taste it. We've no plan other than to never have a fucking plan."

The lack of a game plan tied in with the state of the musical market, which was in flux at the start of 2003. A new, unpolished league of garage-rock bands led by The Strokes, The Hives and The White Stripes had taken control of the charts from once-fashionable nu-metal acts such as Staind and Papa Roach, a development which had not escaped the attention of QOTSA. In true Queens style, they welcomed the first of the new/old breed to the stage: "I think that people's ears are now ready for records that are much rawer-sounding," said Homme. "People's ears were never really ready for The Cramps or The Stooges or Hasil Adkins. With records like ours, The White Stripes, The Strokes, the way they sound – forget if you like the music or not – it seems like the public is ready for raw. And I like that [people's] ears are finally in tune with what music sounds like when you're standing right in front of it. And they've done away with overproduced music made by people in giant shorts. But, really, I don't care until it's time for me to listen to music. Because I spent so much time on stuff I didn't like, I had to realise what the hell I was doing. It seems like a better idea to be for something and now there's finally a few things I can be for. We played with The Hives four years ago, and they were great then. Now, there's that thing we call the Nirvana Theory, where people say they don't like someone because they are doing well, which I find equally dumb-assed. All of a sudden that same record isn't good any more? I understand when to hold on to your favourite band, as opposed to one that's been around for a while. And we're not a new band."

The once much maligned stoner-rock genre had survived, however, albeit in a different format. Sometime Kyuss members Brant Bjork and John Garcia had recorded their latest albums in LA and Cincinnati respectively – not in the desert. Josh Homme indicated that the Desert Sessions might be coming to an end after the next volume, *9 & 10*, perhaps because Rancho De La Luna studio owner Fred Drake had finally died of the diseases which he had fought for years. Homme and Queens guitarist Troy Van Leeuwen had recently contributed to the second album from DJ Shadow and James Lavelle's experimental trip-hop project U.N.K.L.E., recording six hours of sessions for what Homme labelled "the bad-ass tune on the new U.N.K.L.E record". He explained: "They just have a dark way of making you still be able to dance, which is nice. We all do things outside the band, just like a merry bunch of minstrels skipping through the countryside . . . breaking off and doing other things. It makes you really glad to come back to the band. It's sort of like an important adventure for everyone else to go out and discover things and bring that ship back."

Homme seemed to be looking for another experiment to try out after the third Queens album. He even appeared to be developing some tolerance: "I used to immediately laugh at all of those new hard-rock bands without even listening to them," he mused. "But I really like what System Of A Down are doing with bizarre arrangements and crazy vocal lines. And I like bands like The Deftones, because they are so passionate about their thing that they're about ready to explode. I'm forced to go into other territories to find good music. People come backstage and hear Björk playing, and they're like, 'Is that Björk? What's wrong with you guys?' I have no respect for genre. In fact, I deliberately disrespect it on my own records."

As for the state of the music scene, he ruminated: "The current climate makes me stick out. By the same token, I like to listen to music, and I've been waiting for stuff to present itself that I like . . . I think we go through different cycles. Sometimes we get to a point where we feel we've gone far enough and we decide to add a little structure. It doesn't matter what it is, but eventually you feel like you've been doing some-thing too much. You know that philosophy that says anything that's worth doing is worth overdoing? I don't subscribe to that. The goal isn't to be the heaviest band in the world. In a perfect environment, songs come into your head and that's where you go. You don't make any judgements about them. The less we concentrate on it, the more it will just come out."

More than a few interviewers came up with the idea that the Queens album was doing well because heavy music was the music of the moment. However, Homme didn't buy that theory: "There must be 50,000 bands. I don't necessarily think that [in recent years] the good rock didn't exist. I mean, we've been playing for 12 years – this isn't some overnight thing – and we played with The Hives four years ago. To me it's more a case of, 'Oh, welcome. We've been here partying and you're just showing up.'

"I love Kylie Minogue. That song 'Can't Get You Out Of My Head' is the perfect bubblegum pop song, but it's dark as fuck. Totally dark. She's got cute little horse teeth, and her ass is really high in the air, but she's really tiny."

2003 began with rehearsals for an extended QOTSA tour, which would take up three months between February and May – the most extended jaunt the band had undertaken for some time. Signs that the band had truly settled into the public's consciousness came with the news that Josh was now one half of a celebrity couple with his new girl-friend Brody Dalle, singer and guitarist of some note with a punk-rock band called The Distillers. The Melbourne-born frontwoman and her band were touring with Queens, and the story of how they had come together was the stuff of tabloid fantasy. Dalle's ex-husband, Rancid singer Tim Armstrong, had allegedly criticised the couple in the press after a *Rolling Stone* photo shoot pictured Josh and Brody in a passion-ate, but staged, embrace. Homme was slightly taken aback by the new focus on his love life, admitting: "I'm not too comfortable with that . . . It's been a little weird for me because I'm quite personal about that stuff." Ambiguously, and threateningly, he added: "It's quite hard to have someone say something bad about someone I care about and then not take care of it myself.

"I had this one girl who followed us around asking to get married," Homme told *Playboy*. "Finally, one day she couldn't take it any more that I wasn't even talking or responding to her, so she just came up alongside me and started throwing left jabs and right hooks off the back of my head, screaming, 'I love you!' I started laughing and that's because she hit like a girl. Which was good for me. It was one of those things where I was like, 'God, is that supposed to hurt?' It felt like someone throwing little Nerf balls off my head.

"In Melbourne somebody tried to take a swing at me. I picked up my beer but the table wasn't connected to the top, so when I picked up mine, it acted like a seesaw, and this guy said, 'You blah, blah, blah,' kept swearing at me. I was like, 'Look, I'm sorry, it was an accident, I'll buy you another drink.' I pick up this sweatshirt, I'm like, 'Whose is this, I don't want it to get wet,' and his girlfriend goes, 'It's mine you retard.' And they kept going and kept going, and I went to go buy them drinks and I thought, 'God, they're like strangely overzealous about hating me right now.' Maybe they just thought, 'Hey you think you can come here from America, rock stuff, dude,' stuff. I feel lucky to have my job and I love playing music and I put everything I have into it. I find it extremely easy to justify what I do because I give a shit and I'm doing it. I'm a workaholic, so I can sleep at night easily no matter what anyone from

Melbourne or Iowa or whatever, no matter who it is . . . if someone says, 'You think that you're a rock star,' I can easily sit there and be like, 'You're not bothering me at all.' It's not even denting. I mean ultimately, he took a swing at me, and that was his mistake, you know."

More surreal indicators that Queens were now a full-blown brand came when the single 'No One Knows' was nominated for a Grammy award in the Hard Rock Performance category, the highest honour the US music industry can pay. "It's strange," pondered Homme, "you want people to like your music and you want them to like it for the right reasons and . . . yeah, it's bizarre because we've been playing for a long time, doing this for a long time. It's more strange just to get [a Grammy nomination] regardless of what time frame it is, and the amount of time we've been playing because I don't think we ever think about things like [this]. In fact, I know we don't think about things like that. So it feels like being recognised by someone that you almost never think about. It's kind of hard to describe because it's never in my mind, like, 'Boy, I wonder if we'll get a Grammy nomination.' You never sit there and think about it."

Oliveri was jubilant when he was told. "I was at home when Josh called me and said, 'Hey, man, guess what?'" he chuckled. "Then I said, 'What? No way.' I thought he was lying to me. As it turns out it was for real. It was cool. I never even joked around about the Grammys. I never once had said anything like, 'Yeah, see y'all at the Grammys,' or anything. Obviously, I called my mom and told her about it. That's certainly the type of thing that she's going to be more excited about than you are yourself."

"That was a cool first single," he later recalled. "We didn't expect it to do as well as it did. I'm not saying that we didn't love the song. We love all the songs on the record. But, it could've been any of the songs on the record. I think the reason we went with 'No One Knows' is because it featured the drums and it features a bass part, and the guitar part. It has all these different elements of what the band is. It illustrates that, hey, we can jam, too – not just play structured pop songs. It also represents how much changes with this band as far as music is concerned. We're going to go into weird bass parts and experiment with guitars." Although the band didn't ultimately win the award (which went to Evanescence's goth-lite 'Bring Me To Life'), they shrugged it off, with Nick remarking, "We won by just receiving the nomination.

That's how I saw it. We would never have even dreamed that it (a nomination) was even possible when we started out."

Did all this success mean that the band were now rich? Apparently not, as Josh hinted: "Now we have our assistants call each other and we tell each other we're going to do lunch . . . nah, I'm just kidding. You know, it hasn't really translated into that just yet or anything, I don't know . . . that's the thing, I don't know man, all that stuff seems like really out of my realm. I mean when it comes to just playing and showing up somewhere and having a drink with somebody, that's something I know about and this other stuff is more new to me." Wealthy or not, Homme was bullish about the state of affairs within Queens, boasting: "Man, we're playing the best we've ever played ever as a band and so I think anyone who's seen us before will be like, 'Wow, this is even more, you know?' Which is part of the reason we've always had a revolving line-up, so that each time you see it it's like you've never ever seen it before, and the first-time people I think we're going to knock on their ass."

Were the band themselves pleased with the way the new album had turned out? Nick: "People have been saying that it's an improvement on *Rated R* and tried to dig out of us that we don't like *Rated R* or something. Of course it's a fucking improvement! Have people really developed such low expectations now that bands are meant to do two albums, the second one worse than the first, and then disappear off the face of the earth? Every single thing we've done I have believed in 200%, or why put your fucking name to it? I loved *Rated R*, I loved the debut and I seriously fucking love *Songs For The Deaf*."

As always, Homme played the more restrained foil to Oliveri's outspoken vehemence: "I think that's the first time our dark pop sensibility came out, because before, anything that used to sound like a chorus I'd just censor it out, and now I don't censor myself. I think we lost our punk rock guilt, which was, 'Do well but don't do *too* well.' " He referred once again to Kyuss' 'they' theory': "Will 'they' say we sold out, what will 'they' say, what will 'they' do?' And now we're like, fuck them, you probably wouldn't like them if you met them anyway. And they will never be happy, you know, it's about making yourself happy with your own music. Like when we left the studio with this record it was already a success to us, and now we give it to you and that part of it is beyond our control. It's great to get this Grammy nomination and all these nods from magazines and stuff but really that's beyond our control – we can't make music explicitly for that reason, because music isn't really for that, that's almost like a peripheral thing that happens when you play, or what doesn't happen. I mean that's why it's called *Songs For The Deaf*, we've made a lot of records that have fallen on deaf ears and we know tons and tons of great bands that no one's ever heard that are some of our favourite music."

Homme wasn't averse to a little swagger when the occasion demanded it, promising that the next album would be better still: "No problem, we've already got songs that are better than this record. We don't feel pressure like that because we're always writing all the time. I mean, right now our focus is this record, it's just we have enough songs to blow away this record to do another one – we're always onto the next thing all the time. For lack of a better example, it's like if you vomit, you don't stop and look at it – you keep on going! It's better than *Songs For The Deaf*, it's way better. I think we're onto a new phase . . ."

His words were about to be proved prophetic.

In autumn 2003 the latest *Desert Sessions, Volumes 9 & 10*, were released, notable for the presence of English singer Polly Harvey, whose unorthodox, emotional music had been admired by Homme for a long time. Dean Ween and Joey Castillo also appeared, with the latter remarking, "It's one of the best times I've had. You turn up and Josh pushes record. No one has any hang-ups."

On top of this, two more QOTSA singles were due for release. The first was the hypnotic 'Go With The Flow', described by Homme as a 'straightforward rocker', accompanied by the usual trippy Queens video, created by the British animation consortium Shynola, who also provided videos for U.N.K.L.E. and others: "It's animated," sniggered Josh, "and we're playing chicken with another truck, and we kind of crash into one another, among other things. It's very interesting. I've never seen anything like it."

'First It Giveth' was set to appear in May, promoted with the band's confusingly varied takes on what the song actually meant. Oliveri explained, "It's about sometimes you can be partying, and the party turns so you're alone in isolation. You're in a room by yourself, so first it giveth, then it taketh away." Troy Van Leeuwen took the philo-sophical angle, adding: "Basically, you take something to go up, and inevitably you have to come down at some point – I'm talking about religion here. You get high on God and then the devil comes in and yanks you back down."

July saw the start of another Lollapalooza, which the band would fit in between bouts of songwriting and recording wherever possible. Later in the year there would be festival support slots with the newly anointed biggest rock band in the world, the Red Hot Chili Peppers, at which PJ Harvey would also be playing. In the face of all this activity, it was just as well that the band seemed to have stabilised into a solid line-up. As Nick explained, "We've finally found players that want to stay and we want them to. We haven't had that before. It wasn't that we wanted it to be two or three people, it was that we hadn't found the right people until now. So it's gotta be better now, because bringing in guests who don't know the songs is a different thing. It takes more time with people learning stuff and showing them parts. Plus, all the newer songs are better because our songwriting just keeps improving."

The idea of the next QOTSA album, even so soon after the release of the previous record, was a serious one, it seemed. Oliveri: "There's all kinds of guitar-heavy stuff that's similar to [the self-titled debut album], and some more melodic, poppy stuff with hooks and choruses like *Rated R*, and stuff that's hard, hard, hard and driving like 'Six Shooter' from *Songs For The Deaf*. Plus there'll be stuff that will be unexpected, because we're always trying to experiment with new things so we never end up making the same record twice . . . it's gonna be hard to choose [just] some of the tunes. Do you do a triple record or do you do another 14- or 15-song record? There's a lot to choose from, and you don't want to cut away too much because then it cuts out a style that the band's also good at. So to cut out too much is to cut out too much. To cut out a little would be to cut out too much. So we have to really sift through it and not rush it. We're not even rehearsing the new songs, because if we start rehearsing then we're gonna be playing them live. And by the time we go to record them, we'll already be tired of them. So why sound burned in the recording when it can be fresh and you're still loving it?"

On top of all this there was the much-anticipated new Mondo Generator album, snidely titled *A Drug Problem That Never Existed* on the Ipecac label, owned by ex-Faith No More singer and alternative rock icon Mike Patton. Oliveri had timed it to appear on July 1, just in time for the July 4 weekend. "It's my Independence Day," laughed Oliveri. "It's basically the harder stuff that I do that doesn't work in Queens. I'm a mad young man. I'm pissed off about something, so it's therapy for me to do Mondo. I get to scream out of my head. It's my mistress, if you will. And the Queens is my wife." In case anyone might have missed the point, he added: "I appreciate my wife more when I go fuck my mistress. You know what I'm saying? I can have more fun fucking my wife. She was never quite good to me."

Outside the Queens, Nick wrote songs in a far less structured manner, as his mention of music as therapy would suggest: "It's not a thought-out thing: with Mondo it's just what's coming out, and it's an uncensored version of what I would do. It's just what's worn out, and I leave it alone. Producing is a blast, and it's another avenue for music, and it's really good that Ipecac's putting it out because they're my favourite label right now . . . they're putting out the best stuff right now, and I'm pretty psyched about it because it's great to find a label that just lets you put out your art, and I really need to express myself on that level." Of working with the legendary Patton, Nick explained: "Mike's pretty hands-on, and he's a really busy fellow and isn't afraid to get things done, and it's been very fortunate that there are all these great people that are totally getting stuff done . . . we got to play with [Patton's supergroup] The Melvins Fantomas Big Band, which was like the fastest drummer, and the slowest, heaviest drummer on the same stage together and it was like, 'What!' It was pretty incredible, it was pretty wild and very intense, and a really amazing experience."

The recording of *A Drug Problem That Never Existed* was a fairly rapid-fire experience, as drummer and Kyuss alumnus Brant Bjork (who made up the numbers alongside Molly Maguire on bass and Dave Catching on guitar) explained: "Nick and I recorded the basic tracks in about six hours, in one day. Then he took it, started working with the Queens, and then he would come in and periodically dump tracks and overdubs on it throughout months because he was busy touring. And then he mixed it up, mastered it and sent it out." Bjork was enjoying life away from the big-band treadmill: "Right now, I just play in my own band Brant Bjork and run my label, Duna Records. I'm going to do four shows in California next month, then I'm going to Europe in October. Then I'll probably do an extensive US tour next spring." Asked if he was pleased to have had his face on the compact discs of

143

QOTSA's last two albums, he laughed: "Yeah. You know, there aren't that many double-chin models in the world. And I happen to feel that I am quite absolutely the most famously perfect double-chin model. I'm hoping to bring it back into style."

A Drug Problem That Never Existed is a blend of fast, thrash-metal-style aggro punk ('Meth I Hear You Callin'', 'Do The Headright', 'Jr. High Love'), more approachable Sex Pistols and Stooges-style punk rock ('Open Up And Bleed For Me', 'F. Y. I'm Free', 'Like You Want') and some unexpectedly thoughtful acoustic ballads ('All I Can Do', 'Day I Die'). The album ends with a very Kyuss-like bass-heavy lament called 'Four Corners'. While it's not for everyone, and not even for many Queens fans, it's evidence that, at this point, Oliveri's creative urges were at their peak.

On the other side of the coin in every imaginable way came the autumn release of the Desert Sessions single 'Crawl Home', a collaboration between Homme and Polly Harvey. A heavy slab of riffage and drums (Castillo in particular is on fine form), the song features Harvey's aggressive lead vocal and Homme following it up with harmony backups. 'Crawl Home' was accompanied on the single by a cover of the Prince song 'It' – sounding appropriately unearthly and anchored by Homme on drums – and a version, sung by Josh, of Polly's own song 'The Whores Hustle And The Hustlers Whore' from the *Stories From The City, Stories From The Sea* album. A video was shot in New York by cult auteur Hal Hartley, which Josh described as fairly riotous: "'Crawl Home' is basically about two people who disagree over one idea," he said, "so Polly and I are in a car and the arguing gets more heated as it goes. It's a short song, so it's all about this one argument, but it gets very intense. She's, like, punching me in the head and I'm pushing her around. So it gets physical." As always, Homme was affectionate towards the Desert Sessions concept, remarking, "It helps us remember why we started playing music, because it's really pure and kind of out there. You're doing it for the love of doing it, and you have to leave your ego and your feelings behind. On the other hand, it still has to sound badass. As it pertains to the *Desert Sessions*, I'd like to go to 119 or 120 . . . Eventually we'll get to everyone who plays music."

The Sessions were the first to be recorded without the late Rancho De La Luna studio owner Fred Drake, whose studio had been allowed by his family to remain open for use. "Part of *Desert Sessions* is the vibe –

and Rancho is the vibe," explained Homme. "If Rancho ever closes, then I'll stop doing Desert Sessions, probably. Because, where else am I gonna do 'em? It's a very magical place. Fred had vintage equipment everywhere: old keyboards, Dictaphones, stuff you'd never seen before. And you could play drums by the fire, and sing in the bathroom. Well, you had to, you know? Because it's a house.

"Fred is probably the toughest motherfucker that I've known. He was always sick, from the day I met him. He always had a terminal illness. But he smoked and ate bacon and rode his horse Kashmir and would just fuckin' go. He prolonged everything. He should have been gone 10 years ago. But he just refused to go. He was just pissed off enough to stay around. He was definitely a tough bastard. That's what I liked about him."

Dave Catching: "Everyone leaves, at some point, but we're here in spirit. And Fred was there in February, even if physically he wasn't. I thought a lot about how much fun he'd be having, because he was such a huge PJ Harvey fan, such a huge Ween fan. But he was there in spirit: all the equipment and everything was workin' good. And Kashmir rode by a couple of times."

The album was received with the usual response – that is to say, most people never heard of it, but the chosen few who did worshipped it. An unexpected hitch at British customs in late 2003 almost meant that the 12″ vinyl version didn't make it to the shops – the entire 5,000-unit consignment was seized by customs at New York's JFK Airport. A spokesperson for the Sessions' UK label, Island, had no idea why the records had been seized or whether they would eventually make it to British record buyers. In the end it was allowed into the country and the matter was left unexplained.

In the meantime, Queens Of The Stone Age, Mondo Generator and the associated personnel went about their business. On the surface, it seemed as though all was well in the QOTSA camp, with the two linchpins Josh and Nick rubbing along just as they'd always done. "I'm a boisterous guy when I'm alone, but when Nick's there, I don't need to be," Homme told the press. "We're a great team. He's naturally inclined to blow your head off, so I can be the down guy. He enables me to be more mysterious."

Unfortunately, this idea of dual roles was about to dramatically get out of hand.

CHAPTER 10

2004 And 2005: Still Got A Killer Scene

As the reader will have surmised by now, Josh Homme can party hard when the occasion demands it. But he's also a songwriter, a producer, a bandleader and a man who has steered not one but three successful bands (Kyuss, Queens, Eagles Of Death Metal – four if you include the Desert Sessions collective) through the horrendous logistical quagmire of writing, arranging, recording, producing and mixing songs, then having a record company manufacture, distribute and promote that material, all the while organising tour practicalities with a host of related personnel. This takes a calm, focused, driven and (dare one say it) business brain.

So after a decade of touring the world with a living firecracker by his side in the shape of best friend and bassist Nick Oliveri – a man who attacked life at full speed and with gusto – it's perhaps understandable that his tolerance would crack. Of course, Nick had seen this a few times before: "Josh has consistently hated me," he said, although at the time he was joking. "It's a timing thing, really. When Josh is pissed . . . I know what it's like when I'm pissed, so I think the best thing for any band is [to think], OK, let him be pissed, and try to help later. The last thing anyone needs when they're pissed is someone to say, 'You look angry, dude. What's wrong?' That's what a boyfriend and girlfriend do. There's none of that bullshit. I think that's important, you know? Otherwise the band probably would have broken up a long time ago. For me it works out great because we trust each other musically. And that right there is enough to make any differences in life go right the fuck away, because music is the most important thing to me. In trusting each other musically, I don't bring any songs to this band that I think wouldn't fit or maybe I think aren't my best songs . . . I think that's the cool thing about having an unconditional relationship musically. There's no egos about it, man.

"It's like I've known Josh for so long that we don't let each other's bullshit bother us any more," he added. "He knows my trip, you know. Like if I'm being obnoxious, Josh will be like, that's just Nick doin' his thing. And I understand things about Josh where I'm like, 'Whatever dude, do your thing. It's all good. I'm not your dad. We don't father each other,' you know what I'm sayin'? That to me falls into the unconditional thing. Of course we have our throw downs but very rarely. Neither one of us knows how to back down, so it usually ends up with Josh fuckin' slammin' my head or something. And then I'll try to hit him and he'll probably beat the shit out of me. If you haven't noticed, he's a big motherfucker . . . No, but we don't throw down that way. We just don't trip on each other's vibe, you know? We've known each other for so long it's just like, 'Oh, that's cool. Whatever.'"

When it came to Mondo Generator, the vibe was apparently just as peaceful, as Oliveri concluded: "He's really into it, so that's pretty positive too, but I think because we've known each other for so long we don't judge each other. That's really hard to find, because most people have that judgemental bullshit going on. I know there are things about me he doesn't dig, but he doesn't sit and stress on those things, so it is what it is. We are different and also very similar, which is why we came together to make music in the first place."

All of which made it a total surprise when, in early 2004, the news came that Josh Homme had fired Nick Oliveri from Queens Of The Stone Age.

What is most interesting was the way in which all parties involved viewed the split differently. Josh spoke to the *NME* about it in almost abstract, regretful terms: "Queens Of The Stone Age is a family of intense individuals. Everyone in the band is an individual and that was by design. It was what we were all looking for, to harness the chaos. There's events that always happen. The thing that always brought Nick and I together is that we have different styles of doing the same thing. Nick is probably one of the most unafraid people I know, and I'm not afraid either. And that's the reason we're friends . . . For me it's the hardest thing. I will never talk shit about my bro or anything like that. Nick and I are still definitely that. I love making music and stuff but it's more important to me to be brothers with Nick."

"So why fire him, then?" was the reasonable response from most fans. A management statement gave some form of explanation, reading: "A number of incidents occurring over the last 18 months have led to the decision that the two can no longer maintain a working partnership in the band." Another, less clinical but equally uninformative source was Ipecac co-owner Greg Werckman, whose label had released music from both men. Werckman said that he had spoken with Josh after the last dates of the current Queens tour. "This definitely took me by surprise. [Homme and Oliveri are] both extremely talented people and they seemed pretty much like kindred spirits. They both just love the music and love rock."

The most useful information came from Oliveri himself, who posted a message in February which read, "I just wanted to tell you folks what's really goin' on – good news and bad news. The bad news, which you all know, is that Queens Of The Stone Age, as we all know it, is no more. I heard it's now called 'Queens Lite'. Unfortunately, I was fired." Nick added the news that Mark Lanegan had also decided to jump ship and resume work on his own solo career, although this appears to have been a pre-planned, amicable move and not at all connected with Oliveri's unexpected sacking. Lanegan's management dryly stated, "Mark is officially no longer playing with Queens Of The Stone Age so as to devote more time to his own band. His new album, *Bubblegum*, is finished and will be out in late spring."

"A pure idea has been polluted," Nick said in his posting. "It's funny. A band about an idea? The concept was simple: a rock band, selfless, mindless, ego-free, unprotected, about danger, sex, and no bullshit rock'n'roll. You know what happens when a pure and original rock band gets polluted, poisoned by hunger for power, and by control issues? Things get really out of control. I'm noticing that people start fighting for control, especially when they realise they have no control. And whatever happened to loyalty? The strongest leaders are chosen by their followers, not self-appointed. The best frontmen are chosen by their fans. At one time, the thing I really loved about the Queens was that there were three frontmen, organic and original. I'd never heard of a rock band with three lead singers, with three different voices. My

favourite band is dead." Adding 'QOTSA RIP' and a note that he would be working on Mondo Generator full-time, Oliveri signed off, mentioning that he was heading out to the desert to work on new material and that he'd be appearing on the next Lanegan and Dwarves releases.

The Queens fanbase were mystified, not to say distressed. Not one but two key members had left the band. Only Homme could provide any real answers. Fortunately it wasn't long before he spoke on the subject – revealing as he did so a surprising degree of emotion. He told MTV, "It feels almost like my kid went to jail, or I got out of jail. I can't tell which one . . . Our whole band is full of hard partiers," Homme added. "We have put more people in rehab than Mardi Gras. But when you get drunk, you either get drunk with class, or you get drunk like a slobbering, toothless fuck. And that's just an analogy. It's not just drinking, it's how you live your life."

It seemed clear that Homme had finally had enough of Oliveri's full-tilt behaviour. "He's a tornado, and a tornado just destroys and goes on to the next city," he said. "I'm in the tornado cleanup crew, and all I ever see is his detritus and I'm sick of it . . . We used to have a thing we called 'Jekyll and Hyde' where, whenever Nick did something, we blamed Nick in the press, and whenever I did something, we blamed Nick in the press. But I think Nick started believing our press and thinking that he's gotta be the next Sid Vicious or something. And I think Sid Vicious is a bad-ass, but also I think Sid Vicious is a dumb drug addict who couldn't play bass and never wrote a song, and if he stayed alive most guys would have went, 'This guy's a worthless piece of shit.' And so I don't think that's something to aspire to."

It transpired that Homme had been appalled by an incident in which Oliveri had thrown bottles of beer at Queens audiences: "In the press, he admitted he threw bottles into the audiences, but he's saying, 'I do it for the fans. Isn't that what they really want?' But what Nick really did was come up to me between the first and second song and say, 'This audience isn't good enough – they're shit,' and then he threw full bottles of Corona at them, like a baseball pitcher. Is that for the fans? That's not my style. I get drunk with the fans, I don't throw bottles at them." The final nail in the coffin came when Oliveri destroyed his equipment at a show in Australia, and then got the group banned from a Perth hotel. "You can just put that in a box with the other hotels we've been banned from," Homme went on. "You know Nick's been accused of a lot of things, and basically all of them are true, and I can live with the shit I've done, but I can't be tied to the shit I haven't done."

Having made the tough decision to fire his friend, Josh went to his house to tell him in person. "He was bummed, man," Homme recalled. "It was the only time that an irrational guy was rational. He was going, 'I don't want this to happen.' But when you see a guy winging bottles at the audience, you eventually just say, 'Fuck this!' If you don't, then you're just somebody's bitch . . . I still love the guy, man. And Nick had a vital spot in the band. Nick has great energy. He scares people, I guess . . . You know what? I don't want to scare people. I want to enrapture people with music. And I want them to get the goose bumps when they hear our album. I don't give a fuck if they're scared about looking at us."

Homme wasn't concerned about Oliveri's absence from any future songwriting in the band, explaining: "I write 90 per cent of the music, which I never say, because I always try to stay mellow about it. I wrote most of the music and took care of all of the business, and kept it so our bass player could just play for an hour and a half a day and that's all he had to do. If you're wondering if Queens has no balls, you don't have to wonder. If you want to see balls, go see Nick with The Dwarves, because I understand he's playing with them again."

Asked by *Spin* how a two-member band could still exist after one member leaves, Homme answered with perfect judgement: "That's a good question. Let me try to answer this carefully, so that I don't get fucked. I don't feel like the issue here is anything musical. The issue is more personal. It is about my relationship with my friend Nick. The band started with me having this idea of working with people and trying to take their best songs. I've done it by myself, and I've done it with other people, and I've done it a lot with Nick. So Queens Of The Stone Age is an idea. That's it. I already miss Nick, but I can't be someone's babysitter for their life. There've just been too many incidents where Nick is the tornado who goes on to the next city and expects everyone to clean up his mess. Keeping him out of trouble is a full-time job. And then I got my own trouble, because I like to party and fuck around, too."

With Homme's reasoning behind Oliveri's dismissal on record, the situation seemed a little clearer, except for the fact that Nick pointed out a slight inconsistency, as he told *Musictoday*'s Greg Prato: "He came over my house and I thought he broke the band up. That's what he told me. He's like, 'I don't want to do this any more. I don't care about the name. And I was like, 'Dude, all right man, whatever. I hope you reconsider.' And then I read on the internet a week later that I was fired and he's making a Queens record."

This point has never been resolved by either man, to date, but – as ever – the story soon evolved in an unexpected direction, with Oliveri seemingly relaxed about the whole affair, as he told Prato, "Well, obviously, I went through the mad stage, then the sad stage, and now I'm at the OK stage. It's all right, you know? You can't force somebody to play with you in your band. So unfortunate, since there is a really good chemistry there and I think we should be so lucky to say that we have fans 'cause you only get that, if you do, once in a lifetime. We rolled the dice and lucked out. I stopped dreaming about the stuff we got to do on this last run years ago. With that in mind, it's all right. I got to do things that were pretty bad-ass, man. I know they're making a record now, and it feels weird for me not being down there. It's strange, but it's something that you just get used to: OK, it's not my band any more. It's a shame; it was a good band."

Nick had wasted no time after his sacking, picking up an acoustic guitar and going on the road to support his old bandmate Brant Bjork as a solo act. Inspired by the reception he received Oliveri recorded an acoustic album, *Demolition Day*, and fixed a release date to the end of 2004. "It opens with a song called 'Brown Pussy'," he said, "then goes into a song called 'All That I've Got', 'One More Time In Hell', 'Demolition Day', and 'Paper Thin'. There's 21 songs on the CD and 15 on the vinyl. I put horns on some stuff. There's some pretty cool stuff on it and I'm pretty happy about it. I had Dave Catching play on a couple of tunes, some melody guitar stuff; I had Molly play bass on a song – nothing consistent on the whole thing. It was like, come play on one song. I did bass on a couple of tunes."

The tour helped him through the split, he explained: "At the time, I really needed it. And Brant was my bro who called me up and said, 'Do you want to go on tour?' I thought he was calling me for a bass gig and I was like, 'Yeah dude!' But he's like, 'No, to come out and open up with your guitar – just you . . .' I was sitting at home, kinda tripping about things a little bit – well, a lot – so it was a good thing for me. [It] let me know that I could still go out there, play, and have some fun. It's all good." The shows had also been musically beneficial: "When I got a big old bass amp, drums, and everybody playing, you can hide mistakes pretty easy," he laughed, "but there's nothing to hide behind when you're up there with an acoustic guitar. Which is what's cool about it. There was a new 'fear attitude' to playing live which I really enjoyed, being scared to walk up there myself. 'Cause it's good to be nervous, you should never be too comfortable. It was amazing, a really good time."

By this point, Nick was more puzzled than angry about his dismissal: "I don't know too much about it, to be honest. It's one of those things like, 'So you fired me for what you hired me for?' It doesn't make too much sense. That's like saying I got fired from a rock'n'roll band for doing things that rock'n'roll bands do. I know it sounds cheesy, but it's true. I was just trying to have a good time. I'm sure they're going to make a great record; it's just going to be very different. It's a bummer, but at the same time, I just made a really good record and I'm happy with it. It makes me realise it's going to be all right."

Asked if Homme's relationship with Brody Dalle had anything to do with his actions, Oliveri replied: "I don't think it had anything to do with her . . . But I don't know – you'd probably have to ask Josh that one. But I know things between me and him . . . I've seen bands fist-fight daily and still be on tour. We had a blowout one time on the tour – I may have took things too far or whatever – but there was never any fighting as far as fists or anything crazy. We were out for 16 months or however long, and I had a little meltdown. It happens. You can't be out that long and not be able to vent every now and again. I love it, but sometimes it catches up to you, and it did one night to me. I may have said some things, done some things . . . I'm not necessarily saying that that's the reason why it went down. I don't know, maybe I weighed down on Josh's nerves or something and he just didn't dig me any more. And that's cool, man. I can vibe on that. I don't want to play with somebody who doesn't like who I am, anyway. I'm not going to change; I am who I am.

"It's OK at the end of the day. I had some friends staying at my house after it happened, and I had to tell them to leave 'cause they were bummed and made me think about it more than anything else! I was like, 'Dude, it's going to be all right! . . .' There's nothing I can do about it except keep playing."

Would he work with Homme again: "No," answered Oliveri. "He fired me three times in my life. It's done. I can't be told one thing, strung along – this is your thing, too. It can't ever happen."

At the same time, Homme hit the road with The Eagles Of Death Metal, a back-to-basics move that saw him take on some duties which – with Queens – he would have delegated years before: "I like to keep my toes in the dirt, where they should be," he told Melbourne newspaper *The Age*. "I'm driving the van, tour managing and playing the drums (under his old Queens alias Carlo Von Sexron)." The band released their debut album, *Peace Love Death Metal*, in May and Homme was clearly enjoying the unpressurised situation. More of a garage-rock act than a rock or metal band, the Eagles (including Homme's childhood friend Jesse 'The Devil' Hughes, also known as Mr. Boogie Man, and ex-Deus guitarist Timmy 'Tipover' Van Hamel) had first appeared on *Desert Sessions 3 & 4* and enjoyed the unusual status of an act perceived as a light-hearted novelty that was actually worth seeing. "It's the perfect experiment for people who really shake their ass and dance to rock'n'roll," Homme said. "It's just an unpretentious bad-ass record. That's why I've been doing it so much lately . . . I just sit behind the drums and play rock'n'roll, which is a great change of pace for me. J. Devil writes everything, every lyric and riff, and he's a fantastic songwriter. He and I go through and arrange them, and I lay down harmonies, but it's really his thing. It's the antithesis of the bloated rock-attitude bullshit I've had to deal with recently."

Asked about the band's frankly ludicrous name, Josh explained, "The larger truth is that we're The Eagles Of Death Metal, so we're neither death metal nor The Eagles. We're that missing link between them. We were listening to this band, [Polish death metal quartet] Vader, late at night, and someone said, 'We should play death metal, but like The Eagles.' And we started to conceive of what that music would sound like. We knew one thing would happen for sure: when you heard that music, your ass would jiggle. We're sort of the gatekeeper. We keep The Eagles and death metal from waging an all-out rock war."

As for the band's motive for covering the Seventies soft-rock hit, 'Stuck In The Middle With You' by Stealers Wheel, Homme went into sarcasm overdrive: "It's because we want to put a new face on such a lovely song. That song has a sexy vibe to it, and I don't know if you know The Eagles Of Death Metal's motto, but we're trying to commit everyone to 'Death by sexy'. That's what we say before every show: 'All right, people, death by sexy'."

It was clearly time for all those involved to relax a little. Who knew if Homme was being serious when he described the Eagles' album as "a combination of bluegrass slide guitar mixed with stripper drum-beats and Canned Heat vocals," or when he explained, "Jesse used to write speeches for the local Republican senator, and he's huge into the devil. He's not into Satanism, he's really into the idea of the devil. He calls me on the phone and he says, 'Let's evil,' and we jam. He wears jean shorts and he cuts his shirts into tank tops, which is weird. He's a real character but he writes the best stuff I've heard in a long time."

Hughes – evidently a lover of an interview soundbite in his own right – talked at one point about releasing his own solo album, after he had found himself on an extended songwriting and recording binge: "I don't know how else to describe it, but it's been like this, 'Whoa, I can't stop,' and I wonder what the penalty's going to be . . . I want to release it very limited and just see what people think. It's more clearly guitar oriented; kind of a demonstration of my musicianship and my hillbilly tradition." He added that while Homme wouldn't be on the album, Fatso Jetson's Mario Lalli and – with sublime irony – Nick Oliveri would be. "Nick's on a track or two [and so is] Mario Lalli, and then I incarnated myself into eight different entities and played! So that was an experience – very *Cybill*."

Even more strangely, he planned to release an EP, *A Pair Of Queens*, containing two QOTSA covers: "I was in a hotel room above the Café 101 in Hollywood, and a friend of mine was trying to convince me she hadn't heard Queens' songs," he said. "All I had was my little Roland VS 880 recording device, a guitar, and a drum machine. So I recorded ['Go With The Flow' and 'Gonna Leave You']. It's proof that no matter how bad you suck, you cannot destroy a well-written song. It's a clear ode to my friend Josh Homme, who is my guitar hero. I look up to him musically and I just wanted to say, 'Man, you rule.' It's also a vanity spite, it's, 'I'm owning your song!' "

When the inevitable subject of the next Queens album came up, Josh was serious. He had plenty of new material ready to go, it emerged, and had prepared for it well in advance: "I gotta be honest," he said. "I knew [the split] was coming, so I wrote everything by myself. And it's the best shit I've ever written. My tank has been fuelled by people saying I couldn't do it, and I'm gonna show them they're dead wrong . . . It reminds me of the same, trancey emptiness of the first Queens record. It's no accident everything has come full circle. There's lots of repetition with falsetto melodies over the top. I want people to shake their ass and shut their eyes and just trance out. I want to move people and get the hairs on their arms to stand up." As for the role of a future bass player, Josh confirmed that he would play the parts himself for the time being, just as he had on the Queens' debut: "I don't want to rush into anything with another bassist, so I'll deal with that when the time is right," he said. "Oh man, I'm fielding all these crazy phone calls from people I've never met. They're like, 'Hi, I've got long hair and the look, and I can tear it up.' These guys say things like, 'I got your number through Joe Shit the Ragman and Gravel Gerty.' Man, I just don't care right now. Queens has had lots of members, and I don't mean to suggest that Nick was just a casual member, but because the music has always been made with love we've always sorted ourselves out. And I don't expect that part of it to be any different. We'll find someone who loves music."

As always, the new sessions revealed a different approach from what had gone before. It was announced that two of the guests on the next Queens album would be Garbage singer Shirley Manson and Homme's girlfriend, Brody Dalle. "It was so much fun," Manson wrote on her band's website. "[Brody] has a crazy voice. She can really sing and what's even cooler about her is that she has no fucking idea just how good she is." As for the new QOTSA album: "It's great. Really, really great. You'll love it. And how Josh Homme is not yet a household name is quite beyond me."

Unfortunate events would soon befall both Josh and Nick. A brawl in a downtown New York bar in April forced a Queens show to be cancelled. Josh, Brody and Desert Sessions stalwart Paz Lenchantin were enjoying a drink when, as Homme explained to Launch Radio Networks: "There was a guy that was disrespecting my friend Paz and my girl Brody. I'd asked him nicely to leave and he wouldn't leave, so I put his lights out. You know, he took a swing at me basically, and he didn't fully get the swing off, but I got mine off, and I knocked him out and they took him outside and that was it. My hand was a little swollen, so I couldn't play Philly the next day."

After touring with Brant Bjork's band and recording his solo album, Nick had set up a Mondo Generator tour of the US West Coast, supporting the re-formed garage-rock pioneers, MC5. In the time-honoured spirit of a revolving-door personnel policy, his new drummer was the venerable Kyuss/Queens drummer Alfredo Hernandez. As well as all this, Nick had set up a record label, Tornado (whether this was in response to Josh's labelling of Nick as just that is unknown) and was planning a Mondo single and album as well as a solo record, to be titled *All Is Forgotten*, scheduled for release on Brant's Duna label.

However, in true Oliveri style the Mondo Generator tour was upset by an incident in July in which Nick was asked to leave his own tour bus. XFM Online reported that he had engaged in a fight with a sound engineer during a Mondo show, ultimately breaking the hapless fellow's nose and teeth. An acoustic show was subsequently cancelled, with Nick writing: "I have never in 16 years of playing shows and touring cancelled [a show]. I am extremely angry about this and will make it up to you. The truth is I was asked to leave the bus we have been touring on, and was left on the side of the road in Germany somewhere."

After finding his way back home, Nick underwent surgery for a "very large hernia. The doctor said I've had it for a very long time. I didn't know until recently when part of my intestines started poking through [to] my belly button." A European tour would still take place later in August, however, with the Mondo line-up a power trio consisting of Oliveri on bass and vocals, Josh 'Headly' Lamar on drums and Marc Diamond on guitar.

The shows went ahead, as did late-August sets at the Leeds and Reading festivals in the UK. "It was a blast!" Nick frothed. "The 5678s played at breakfast time and they kicked ass! Got to see The New York Dolls and The MC5! Roxy Saint played before us and The Mark Lanegan Band headlined our stage!" His band were also set to support The Mark Lanegan Band in Australia. Clearly the future of Mondo Generator was, apparently like that of The Eagles Of Death Metal, a wholly viable enterprise: Oliveri's band were evidently making progress. He spent the last few months of the year supporting Lanegan as planned – this time under the *nom de guerre* Acoustic Tornado – and even helped out on guitar with the main band at a few dates. "I was reading off of cheat sheets," he revealed. "It was pretty stressful but in the end it all worked out good!"

Back in the desert, the Queens Of The Stone Age's new, Oliveri-less line-up was starting to make headway. Back from the Eagles tour and ensconced in the studio, Josh Homme (or, more likely, his record label) decided to keep the Queens' name on people's lips by releasing a six-track Queens EP in late 2004. The songs – 'Who'll Be The Next In Line', 'Wake Up Screaming', 'No One Knows' (remixed, not altogether successfully), 'Most Exalted Potentate Of Love', 'Born To Hula' and 'The Bronze' – had all appeared as B-sides before, notably on the UK *Rated R* bonus disc, but as an awareness-building exercise in the USA it worked admirably, priming fans for new Queens product in 2005. This was helped along by Homme's announcement in October that he had been working with yet another special guest – ZZ Top guitarist Billy Gibbons – and that the results were "awesome . . . so un-Santana-with-that-guy-from-Matchbox Twenty (a reference to the recent superhit 'Smooth', recorded by the rejuvenated Carlos Santana and the rather faceless M20 singer). Gibbons was playing shit that made our jaws drop." As for the new album, Homme told *Rolling Stone*: "Honestly, I think it sounds more like our first record, but there's elements song-wise that are unlike any of the records . . . It's almost like part of the record is songs for daytime and part of the record is songs for night-time. We've got one song that's a bit twilight."

Rumours filtered through that the new Dwarves album, *The Dwarves Must Die*, featured a song, 'Massacre' with the lyrics, "This one goes out to Queens of the Trust Fund / You slept on my floor / And now I'm sleeping through your motherfucking album". Oliveri, who played on the song, was alleged to have been heard laughing in the background. On November 11, a leading rock magazine's online report stated that Homme had been involved in a bar brawl with Dwarves singer Blag Dahlia, ultimately hitting him over the head with a beer bottle. Homme rejected the story, with a report on his own website authored by 'Dr. Insider' stating: "When asked about hitting Blag with a bottle, Josh responded with, 'Why would I need a bottle to kick Blag's ass? I mean, who couldn't kick Blag's ass? Seriously. I merely tapped Blag in the eye because he pushed me. A full swing it wasn't. You see, I was just messing with him. You know, pouring beer on his head and dancing 'round him singing 'What chu gonna doo, Blaggy boo'. This is the guy that hits audience members in the head with his mike and shows them his teenie weenie . . . And the best part is . . . wait, I have a trust fund? Awesome. Why am I workin' so hard? I'm officially retired . . . Until next time, check your facts so it looks like you know what you're talking about, stop being the type of person everyone wants to slap and keep rappin' old whiteboy."

In January 2005 the announcement came that the fourth Queens Of The Stone Age album would be entitled *Lullabies To Paralyze* and would be released at the end of March. Guitarist Troy Van Leeuwen posted a message on the Queens' website which revealed something of the nature of the new record: or at least that the band's sense of humour was intact. "I know March may seem far off, to me anyway, but when the creative engine is chugging at full steam, it's hard to stop. In other words, songs are still being recorded as we speak. We've just put the finishing touches on 'The Fun Machine Took A Shit And Died', which I think is a good title for a tune so strange. The session started out relatively normal, but then took a turn for the bizarre, once long-time friends Dean Ween, Chris Goss and Jesse 'The Devil' Hughes scarred this song with their musical branding irons." The new Queens bass player, it was announced, was long-time Desert Sessions collaborator Alain Johannes of the band Eleven.

Speculation grew about the nature of the new record, especially after Nick Oliveri posted the following (on February 20): "Josh came to my house, and gave me the new QOTSA record to trip on. It's good but I can't help but know I could have added what is missing." Nick had, as ever, been keeping himself busy, mentioning that he had recorded a song for the new Turbonegro album called 'The Final Warning' and that he was one of the many artists who were queueing up to make music with Amen singer Casey Chaos: "I might do a project with Casey called Suicide Pact," he enthused, "we thought it would be good to fuck some shit up together, since that is what we would be doing anyway!"

As for the Queens, a slight blip came about in March 2005 when a European tour was cancelled after Homme developed a lung infection. According to the band's website, doctors in Holland initially treated Homme for flu, but he later began coughing up blood. "We've toured with everything from broken ankles to bruised livers, but simply weren't prepared for this relentless attack of teeming bacteria," the band said. "Our fans know that we ain't pussies and that this is an obvious downer for everyone involved . . . so, for those of you with any unused tickets, hold on to them. We'll be back as soon as possible to make up these shows, and when we do, we'll have something special for all of you with an un-ripped ticket. We ain't in the habit of cancelling, and we don't forget."

Despite illness and the imminent arrival of *Lullabies*, Homme was still active on other projects, in this case the next Eagles Of Death Metal album, which would be titled *Death By Sexy* and feature guest spots from associates such as Mark Lanegan, Joey Castillo, Brody Dalle and singer Wendy Ray. "Brody and Wendy make up a little part of the Eagles called the Eagle-ettes," Jesse Hughes said. "They're like our answer to The Marvelettes.

"In order for the first album not to seem like a fluke," he added, "this one needed to step up and expand. It accomplished that goal. I think we've got, like, five singles on it." The record was due for release in the summer of 2005.

Meanwhile, time was healing a few wounds. In early '05 it was reported that Homme had told the press of Oliveri: "Oh, we've been fine for eight months. It's one of those things where I don't expect people to understand, because, you know, I know some people don't, and I don't expect them to, and it's just like that . . . What's important is that he and I are friends. I mean, that's why I needed to move on in the first place, to be able to be friends, you know? I'm gonna play music no matter what, and so is he. But I'd rather be able to go have a few beers with Nick."

When *Lullabies To Paralyze* was revealed to the press and public, it displayed a different face of QOTSA. As Homme had warned, much of it sounded like the open spaces of the first Queens album, but also noticeable was a first-half versus second-half division where the first handful of songs were more upbeat than the darker, much more progressive and experimental back end. At the time of writing – two days after the record's release, with a single, 'Little Sister', ascending the charts – it's too early to predict how the record will perform, commercially or critically. However, it's an interesting experience, with the full range of the Queens palettes on display: although it's not as expansive in its concept as *Songs For The Deaf* or as packed with

159

hooky singles as *Rated R*, it seems to have something of the creative essence of both.

It begins with 'This Lullaby', a short, Tom Waits-like dark ballad with Mark Lanegan's breathed, throaty vocals setting the scene. 'Medication' is a straight pop-rock tune with a busy bass, perhaps a deliberate dig at anyone who thought the album would be lacking in that department. The heavy, sand dune lament of 'Everybody Knows That You Are Insane' is the album's first real high point, with its deep, Pink Floyd-like atmospherics and wailing guitar leads utterly ethereal. 'Tangled Up In Plaid' is a little weird, with its questioning central riff, Josh's falsetto and the distorted vocal sound making uneasy bedfellows. It's interesting that at four songs in, with three of them featuring Homme's vocal, the listener still half-expects a blasting Nick Oliveri punk song to appear.

'Burn The Witch' is pure Deep Purple, with a scratchy riff and creepy vibes that hark directly back to Lanegan's freakout on 'Hanging Tree', while the excellent, jittery 'In My Head' comes closest to the singable pop fodder of 'Lost Art Of Keeping A Secret'. Its twisting, piano-laced riffing is simple, memorable and easy to sing: Homme's pop sensibilities in full flow. They're also present on the first single, 'Little Sister', a Foo Fighters style snare-heavy workout that has shades of Dave Grohl all over it and marks the end of the accessible first half of the record.

'I Never Came' is a melodic, subtle guitar and vocal tune that sits perfectly on the record, with Homme keeping the lights and levels low. 'Someone's In The Wolf' is both darker and deeper, moving un-predictably from riff to riff and providing an uncomfortably shifting bass and long, textured vocal lines that come straight from Kyuss. 'Blood Is Love' is more jagged, sliding into a miasma of jammed noise that doesn't really say an awful lot but does remind the listener of the band's desert roots, whereas the heavy jumps and crashes of 'Skin On Skin' are an odd combination of industrial noise and vintage Sabbath riffage. 'Broken Box' doesn't make things much easier, even if it does have the patented trance riff that Queens do so well, and the plinky piano that gives so many of their songs an edge of sarcastic cool. 'You Got A Killer Scene There, Man . . .' has a vocal hook that sinks deep into the listener's mind, but (to me at least) is spoiled by a droning piano monotone that sounds like Edwyn Collins' dirge hit 'A Girl Like You'. Finally, 'Long Slow Goodbye' returns to vintage Queens territory, with a falsetto note hit by Josh that lends the song a welcome blues-at-the-crossroads feel. There's a hidden track – a sumptuous, entirely overblown and unnecessary but fabulous orchestral brass section which sees the record out with wonderful pomposity.

Is *Lullabies To Paralyze* a good album? Yes, it is. Is it a *Blues For The Red Sun* or a *Rated R*? Probably not. But it's new-sounding and the obvious result of many months of experimentation with new influences. And that, with all that Homme has been forced to deal with since his remarkable band came to prominence so rapidly, is probably as much as we can expect.

With a slew of live dates in Canada in the spring and a host of touring commitments to come later in the year, as things stand Queens Of The Stone Age are truly poised to conquer. But the new album is not an easy one, and time may prove that this was something of a crossroads.

But does Josh Homme care about that? Let the last word be his.

"We're asked a lot where we fit in," he once mused. "Whether we feel isolated, who we consider like-minded. Well, we've never felt kinship with anyone other than bands who are honest; bands who you feel are unique and are doing their own thing, with their own voice and with nothing else on their mind but getting as close to spitting themselves out as possible. None of those bands sound like us. They sound like them. You can immediately identify it's them because they don't give a shit about matching what's going on, just about giving themselves to the music. The fact that that might make us a rarity at the moment doesn't really bother me. I'd just rather be having a good time being in a band than fucking worrying all the time. It doesn't look like much fun being 'successful' any more. I'd rather play with people I love and make music I can feel totally proud of. That's never gonna be a strong enough selling-point to turn it into the kind of 'movement' you guys in the press are always agitating for. But it's gonna make music you can fucking get your rocks off to rather than just buckle under the weight of hype.

"The Queens is an exercise in something," Homme concludes. "I'm not gonna force it along, because it can't be so wide that you don't know what's happening. When you're a band, you need to move slowly in order to hold hands with whoever is into you. We have a song on this record that I've had for eight years; it just wasn't ready. Even though I've been writing stuff like that for a long time, I had to wean everyone else onto it. Now I can do it in Queens whenever I want.

"I love making records. It's my favourite part – the sounds you chase in your head are actualised in front of your face. And I'd like to have done everything, or tried to do everything, by the time I'm dead. No one can tell you what to do."

Interview With Nick Oliveri

March 2005

The following is a conversation the author conducted with Nick Oliveri – the madman, maverick and all-round rock monster – via his cellphone. Nick was at the South By Southwest Music Festival in Austin, where (coincidentally) he had first hooked up with Josh Homme just before being enlisted into Queens Of The Stone Age, some eight years before. The night before the interview, he had been to see Queens play a set – and it seemed as if a weight had lifted from his shoulders.

"I just wanted to make sure my old mates were doing good. It was good, I enjoyed it. I wanted to get up there, of course, because I love the tunes, but it was fun to sit back as a spectator and just chill. I've got some new Mondo stuff in the works, so everything's going good, everything's awesome."

Josh has been complimentary about Nick in the press lately and has referred to you as a 'brother' on more than one occasion. Is the friendship still there between you?

"Absolutely, man, we were just hanging out last night and seeing what was going down and whether we'll be collaborating on this new Mondo record or not. I think I'm gonna end up doing it myself because the time frames between his band touring and my band touring might be hard to make it happen."

Who's in Mondo these days?

"The Winnebago Deal band members are my band in Mondo Generator now and I'm really excited about that. They're younger guys and
they're excited about playing and light a fire under my ass to make me
do stuff as well."

Now you're an old fart, you mean?

"Yeah, I'm an old fart . . . I'm 33, and they're like, 'You're 33? Jesus!' Ha
Ha! The last Mondo tour I did, the drummer Josh was born in 1984. I
was like, 'Are you fuckin' kidding me?' They're like, 'Who's this Kurt
Cobain?' You show 'em vinyl and they say, 'What's vinyl? You mean,
vinyl clothes?' 'No, dude, no . . . Let's not go there, man!' Heh heh."

*Brant Bjork said that when you were at school together, you were a kid from the
wrong side of the tracks who smoked and drank all the time.*

"That's probably right, yeah. I was born in Los Angeles and my family
moved out to the Palm Springs area because my mom got a job
advancement in this supermarket where she still works. It was like a
building city, a city on the way up, with all these new stores going up.
So that was the only reason we moved there. I was wearing cool clothes
while all the other kids were wearing Levi's, you know. Sears brand
pants everywhere. I was 12 years old."

Was it a drag to move out of the big city into the desert?

"Yeah! I didn't want to move there. I was glad we did in the end,
because I probably wouldn't have played in the bands that I did play in.
I wouldn't have been in Kyuss and I wouldn't have been in Queens
and I wouldn't have played with Homme."

You would have been in an LA hair-metal band.

"I would have been in an LA hair-metal band for sure! I would have
leaned more towards the Hanoi Rocks end of the hair thing and the
New York Dolls-driven end of it rather than the Poison-driven thing,
ha ha."

The beginning of that movement – the first Mötley Crüe albums and so on – had some credibility.

"Absolutely. A lot of those bands came from The Ramones school and The MC5."

When you joined Kyuss, you were the most into metal of any of them?

"Oh yeah! I was big-time into it. I was probably one of the few people in the Coachella Valley area that had [death metal pioneers] Possessed's *Seven Churches* when it came out, on Dark Angel records. I had the imports before they were out in the States! I was a record collector and a music lover from a very small age. I had everything. If it was fast and evil, I was there, man, I was into it. So that's how I got into punk rock, too – the speed of it. The crossover movement, you know, DRI and Cro-Mags, were very important records in my life. On the *Age Of Quarrel* record, they did a video for the first song, 'We Gotta Know', and I'm actually in it, because I went to see them play. I'm a long-haired kid at the beginning, before the music starts, I jumped in front of the camera and went, 'Yeaah!' "

I knew all of Kyuss were punk freaks, but I assumed you brought more metal influences into it.

"Yeah. Josh and Brant were listening to Black Flag and stuff I still love to this day, but I was also listening to Sabbath. I was into Volume 4 and those guys were My War, you know. We met in the middle. Both bands are equally heavy, but I think Sabbath is at the root of it all, and I always went for the roots of things, to where it started."

Josh always claimed not to have been into Sabbath.

"It was funny, man, he was heavy like Discharge was heavy."

But his guitar sound was pure Sabbath.

"Exactly! I was like, 'Man, don't lie to me, you're a closet Sabbath fan. You gotta be, because you got Iommi's influence.' Which is not a bad place to get it from."

164

He's grown into his looks: Josh Homme, modern alternative rock's poster boy. DALLE/PHOTOSHOT

A popular touring incarnation of Queens Of The Stone Age, with drummer Gene Trautman, sound engineer Hutch (the fifth Queen?) and lap-steel player Dave Catching pictured between Nick and Josh. FOTEX AGENTUR GMBH/REDFERNS

QOTSA at Rock In Rio III in January 2001. Guitarist and keyboard player Brendon McNichol, a Masters Of Reality and Desert Sessions alumnus, appears between Trautman and Oliveri. LFI

Nick Oliveri at the Inter Continental Hotel, Rio De Janeiro, Brazil, January 2001 – wearing shorts, unlike his stage appearance some days later. GEORGE CHIN

Never backward in coming forward, Nick Oliveri strips off on stage. Again. The 'Kango' (see text for explanation) is thankfully not pictured. STEWART TURKINGTON/REX FEATURES

Nick and Josh with temporary drummer Dave Grohl, sometime of Nirvana and now of Foo Fighters. "When he tells me he was in Nirvana," recalled Josh, "I say, OK, go buy me something." JOHN McMURTRIE/RETNA

"I was put on this Earth to play drums," enthused Grohl. Judging by fans' and critics' response to Songs For The Deaf, he was probably right. LFI

QOTSA pictured on *Later With Jools Holland* in October 2002. ANDRE CSILLAG/REX FEATURES

The post-*Songs For The Deaf* Queens line-up, with Mark Lanegan (far left), drummer Joey Castillo (centre, standing) and guitarist roy Van Leeuwen (far right). LFI

Nick Oliveri onstage with Mondo Generator in August 2004. Note his 'Freitag 4:15' tattoo, a permanent reminder of the day QOTSA played their worst gig ever.

Josh Homme, making the most as ever of the cards life has dealt h
JOE TORENO/RETNA

John Paul Jones, Dave Grohl and Homme as Them Crooked Vultures, a slick jam band that scored huge success.
NICK STEVENS/PHOTOSHOT

Them Crooked Vultures appearing on *Friday Night with Jonathan Ross*, London, December 4, 2009.
BRIAN J. RITCHIE/HOTSAUCE/REX FEATURES

roy Van Leeuwen (guitar) and Jon Theodore (drums) of Queens of the Stone Age pose backstage with the Grammy Charities Signings uring the 56th Grammy Awards at Staples Center in Los Angeles, California, January 24, 2014. MAURY PHILLIPS/WIREIMAGE

The look of a man who knows exactly where he is going, even if we don't know what it will sound like when he gets there; Orange Warsaw Festival, Poland, June 13, 2014. EAST NEWS/REX FEATURES

Was the desert-party scene already up and running by the time you moved out of the city?

"Yes, but the thing is, it was Mario Lalli from Fatso Jetson who started this thing. He'd throw parties and actually go and get a generator and play out in the desert. He's the man, you know, he's the founder and the father. I saw Across The River play at my high school, Indio High School, when I was in ninth grade. This must have been 1987. I was meeting some girl over at the smoking section and there was a band playing there – at school, with a generator! They just went and set up at school – didn't ask the principal, didn't do shit – just set up and as soon as the lunchtime bell went, they just started jamming. It was Alfredo Hernandez on drums and Scott Reeder on bass and Mario on guitar and Mark Anderson on second guitar. It was bad-ass."

It sounds like quite a progressive school, if that was allowed to happen.

"Totally. They had off-campus lunch, you could go to McDonald's or whatever the hell they had down the way, and do your thing."

How did the desert parties get publicised?

"It was a totally word-of-mouth thing. You couldn't tell your parents, they weren't allowed in, and nor were the police. We looked at the parents as police, so we didn't ever, ever tell them where we were going! They got to be really big parties, and sometimes you would get busted because too many people got to know about it and the cops would find it. It was a good time! If it was kept down to a couple of hundred people, it would be a good party and it would last for as many days as you wanted it to. The cops usually couldn't find us. We were literally in the middle of a canyon, in a cove between some mountains in the desert, where even the lights we had to play by would be dimmed by the mountains surrounding us. We'd just go and play and the sound would bounce off rocks and sand, it was pretty wild. Sometimes it would sound really bad and sometimes it would sound really cool! It was more of a visual and a vibe and a 'we were there' rather than a 'this sounds great', you know? The wind would be blowing and you'd be like, 'I can't hear my guitar!' It would be turned up to 10 and you'd be going, 'What?' You could hear it like four miles away.

"You know the reason it started? Because we didn't have a live venue in Palm Springs, not until Sonny Bono became mayor, anyway. There was no live music. When he came in, he changed the city ordinances to having live music, so you can actually go and play a club now. Back when I was a kid, the only place your band could get a gig was out in the middle of the desert with a generator. Or a house party."

It sounds like a grim place for a teenager to live.

"It was. You tried everything at a really young age because you were searching for stuff, big time. It was like, man I need to try something quick. And you're ready to try stuff because you want to get out of there. It's like, if being alive is these old people, I want out."

Is the scene still going?

"Well, I think the kids nowadays are more into the house/rave/ecstasy thing, rather than the hard rock, 'take a couple of kegs into the desert and play' kind of thing. Also, I think the last time they tried to do one of these things up at the nudist colony at Desert Hot Springs, a kid got stabbed at the pool which they use. The Nudebowl, they call it. Now, with the gangsta rap thing, kids in suburbs like Palm Springs think they have to prove themselves. They think that the hip-hop guys in the city are killing each other – they're really not, but the kids in the suburbs think they are – so they have to prove that they're as hard as the city guys, so they're stabbing each other and doing stupid shit. And it's silly, because it was such a good time for me growing up. So after that, the authorities came and filled in the pool, and the scene doesn't really exist any more. It's a shame, man."

Was it an easy decision to leave Kyuss for The Dwarves in 1992?

"Basically Blag Dahlia called me and was in a pinch for a guitar player. I was wanting to play faster and Kyuss was getting more spacey, with longer songs and more jamming, and I love that stuff to this day and I was still pretty good at it, but I prefer more focused songs. Quick, short, and let's go! Now I kinda mix them both together, but at that time in my life I was going fast, fast, play faster! So I was moving in a different direction at the time anyway. It was a better choice for both parties."

Did you just tell them you were leaving one day?

"I think it was a decision that they made. Ha ha ha! I was fine with the melding of styles, which is basically what Queens came from, but maybe when you're young you're not ready to meld everything. I was like, 'OK cool,' plus Blag had asked me to join his gig, so I was like, 'I've got somewhere to go, it's cool.'"

Do you ever listen to Blues For The Red Sun?

"You know, I haven't listened to it in years, and I just put it on recently because someone was over at my house and wanted to hear it. It's good, I like it. I wondered if it would still move me and get my head rockin', you know, and it did the trick. My favourite Kyuss album's always been *Sky Valley*, just because I'm not on it. Brant's still there too, and I like Alfredo's drums, but the one with Brant and Scott Reeder has always been my favourite one."

What did you think of the Kyuss best-of Warners put out in 2000, Muchas Gracias?

"I thought, this is the best of? You don't even have the singles on this fuckin' record! That was kinda strange. They should have called it *B-Sides And Rarities*, because there was live tracks and stuff on there. If the band put together a best-of it would have a whole different track list. But I guess the fans picked the songs, which is kinda cool."

Do you still see John Garcia?

"Yes, whenever I can. I'm a huge John fan. I buy all his records. He probably doesn't even know I have all his stuff! I got everything, from Hermano, to Unida, to Slo-Burn."

I assume he was John G. on Cocaine Rodeo?

"Totally. I said, 'Shall I put your name on it,' and he said, 'Just put John G,' because he was signed to a different record label and he thought it might give them a reason to give him hell."

That album was the nearest Kyuss have ever come to re-forming.

"You recognised that, man? You're one of the few people who have ever recognised that. Yeah, I got the original Kyuss in the studio for the first time in like seven years. The original *Wretch* line-up together in the studio, it was good."

Was the old chemistry still there between you?

"Oh yeah. The songs we did were first takes, just jamming. I showed them the songs and we went off on an improvised jam, and we captured it on tape. That album, I was shopping cassettes around in 1997, saying, 'I gotta get someone to put this thing out,' but the band ended up dissolving and I did the Queens thing. But Greg Anderson from Southern Lord Records said, 'What did you do with that Mondo stuff?' And I said, 'Nothing' – so he said, 'Dude, let's put it out!' I was like, 'Really?' He brought it back to life and had it resurface again."

Who's been your favourite drummer to play bass with?

"Brant Bjork is the easiest drummer that I've ever worked with because he was the first drummer I ever worked with. He understands my songwriting, and he's a songwriter too so he understands why I'm going to a bridge or a chorus here. Rob Oswald who played on the first Mondo album, he was a slamming drummer too. But Dave Grohl and Joey C probably tie for the best, most bad-ass drummers I've ever played with. I've been very fortunate on the drummer tip."

What was so good about Grohl's playing?

"Dave is hard-hitting and precise. He's almost programmed to play. Like, even if it's just a crazy fill. You think, 'Holy shit, how did he play that exact thing every night of the tour and never make a mistake' – the exact same drum fill, for the first part of the chorus, the second part of the chorus and so on, all with different drum fills, and he'd do them the same every night, precisely. He made this one mistake one time on the whole tour – *one time*, the guy made a mistake! – he dropped a stick in the song 'Avon', and he fuckin' laughed at himself. I knew he was leaving that night – I said, that fucker's quitting, isn't he? That sonofabitch! Ha ha ha ha! He's probably the best drummer I've ever played with – period."

Is Mondo Generator now your full-time band?

"Yeah. It started out as a project and it's now my first choice band. Queens was a partnership, and when you work good with someone it doesn't matter anyway, but it feels good to make decisions for myself and my own band."

You seem to be quite relaxed now about the way you were fired from Queens.

"Yeah, I was pissed off at the beginning, know what I mean? But going to see them last night was a breath of fresh air for me. I know what we did together. But they rocked. They came to bring it, and everybody rose to the occasion. I know what it can be, and I know what it is now, and it's good, and I'm stoked, and I know what I've got going, and it's good we're getting along. That's the main thing because at the end of the day you can't force people to play with you who don't want to play with you. There was some headline in England about it which was totally false – like 'I will play with you, let me in!' kind of thing – which came about because I'd said, 'Yeah, I know a band I played bass in,' or some totally passing comment, right? And the headline was, 'Nick's begging Josh for his gig.' I was like, 'Holy fuckin' shit! What happened?'*

"I think the whole thing that happened with Queens got blown out of proportion. I think everybody involved with the Queens is still having a good time, if you want to break it down that way. I think that was something that got turned around in the press a little bit. Uh . . . the reasons for the split and everything were different things."

Do you ever miss being in Queens?

"Oh yeah – there were moments last night when I was like, 'Goddammit, gimme that bass!' Ha ha ha ha ha! Of course I'm gonna miss it at times, but I also miss some girlfriends, know what I mean? It's one of those things. Like, I miss my old car, man!"

* This was a reference to an interview with Billboard.com in which Nick was quoted as saying, "I told him last time I was hanging out with him, if anything falls through and you need somebody, you know where your bass player is, dude – you know where the bass player for that band is. So pick up the phone . . . it ain't about a money gig thing for me – I know which band I play bass in."

Hearing some of your bass parts – like the start of 'Feelgood Hit Of The Summer' – must be hard?

"Yeah, yeah, totally. They did 'Better Living Through Chemistry' last night, and it's got my bass part, but it was cool. Alain kept it pretty close-knit to how it's supposed to be played. The band were good. I love watching Joey Castillo play drums."

So here's the killer question. Will you ever work with Josh again?

(pause): "I'm sure we'll work together some time in the future. I can't say yes or no, but I'm sure that we will at some point in our lives."

CHAPTER 11

2005–2009: Vulgar Vultures

THE first inkling of a potentially momentous alliance of Josh Homme with other rock figureheads came as far back as 2005, when Queens' old collaborator Dave Grohl told the UK's *Mojo* magazine: "The next project that I'm trying to initiate involves me on drums, Josh Homme on guitar, and John Paul Jones playing bass. That's the next album. That wouldn't suck bratwurst."

Homme and Grohl playing together was an old concept for Queens Of The Stone Age fans – but with a member of Led Zeppelin? Unlikely, people thought, and went on their way.

In any case, there was plenty of Queens-related action happening that didn't require the addition of a classic rock legend. A tour in support of Nine Inch Nails, then approaching the end of their most creative career phase, occupied the autumn of 2005, along with the release of *Over The Years And Through The Woods*, a live album and DVD that included footage of Queens as far back as 1998, already an age ago in the perception of many of their more recent fans. Followers with longer memories were enthralled on December 20 when sometime Kyuss singer John Garcia appeared on stage with Queens: he sang on three Kyuss songs, 'Thumb', 'Hurricane' and 'Supa Scoopa And Mighty Scoop', marking eight years since he and Homme had performed in public together.

Public appetite for Kyuss's material was as strong as ever, a decade or so after that band's dissolution, but the idea that those songs would actually be toured and played by a group of musicians seemed fanciful. As anyone paying attention to the ex-Kyuss members in recent years will now know, however, unlikely scenarios have a tendency to materialise if enough time passes, right?

The overall picture, then as 2005 rolled into 2006, was that a veritable frenzy of activity surrounded Queens Of The Stone Age, and more specifically Josh Homme. In April Eagles Of Death Metal released a second album, *Death By Sexy*, on which the focus was obviously more on wry comedy than serious musical statements. However, there was nothing unserious about the subsequent Eagles tour, which saw the band support the Strokes (remember them?), Peaches and Joan Jett. They even opened for Guns N'Roses on one occasion, then as now a band composed of founder member Axl Rose and a bunch of hired hands.

Despite the focus on Homme's side project, fans never stopped talking about a new Queens album, with conversations triggered among the faithful by the occasional snippet that appeared in the media of new music. For instance, Death From Above 1979 bassist Jesse F. Keeler stated on Australian radio station Triple J in June '06 that he would be playing bass on the next Queens record, although this was swiftly retracted, with conflicting schedules cited as the reason.

In fact, Homme was coy on the subject of which musicians would appear on his next album, snubbing an inquisitive *NME* writer with the words, "That's not a healthy question. You'll ruin the surprise. We've gotta keep our cool." He also mused on the subject of his ever-changing band line-up with *Ultimate Guitar Archive*, saying: "Long ago I lost the opportunity to be in U2 – where it's the same four guys. I respect that, but at the same time this is the search to try to take advantage of playing with certain people, even if they can't stay, and then there's other times that you need to humble yourself at the altar of music, and if you don't . . . [makes a throat-cutting motion]."

It took until February 2007 before concrete details of Queens album number five emerged. *Era Vulgaris*, as it was named, was set for release that June and would feature regular guest Mark Lanegan plus Strokes singer Julian Casablancas and Nine Inch Nails mainman Trent Reznor, the last of these in a remix role. Homme and Troy Van Leeuwen would handle guitars and bass between them, and Joey Castillo remained on drums as usual. From this point until the summer, Queens promoted the album in the way of the modern world, revealing snippets of audio and video on Youtube and their website. A fansite, thefade.com, offered a competition in which entrants could snag a 'special package', which turned out to be a CD called *You Know What You*

Did with a single track, 'Era Vulgaris', which only appeared on the UK edition of the album.

With this collectable item came a letter which read, with typically sardonic humour: "Hello friend, thank you for accepting this gift. Included you will find the will to dance & the song ERA VULGARIS. It was pulled from the new album (of the same name) so that it could be to you and become an example of how we think 'from now on' should be. As in – we do for you, you do for us. So to start this relationship off, we have done for you. Now we ask this in return. Share this with friends you think we (you & us) would enjoy. Upload it and spray it like time released graffitti [sic] on the websites of places it does not belong. Is it a new recipe on Rachel Ray's site? Is it a new Nickelback song on their board? A secret Gov't document? Video game cheats? Sex site password? Fuckin' whatever? You decide. Then tell us how you shoved this song into the guts of the internet & we (both) can smile wide with pride at our new relationship. Oh, but not till after midnight tonight . . . from now till then, is just for us. Can we trust you to wait? Relationships are built on trust. Enjoy! 'Dr Insider & QOTSA'."

A song, 'Sick, Sick, Sick', was leaked into the web shortly before being released as an official single. Minimalist and catchy in the way that all the best Queens songs are, it was the obvious song to introduce the new album and was followed by '3's And 7's', an amusing if not particularly essential bit of upbeat riffage. The video for 'Sick, Sick, Sick' kept the kids happy, with its slick, slightly nauseating footage of the band – with a new bass player, Michael Shuman – performing in front of a woman stuffing herself with food interspersed with shots of raw meat being fondled and then minced.

Asked about Queens' fairly headbanging performance in the clip, Van Leeuwen explained: "It was an opportunity for us to all out-ham each other. And there was definitely some carnage at the end of the shoot. I had just got this brand new Missoni suit I was wearing down in this dungeon that was wet and muddy. I went down! I ended up on my back. It was rad. I slipped on the water. Our new bass player hit his head on this cement beam and had to get staples."

He added: "It was the very last take of the night. If you watch closely you're going to see [Shuman's head injury]. Josh smashed his stuff, the drums got disintegrated. It was carnage, definitely. The director, Brett Simon, gave us this treatment for a song on the last record called 'In My

Head'. We really wanted to do it but it just happened to be the only time we listened to the record label, and it was such a fuck-up on our part. The video we ended up with for that song is so lame! It was three of us against a green screen with effects added later. It was like a fucking Gap commercial. It was terrible. Just terrible. We were on the road so we weren't in control of it. But, long story short, this video concept was originally supposed to be for 'In My Head' but then when this song 'Sick, Sick, Sick' got picked as our single we decided we still really wanted to do this. It was an opportunity for us to tell the director, 'We like your vision, do your thing. You're the director, we're the band and we'll do our part, but it's your art.'"

Era Vulgaris had taken almost a full year to record, it emerged, with long-time Queens collaborator Alain Johannes recording and mixing while Homme and Chris Goss produced under the 'Fififf Teeners' tag. "We basically started a year ago," said Van Leeuwen. "We didn't really have anything written. So it was a long process. It was the longest I've ever taken to make a record, frankly. I've made records over the process of a year, but this was the first time it's ever been my total focus for that long . . . one of the only rules [was] that the vocals and the melody need to be supported. But other than that, especially with this record, there are no real rules at all. It was like, I'm gonna play a bunch of keyboards. I'm going to re-introduce the synthesiser to the band and make it sound like a broken robot. It's about finding a way we can express ourselves through music by not just playing notes. Like creating sound and space."

Sound and space is indeed what this album is all about, along with Homme's lilting vocals and staccato riffs that sounded more electronic than organic. Opening cut 'Turnin' On The Screw' begins with an atonal guitar figure than is more than a little reminiscent of 'Leg Of Lamb' from *Songs From The Deaf*, accompanied by a slow, deliberate vocal line and layered harmonies. 'Sick, Sick, Sick' ups the ante with its knowing, unicellular guitar line, while 'I'm Designer' is the perfect vehicle for Homme's oft-voiced distaste for the shallower end of modern culture. So far *Era Vulgaris* stays well clear of any Kyuss-indebted heaviness, preferring to dance around on fragile, cob-webbed melody lines with plenty of space to breathe, and 'Into The Hollow' is where this approach reaches its zenith: its bass, drums and guitar lines tend to be economical and subtle rather than bludgeoning.

'Misfit Love' and 'Battery Acid' step up the urgency levels a little, but not much: this album continues to keep its sleek distance. 'Make It Wit Chu' (a song which had previously appeared as a Desert Sessions track) is more revealing, addressing the subject of sex with the gentle sarcasm that Homme has always preferred in his songwriting. "We all feel that if you're going to be in a rock band, sex is a big part of the music," said Van Leeuwen, "so we're always trying to put that into the music. There's a lot of that on this new record. We figured things out as we were in the studio because we didn't really have anything written besides that song 'Make It Wit Chu'. So in order to kind of tap into stuff, you have to find stuff in the moment."

After '3's & 7's' comes 'Suture Up Your Future', an unhurried, heavily-produced song in which Homme's dreamy vocal lines overlay a simple, hypnotic bass and drums backing. Of all the tunes on *Era Vulgaris*, this one is the most prepared to stretch out and envelop the listener, the polar opposite of 'River In The Road', a quick-paced, urgent song more than a little indebted to the classic post-punk sound. The album winds up with 'Run, Pig, Run', a chaotic mash of tinny guitars and Dr Seuss-style humour.

Era Vulgaris is a solid album, but it requires some investment of time to appreciate what Queens were attempting to say with it: no cheerful rock/pop hits jumped out from its grooves in the same way that they had on the first three Queens albums. Despite its year-long gestation, the overall feel was jammed, even improvised in parts, with the rhythm section required to hold up the song while Homme delivered his vocal harmonies, always one of the band's strong points. Then again, the idea of a Desert Sessions-style ensemble of talent convening to make records like this is an attractive one. Some of the contributions were significant – those of Johannes and Goss, for example – and others, such as Julian Casablancas's guitar playing on 'Sick, Sick, Sick', less so. Others were noteworthy for their incongruity, such as Primal Scream singer Bobby Gillespie's contribution to a bonus-track cover of Brian Eno's 'Needle In The Camel's Eye'.

"He's so great, man. I loved it," enthused Van Leeuwen. "We were doing this version of 'Smokestack Lightning' for, like, two hours. It was so rad because we don't like to jam that long. But it was so entertaining to watch him sing. He was writing on the floor. It was rad. I was like, 'Wow, this guy is so into it, so we're just going to keep going.'

We were like the puppet masters to him — us just playing music and him going nuts."

I interviewed Homme in London as *Era Vulgaris* came out, having been commissioned to write an extensive Queens feature for a magazine named *Music Mart*, which later switched its title to *Performing Musician* before going belly-up, as rock magazines are wont to do. Meeting Homme and Van Leeuwen, I was struck by the former's enthusiasm and energy as he talked, working his way rapidly through a pack of Marlboro Lights. As I wrote, pretty shallowly in retrospect, "He's so ginger he redefines the term: even his eyelashes are as yellow as straw — but any thoughts of schoolboy mockery you might be considering don't last long when you notice how massive he is. At almost two metres in height, he'd kill you easily, even though he laughs 'Hey, I saw you in the lobby. Our eyes met like two lasers!' as we walk through the door."

The interview continued as follows: "So let's talk about live performance, a subject that isn't merely close to Josh's heart — it's his life. QOTSA are in the UK to play a small club show for a lucky few of the faithful, a change from the usual midsize venues. The point of the gig tonight is to showcase songs from the new album, *Era Vulgaris*, so Queens won't be trotting out 'No One Knows', 'The Lost Art Of Keeping A Secret' or any of the other chart-shafting hits they've released since their arrival on the music scene in 1998.

"Although Homme is depressed by the realities of touring away from his infant daughter and wife, Spinnerette frontwoman Brody Dalle ("It's the hardest thing I've ever done. I'm struggling on day three. There's no way round it, but I was a child before, and now I'm a man, because I'm out here for my family"), he can't wait to hit the stage. As he explains, "Ultimately the live experience is about doing something you'll never forget. We're gonna do something special tonight. It'll just be — whoo, look at this! [mimes whipping open his jacket and exposing himself]. We always play 'No One Knows' and 'Go With The Flow', although we're not going to tonight, because it's about our new record. You know, after this we're coming back, and then after that we're coming back again, and after that we'll probably come back again…"

"Troy Van Leeuwen nods in appreciation. Dressed in impenetrable shades and a snappy brown pinstripe suit, with black, Trent Reznor-style hair flopping over his face, he's the epitome of the

modern LA rock star – apart from the fact that he seems like a genuinely nice guy, that is. Asked if sweaty club gigs are more fun to play
than QOTSA's usual arena shows, he observes, "I think there has to be
a balance. For me, playing a small, intimate show – where you get the
chance to be really sweaty and right in the crowd's face – there's a great
energy there. It's fun when everyone's packed in."

"Homme agrees, adding: 'It's always a cool picture. People leaning
on each other, all elated and sweaty. It's what you go through together.
Shows like that feel like we did something massive.' He pauses to take
the piss out of Van Leeuwen: 'He'll wear a suit through the entire
show. He's a stylish motherfucker!'

"Although tonight's show is an exception because it's an unusually
small venue, the standard Queens gig takes a lot of creative effort from
all sides. QOTSA are in the unusual position of having a sound engineer who is as valued as any of the band-members, as Homme says:
'Our sound man, Hutch, has been with us since I was 18. He's very
much a member of the band. We used to include him in group photos,
because he does the sound as well as a lot of the artwork. He's such a
part of the band that we stand together and say, "What do we want to
do?" Our light guy's the same – we sit together and say, "Oh, you
know what would be rad? Or, you know what I saw once?"

"'Rad' stage designs go as far as home-made gear, explains Homme:
'It's always been a bit of a home-brew. The guys make a lot of stuff.
Hutch and the lighting guy Dan were out in the Joshua Tree desert
making apparatus that I don't want to talk about yet, because it's so
cool and it won't be on these shows. It gets done in the desert because
Hutch lives out there, and that's where his welding tools are.

"Talking of the desert – a prevailing theme of Homme's career,
especially for his pre-Queens outfit Kyuss, whose influence on the
stoner-rock scene was incalculable – Josh's ongoing *Desert Sessions*
side-project looks set for immortality. Twelve volumes of collaborative
music have appeared to date, featuring artists as diverse as PJ Harvey,
Chris Goss of Masters Of Reality and Screaming Trees' Mark Lanegan
(who also doubles as a member of QOTSA). "The *Desert Sessions* are
gonna go on forever," says Homme jubilantly. "There's no reason to
stop them. It's just a mix tape – the longest-running mix tape in existence. It's awesome: doing them is just a matter of making the time
frame come together. I was really wanting to do one before the new

album came out, but we didn't put a time frame on it and so it consumed what would have been a *Desert Session* recording time.

"As well as designing a unique live show, Queens Of The Stone Age are also known for chopping and changing their setlist with a frequency that would level less-rehearsed bands. 'We never have the same one!' says Van Leeuwen, adding: 'There's a master list of all the songs, which is probably up to about 50 by now – but we just try to think what would sound good first, what would sound good last, and where the flow is going to go.' Homme mocks the idea of deliberately choosing the most crowd-pleasing songs: 'Oh shit, you're supposed to do that? No, we know what songs work first, and which are the huge closers. In fact, there's only a couple of closers that we really have. We'll play any song from any record. We don't leave any men behind. And I think our crowd's used to that. I hope they are, anyway…'

"Not all crowds are so forgiving, though: Homme has never forgotten the dreary experience of playing the Ozzfest mega-tour way back in 2000, with his brand-new band the subject of much ridicule from the nu-metal-loving jocks in the crowd. When we ask him if there was anything good at all about playing in the court of Ozzy, he sighs: 'No. We literally had nothing going that summer, so we did it. We're a hard rock band, not a metal band, and we were third on the bill. Our show was at one in the afternoon!' However, Homme dealt with the horrific time slot in a typically uncompromising manner: 'Every day I would stay up all night and go to sleep after the show, so it was the end of my day. It was so I could be like [adopts stoned, drunken voice] "You know whaaat, maaaan?"… and also that environment wasn't exciting, so the idea was to catalyse some excitement out of it.'

"Of playing live, Homme insists: 'You have to do it for *you*. I've played for people who hated us, but it doesn't really matter. I don't want them to hate us, but if they all collectively do, I'm not gonna go "Come on guys, be nice!" Being nice has never really entered into the gameplan.' In fact, Homme welcomes a bad crowd sometimes, explaining with malevolent glee: 'We were on the heavy metal day at Rock In Rio! It was Iron Maiden headlining, with the reformed Judas Priest and Sepultura. The promoter was like, "Do you want this gig?" And we said, "Well, we're not a metal band" – and he said, "You are if you want to come to Brazil!" So we said, OK… anyway, the crowd vehemently hated us. But we played our full set, even though I got hit with stuff. Often, if someone misses with a can, I'll pick it up and throw it at myself, because I don't want someone's bad aim to get in the way of a good time.

"You have to admire any musician who can handle an evil-tempered crowd, right? But Homme does have his limits. Queens once played a show that was so bad that – wait for it – the entire band went off to a tattooist's afterwards and had the date inked onto their bodies to remind them never to be so bad again. You've probably played a bad gig – who hasn't? – but I'll bet few of you reading this were so gutted that you needed that permanent a reminder . . .

"Homme lifts his shirt and shows us the tattoo on his chest. It reads 'Freitag 4.15', German for Friday 15 April, when the gig took place at the Rock Am Ring festival in 2001. 'Mark Lanegan, Hutch, our bassist at the time Nick Oliveri and myself all have the same tattoo – and we all deserve to have it,' he smiles, although it's obvious to this day that he's still annoyed by that far-off event.

"'It was our first show in Europe and it was really difficult,' he begins. 'I didn't go all the way to Germany to blow it like a balloon salesman, but we suffered from insurmountable odds. I had a dislocated ankle and was on enough Vicodin to kill a set of twins. I started off sitting on a chair to play, but I thought "I can't sit down and do this", so I stood on one leg for an hour. I was supposed to be wearing a cast but I just did it barefoot, trying to hit the pedal switches with both feet at the same time. So the sound was all over the place and the pain was making me sing like [agonised wail] "Aiieeee!" And that was just the first line of the first song.

"It got worse, he adds: 'So Mark Lanegan went up to sing – and the mic cord wasn't plugged in at the other end. Then I got handed guitars with the wrong tunings, because it was the tech's first day. Finally, Hutch couldn't get the intro tape to stop when we started playing the first song. Everything that could happen, happened.' He needed the tattoo, he says, 'because it was a total train wreck, and because before that day and ever since that day, I've never experienced anything like it.'

"Asked if the experience was captured for posterity, Homme replies grimly: 'Yes. There's audio bootlegs of it all over the place. It was filmed, too – I watched part of it, and what's interesting is that it's not as bad as it felt. You can hear the intro going over our first song, and you see me throwing the chair into the audience. You can hear me go "Fuck this chair!" and it's the only time the audience goes nuts, like "Yeah!" – because after that it was obvious that I was hopping on one leg.'

"Dial up Youtube, search for 'queens rock am ring 2001' and you too can have the pleasure of seeing Josh limping around the stage in a bad mood, wincing in pain and watching as his gig spirals downwards into disaster. However, what you *won't* see is the backstage aftermath – featuring Homme connecting with two annoyed fans. As he recalls: 'After the show, when I left the stage I was on crutches and it was raining, so when I came down the stairs I went [mimes slipping crutch] "Aaargh!" and almost toppled down the stairs in the puddles. I was so fuckin' angry, dude! And then this German couple comes up and said "We drove eight hours to see you. It was sad". And I immediately went pow, pow, hitting them with this crutch and shouting "Go away!" I'll never forget it.'

"All of which begs the question of what Homme would do if QOTSA ever played an even worse gig. What's worse than a tattoo? A genital piercing? 'That's never going to happen,' he replied, 'because we've had many things similar to that happen, and we've overcome them by reshifting and refocusing. And we know to hold the gig up for a minute and stay cool, while someone is running around behind the scenes shouting "Holy fuckin' shit!" Also, something like that wouldn't affect me in the same way that it did back then.'

"Well, it was six years ago, after all. Homme and his band are three albums, a gaggle of band-members and several world tours older and wiser nowadays. The future of Queens Of The Stone Age seems assured, as long as people still turn out to see them – but it's interesting to note that a significant portion of the Homme fanbase isn't as interested in his future as in his past, and specifically in Kyuss, who are the constant subject of reformation pressure.

"'The offers come in all the time!' sighs Homme, adding: 'The money is crazy, too. No, I'm never tempted. We had John Garcia guesting with us on stage once in 2005, which was awesome, because I love John. But I don't really care about the money, I never have. That's not what Kyuss was about, so to punctuate the end of our sentence with that would be blasphemy. Kyuss fans are so fuckin' rad, they're fuckin' badass – but to me, reunions are just not necessary. It's not what it was, it's what it *is*, and Kyuss was this really magical thing – and if you're weren't there, well, you just weren't. That's the luck of the draw.'

"Unlike many musicians from long-lost bands, Homme has little patience for fans who might complain that they missed out the first time around, insisting: 'It was such a great thing for me – I'm totally satisfied. I don't feel the urge to do it for somebody who didn't have the opportunity to see us, or just didn't take the opportunity to see us. I'll let other bands alter their great legacies. Kyuss has such a great history that it would be a total error. Doing it would open up a can of worms that the fans ultimately wouldn't want. Very rarely, a reformation is worth doing – I'm very glad that I got to see the Stooges live, for example – but the odds are not good, because the reason is usually not good. I like that nobody saw Kyuss and that it was largely misunderstood. That sounds like a legend forming to me. I'm too proud of it to rub my dick on it.'"

I was delighted with this interview and its many gold-standard soundbites, especially the final one about Kyuss, which was widely quoted and is still his default comment about a possible Kyuss reunion on internet encyclopaedia sites beginning with W. But the more significant impression of Homme which I took away with me that day is simply how driven the guy is. This was underlined shortly afterwards when Queens took to the road on their so-called 'Duluth Tour', named after the small town in Minnesota which was among many similarly-sized locations on that jaunt.

Dates in the UK and Australia took the band into 2008, a year of extensive touring that wound up at the summer festivals and which culminated with Homme's announcement that a new Queens album would be shortly in the making. This was ultimately delayed, however, by other activities such as an Eagles Of Death Metal album, *Heart On* (ah, comedy gold) and a subsequent tour – and more impressively, by the emergence of the supergroup to which Dave Grohl alluded at the start of this chapter.

Homme's wife Brody Dalle commented in July 2009 that "I'm not at liberty to talk about it . . . but I think [the project] is pretty fucking amazing. Just beats and sounds like you've never heard before." Apparently Homme, Grohl and John Paul Jones considered the name 'Caligula' for their new band, but when this name proved to be taken already, the landed on an idea based on a bird: appropriately enough, a desert bird.

CHAPTER 12

2009–2014 And Beyond: Keep Your Eyes Peeled

SURREALLY, it emerged in 2009 that none other than an ex-Beatle had expressed an interest in the as-yet-untitled supergroup. As Paul McCartney told *The Daily Mail*, he had met Dave Grohl at an awards ceremony, and the subject had come up. "We went out for a bite to eat afterwards and Dave told me he was starting this band with Josh," he said. "I asked him who was playing bass and he rather sheepishly told me he'd approached John. So you read it here first; Paul McCartney was nearly the bass player in Them Crooked Vultures."

Them Crooked Vultures, whose name meant nothing in particular according to the members, attracted vast amounts of attention right from the start of their short, but spectacular, career to date. The second half of 2009 saw a large amount of coverage devoted to the trio, especially once they debuted original material at a show in Chicago on August 9. The attraction of the band was rooted in their unique make-up: a member of the legendary Led Zeppelin, whose already-monstrous profile had been raised even more two years before at the Ahmet Ertegun Tribute Concert in London, in partnership with the two leading lights of modern rock: what was not to like?

Perhaps not the music, at least if you were expecting something completely new. When the first – and so far only – TCV album came out on November 9, it was a lot of fun for sure . . . but not at all groundbreaking. As more than one critic pointed out, the music on *Them Crooked Vultures* could have comfortably appeared on more or less any Queens album to date. Aside from some unorthodox vocals from Homme, who explored a higher range than usual from time to time, and a jammed feel based on Grohl's 'tight but loose', John

182

Bonham-indebted drum sounds, the album sounded like a bunch of cool grooves and moderately Zeppelin-influenced riffs. John Paul Jones, always the master of economy, delivered an effortless set of bass parts, locked in perfect unison with Grohl's drums and Homme's guitars – the role which he had established with so much success four decades previously. It is to Jones' singular credit that he can still switch styles, genres and roles with ease, just as he did with Led Zeppelin; playing mandolin with bluegrass Americana star Gillian Welch, bass with Norwegian avant-garde improvisers Supersilent, producing and arranging for anyone who captures his fancy yet still able, when the mood takes him, to weigh in with the thunderous bass that under-pinned so many Zep classics.

Being charitable, let's identify some high points on the Vultures' album. One song, 'Reptiles', was a tremendous blast through all the best rock trademarks, with guitars and bass a wall of synchronised sound. The first single, 'New Fang', had its moments too, notably Jones' melodic line and the layers of guitars and vocals: it's one of Homme's gifts that he can mesh so much musicianship and still avoid making a song sound overbusy. The rest of it? Fine, just fine.

Audiences loved Them Crooked Vultures, whatever the critics may have said. Sweeping through the European festival circuit and support-ing the Arctic Monkeys (whose album *Humbug* Homme co-produced the same year), the trio sold out their UK tour dates in December in a miraculous 12 minutes. America appreciated the Vultures too: in Feb-ruary 2010 they played on *Saturday Night Live* and *Austin City Limits*, followed by *Jimmy Kimmel Live!* In April. So much hype, so much attention: another summer of festivals welcomed Them Crooked Vultures, all on the strength of a reasonable album and a stellar cast of musicians.

As TCV's initial campaign came to a close and Homme prepared for a knee operation in the autumn of 2010, an unexpected whiff of nostal-gia was detected when Kyuss singer John Garcia announced a Euro-pean 'John Garcia plays Kyuss' tour for the summer festivals. Nick Oliveri and Brant Bjork joined Garcia on stage at the French Hellfest event, the first time that these three-quarters of the *Blues For The Red Sun* had played together in several years.

Homme kept quiet on the subject. For now he had other things on his mind, namely going under the knife for his knee surgery, a routine operation. In some ways this part of his personal chronology turned out to be a turning-point in his life, never mind anything as inconsequential as a career . . .

Due to complications in the operation, Homme's heart stopped for a short period. Revived by the medical team with a defibrillator, he woke to find that it had been an extremely close call – the proverbial 'died for two minutes' reported by rock stars from Nikki Sixx to Phil Anselmo, although in those cases the near-death experienced was the result of drug abuse. Homme was just getting his knee fixed.

"I woke up and there was a doctor going, 'Shit, we lost you'," he said later. Plunged into depression, and a struggle with the dreaded methicillin-resistant staphylococcus aureus (MRSA) infection, Homme thought that his career was over. His 13-day stay in hospital was followed by an extended period of recovery at home, in which he felt no creative urges whatsoever. "I couldn't get up for four months," he recalled. "When I did, I hadn't got a clue what was going on."

"I didn't want to play music anymore because I died on an operating table," he added. "I didn't give a shit about little things anymore, and music had become a little thing . . . So I'd call up Trent [Reznor] and we'd go and have coffee and talk for five hours about other things. It became part of the process of feeling whole again."

Recovering his mental and physical strength by early 2011, Homme began tinkering with new music. A full year of musical commitments awaited him and the band, although his first efforts at creating new music were a little half-hearted, he explained later on. "The wife and I have a little shack out the back of our house, so I put a little studio in there. She encouraged me to go in there as much as possible and told me not to worry about what I wrote . . . So, I went in and the first song I wrote was 'The Vampyre Of Time And Memory'. I hated it. I thought, 'Who wants to hear this?' Then Brody reminded me, 'Who fucking cares?' You've got to start somewhere, and the bottom can be a really great place'."

As Homme got his act together, John Garcia, Nick Oliveri and Brant Bjork announced that they had formed a touring band, Kyuss Lives!, which would be performing dates in Europe. The singer made it clear that this was not intended to be a 'new' Kyuss, explaining: "There is never going to be a Kyuss without Josh Homme . . . hopefully in the future him and I can get together and do some writing."

In early 2011 Queens released a remastered version of their self-titled debut album and played it in its entirety on tour, a favourite trick of dozens of bands over the last decade or so. The usual round of festivals cropped up that summer, including Australian events, an event in Wisconsin celebrating 20 years in business for Pearl Jam, and the UK's Glastonbury. At the last of these, Homme told the crowd: "I wanna play so loud that Beyoncé [Knowles, playing on the adjacent Pyramid Stage] can feel it in her fucking bones." Reminded of this afterwards, he laughed: "Ha ha ha! I [said that]? The chances are she might have done. We found out no-one wanted to play against Beyoncé. They asked us, and I was like 'OK, hell yeah'. It was great. Or maybe I was just on ecstasy and I didn't know the difference. I walked onstage and was like, 'Wow! Hey everybody! How you doing?'"

After a solid year of touring, Queens retired from the road to field questions about Them Crooked Vultures – who insisted that they would return sooner or later, although they are yet to do so – and in Homme's case, to consider the problem of Kyuss Lives!, who had announced that they would be recording an album. In March 2012 he and bassist Scott Reeder filed a federal lawsuit against John Garcia and Brant Bjork, citing 'trademark infringement and consumer fraud' over their use of the Kyuss name. Oliveri quit the band shortly afterwards to return to his own projects.

Asked about the lawsuit by *Rolling Stone*, Bjork explained: "Josh filing this lawsuit is not an issue of today… it's an issue that began over 20 years ago. That is why the band was short-lived. Josh and I were the creative force within the band and after the completion of our second record, *Blues For The Red Sun*, we developed an opposing view on how the band should exist and operate. In 1992 Josh discovered publishing, which is the financial revenue stream for songwriting. After that, he wanted to write all the songs. As a drummer, I couldn't make him play my songs. I wasn't going to compromise my heart and soul and play drums for Josh to make money in a band I started. So I left the band. I was a confused, angry and sad 19-year-old idealist who sacrificed my love of my band for what I believed in. Two-and-a-half years later, Josh would break up the band after John [Garcia] confronted him about the same thing; his need to control the band for personal gain."

Several months passed before the lawsuit was resolved, when a judge, S. James Otero, ruled partly in Homme's favour in the United States

District Court Central District of California. His ruling permitted Garcia and Bjork to tour as Kyuss Lives! as long as the two words of the band name were of equal prominence, but he also suggested that they change their name entirely and banned them from releasing audio recordings altogether under the Kyuss Lives! banner.

To wind up this sorry tale, Kyuss Lives! played shows under that name for another year before renaming themselves Vista Chino. Signing to the Napalm label in 2013, the trio of Garcia, Bjork and guitarist Bruno Fevery recorded an album, *Peace*, which featured long-lost Kyuss member Chris Cockrell as a guest. "I think a lot of people, especially Josh Homme and Scott Reeder, expected us to fail, and we didn't," said Garcia. "We're here at the other end. This is where we're supposed to be. It just took us a little bit longer to get here, and we're in a good spot. The tour is starting. We're going to be on the road up until the end of next summer, and there's already talk about another record."

Back to 2012, and the now-rejuvenated Homme plus the usual crew of Alain Johannes, Troy Van Leeuwen, Dean Fertita and Michael Shuman began recording their sixth album. Drums were performed by Dave Grohl, as Joey Castillo had been dismissed from the band for reasons which remain unknown. "Some people think I must be a jerk because I fired my best friend," explained Homme, "but the truth is I went to his house, stared him in the face and I told him how I felt. Can you do that?' . . . By the time you get to your sixth record, some of the benefits of being in a band are grander than ever, but some of the obstacles are just massive. You deal with these lateral subjects and all that is left is the elephant in the room."

On the subject of Queens' fluctuating line-ups, he said: "To be honest, I never deliberately changed it. With each line-up, I've always thought, 'I hope this one lasts forever'. It's such a difficult thing to find really talented people that accent everything really well and you can live with after. Each time someone has stayed or been thrown from the cart, it's been a group decision. Whoever's in Queens, that's the group, you know? I know it's got to look from the outside like I'm this tyrant who runs it, but we don't play a song unless everyone supports it. There's no point in doing something if someone isn't backing it . . . when it comes to people, if I'm coming to your house to tell you it's time to go, you've probably been fucking up for at least a year."

Nick Oliveri provided guest backing vocals, while other contributions came from Trent Reznor, Scissor Sisters frontman Jake Shears, Brody Dalle and, unusually, Sir Elton John. As Homme explained, Elton's assistant, who happened to be a friend, had played some Queens material for the veteran ivories-tinkler, who liked what he heard. When Elton called, Homme assumed that someone was playing a trick on him.

"I'm shaking hands with Elton John," he told *The Guardian*, "and all the while I'm covering up some gaping social wound because I just fired my drummer four days before. But, you know, what's a little blood among friends? Elton walks in with a big smile, dressed to the nines, arms wide open. So you just go, 'Well how the hell are you doing, babe?' I think it's obvious to him that he creates a certain amount of mania. If six people go to an area before you do just to check shit out, like they did to my studio – and the people that came first were pretty tough motherfuckers, which I enjoy – then there is a certain mania. Whenever I'm in London or Paris and everything is refined, for some reason I feel like a cowboy. Like a dirty American. I love that feeling of being inspected."

The new album, called . . .*Like Clockwork* as a snide reference to the dire circumstances in which it was created, was preceded by a contribution made by Homme, Johannes, Chris Goss and Scott Reeder to the soundtrack of *Sound City*, Dave Grohl's affectionate documentary about the famous American studio of the same name. Homme, who recorded with Grohl and Trent Reznor, also appeared in the film.

Despite the depressive nature of its origins, . . .*Like Clockwork* outperformed its creators' expectations, becoming the first Queens album to debut at number one in the USA. Homme had mixed feelings about the record, he confessed, as it had been so deeply influenced by the gruelling events of 2012. "There's a part of me that's releasing this record, and I do mean releasing it – and saying 'Goodbye!' to it, in a way that I never have before," he said. "I'm saying 'Thanks for kicking my ass, and I'm so glad to see you go. I deserved it, I needed it, and I got it. And I don't want to do that again, if that's cool?' Now I'm not complaining, that's just part of the gig. I wasn't complaining then and neither were the guys, but I had to ask them 'if you want to make a record with me right now, in the state I'm in, come into the fog. It's the only chance you got'. It brought us much closer, because you never really know someone till everything goes wrong."

He added: "We're trying to hang our toes off the edge here, because the music is totally honest and real – that's where you can fail. But I'd rather fail and die by my own sword than let somebody else choose or play it safe. I just feel like musical safety equals death. You want me to make the same record I made before? Don't hold your breath; because you're probably gonna pass out."

. . .*Like Clockwork* is a dark album, all right, which perhaps explains its popularity in an era when dark is often perceived as cool. The opening track, 'Keep Your Eyes Peeled', sets out the stall immediately, with its withdrawn atmosphere and chilly tones, making 'I Sat By The Ocean' – a more traditional guitar-and-crooning song in the familiar Queens mode – seem almost warm in comparison. Homme's much-maligned 'The Vampyre Of Time And Memory', although its title makes it sound like something from the *Twilight* soundtrack, is a sweet piano ballad, is a song that demands to be heard over and over again, with its carefully-crafted build and dynamics.

'If I Had A Tail' and 'My God Is The Sun' are less accessible. Angrier, more abrasive songs, they're unforgiving to anyone looking for a casual listen: they demand attention, and not in a fun way. Such are the fruits of depression, although 'Kalopsia' revisits the same territory as 'The Vampyre . . .', offering something of a respite from the harpies inside the composers' heads. 'Fairweather Friends' is more straightforward, while 'Smooth Sailing' explores the twisted blues form not unlike the sound established by Them Crooked Vultures.

. . .*Like Clockwork* winds up with its longest and most thoughtful song, 'I Appear Missing', an unhurried descent into musical darkness, full of Homme's anguished emotions. Backed by a plodding bass part and ethereal, echoed guitars, the song seems to sum up the ethos behind the entire record: without wanting to read too much into a single track, if you needed to ask where Queens were at this point in their career, the answer is encapsulated here. After that, the title track adds a simple, effective full stop to the album, easily one of Queens' most atmospheric to date. A piano part plus a questioning, spiralling guitar line support Homme's querulous vocal with great efficacy: it's an awe-inspiring listen.

Back to mundane reality, a performance at the UK's Download festival came in June 2013, and as always Queens Of The Stone Age stood out from the rest of the headbangers simply by their nature. Asked about this Homme shrugged: "Well, we're outsiders everywhere we go, and that hasn't changed . . . If the question is 'Can we just throw down, bury the needle and run over you?' You bet your fuckin' ass. And I suppose we'll do a little bit of that, but I also suppose that we're being asked to be there to be something of a ginger on the palate. I think we take a risk, is what we should do. These are the days where, if you aren't just who you are, you die. Before, you could sort of fake your way through all this stuff, but these are the days that are made for bands like us. And Motörhead, too. I mean, Motörhead is who Motörhead is; Lemmy is the king shit of fuck mountain. Why? Because he's always himself; I think you just take a cue from that."

Queens performed a slick, confident set that day, although other events that summer were less smooth: at the Made In America festival, owned by megastar rapper Jay-Z, Homme was less than pleased. The band were supposed to be frisked by the event's security personnel on arrival, a process which the singer refused to endure. "He has his security frisking the bands on the way in. I just told them, if you open up my bag I'm not playing, so I guess it's up to you whether we're playing or not," he said. "The idea they frisked all my guys, means you're in some different place, no-one has ever done that [to me] . . . He also gave us some champagne and wanted us to take a photo with it. And I thought that's not a gift, that is a marketing tool. So I destroyed it. Because I thought it was rude overall. And you shouldn't frisk my guys, you should fuck off."

The heart warms to that last comment, because it shows once more than Homme isn't merely playing at this rock-star game: he means what he says, and he still has principles. As he once said, "I thought for so many years that 'rock star' was such a bad phrase for me. Buying into the DIY punk rock spirit, you realise, 'Wait a minute, this is just as fucked-up as anything else'. What's important to me is what my grandpappy always used to say to me, which was, 'If you're going to be different, you're going to get hit by rocks. So you should learn to like rocks'."

He added: "To me, that is the thing that needs to be a mantra. People, especially in this day and age, their opinion comes lightning fast before they've even had a chance even to think of it. If everyone's opinion stewed around for as long as it took to write a song, I think people's opinions would be worth listening to more. But now, more than ever, when it comes to music, people's opinions aren't even worth listening to half the time, because they're lightning-fast judgments from an arbitrary place, most of the time."

Let that pithy statement stand as the last in this book. Long may the Queens reign.

Sources

CHAPTER 1

Homme: "I started out taking polka lessons . . . I'd rather sit out on the porch and strum the thing." (*Guitar For The Practicing Musician*, August 1994)

Homme: "I've always been a huge fan of Black Flag . . . I'll play anything that's around." (Guitar.com, 2000)

Homme: "My parents would only buy one record . . . I haven't done that since." (*Rolling Stone*, January 2003)

Bjork: "Yawning Man was the greatest band . . . great musician, had his shit together." (*LA Weekly*, August 2002)

Garcia: "I was a normal kid . . . and fuck people up!" (*LA Weekly*, August 2002)

Homme: "People say, I got into music for the girls . . . without anyone fucking with you." (*Rolling Stone*, September 2000)

Oliveri: "We were literally in . . . seventh or something." (Martin Popoff, 2000)

Homme: "Nick played guitar . . . we did have the balls to keep Nick in." (*CMJ*, September 2002)

Oliveri: "Punk rock kicked me in the balls . . . I don't wanna be in the metal scene!" (*Orange County Register*, October 2002)

Bjork: "Nick was the guy . . . he just can't be stopped!" (*LA Weekly*, August 2002)

Homme: "Nick was the guy in high school . . . thing in our faces." (*Rolling Stone*, January 2003)

Oliveri: "When I was a kid . . . you know what I mean?" (Martin Popoff, 2000)

Homme: "In hindsight . . . that means you love music." (*CMJ*, September 2002)

Bjork: "My dad is a judge . . . well-to-do family." (*LA Weekly*, August 2002)

Homme: "There's a bunch of small towns . . . all locked together." (*LA Weekly*, August 2002)

Bjork: "The high desert . . . real small towns." (*LA Weekly*, August 2002)

Homme: "I was born and raised in the low desert . . . one in every desert town." (*LA Weekly*, August 2002)

Homme: "When we went to throw a party . . . destroyed it all after 10 minutes!" (*Remix*, May 2001)

Oliveri: "We'd drive four-wheel-drive trucks . . . But it was worth it." (*CMJ*, September 2002)

Homme: "It had moments of true beauty . . . this is definitely not it." (*LA Weekly*, August 2002)

Garcia: "They were playing . . . you want me to really sing!" (*LA Weekly*, August 2002)

Homme: "We didn't have enough money . . . the gig would start." (*LA Weekly*, August 2002)

Homme: "That was the main thing . . . it's so bad-ass." (*LA Weekly*, August 2002)

Oliveri: "We played original songs . . . that meant we had a band." (*Cleveland Free Times*, September 2002)

Garcia: "The majority . . . my entire life." (*LA Weekly*, August 2002)

Goss: "I have enchanting memories . . . doing a war dance." (*LA Weekly*, August 2002)

Oliveri: "Those were pretty wild times . . . It was cool." (*Cleveland Free Times*, September 2002)

Homme: "If people see you for free . . . That's a real slice of life." (*Kerrang!*, 2000)

Oliveri: "We had a big punk rock influence . . . That was the little trip we were on." (Martin Popoff, 2000)

Homme: "It was weird because . . . 13 or 14 straight shows." (*Billboard*, January 1994)

Goss: "I went apeshit . . . This was coming from *them*." (*LA Weekly*, August 2002)

Bjork: "We would go into LA . . .we were punks." (*LA Weekly*, August 2002)

Homme: "I used to work at raves . . . around his neck and shit." (Nick Anderson, August 2002)

Bjork: "We were very lucky . . . rad in a club." (*LA Weekly*, August 2002)

CHAPTER 2

Long: "I did tons of stuff on them . . . for two months." (*Billboard*, January 1994)

Garcia: "The Dwarves were the first band . . . rabbit blood." (Keith Ingersoll, 1995)

Homme: "Their songs are like, 'Fuck You Up And Get High' . . . with both hands grab her by the hair . . ." (Keith Ingersoll, 1995)

Homme: "Chris was a godsend . . . get it out of the board." (*Billboard*, January 1994)

Oliveri: "It was great, you know? . . . possibly blow their speakers?" (Martin Popoff, 2000)

Homme: "Our first record, *Wretch*, doesn't sound like us at all . . . Like minds attract each other." (*Guitar For The Practicing Musician*, August 1994)

Homme: "The volume of our music keeps our ears clean . . . it's all over you." (*Guitar World*, 1994)

Garcia: "'Green Machine' is actually . . . so Caterpillar March." (Martin Popoff, 2000)

Homme: "The more you don't know what we're personally thinking . . . stuff just fucks up the music." (*Guitar World*, 1994)

Homme: "There's some great bands . . . this is what we sound like when we grow." (*Guitar For The Practicing Musician*, August 1994)

Reeder: "I hope so! If there's gonna be five people . . . bongo drums. Every concert should be an event." (*Guitar World*, 1994)

Homme: "Sometimes I talk to a guitar magazine . . . Yeah, here's a pen, write it down." (*FFWD*, 1999)

Homme: "I bought it on consignment . . . I tried to buy this goldtop Les Paul and I just couldn't." (*Guitar For The Practicing Musician*, August 1994)

Homme: "If you pick up a used guitar . . . instead of a lot of pedals." (Guitar.com, 1999)

Homme: "I go through phases . . . playing the song the same every single time." (*Guitar For The Practicing Musician*, August 1994)

Homme: "They had heard *Blues* . . . being in Australia alone was amazing." (*Billboard*, January 1994)

Bjork: "We were like, who's gonna know us . . . where do you go after that?" (*LA Weekly*, August 2002)

Homme: "We grew up playing together . . . peaked together." (*Guitar For The Practicing Musician*, August 1994)

Hernandez: "Minutemen, Black Flag, DC3, Meat Puppets . . . when I started getting into punk." (*RIP*, August 1994)

Homme: "Fredo's a tight drummer . . . He's changed the way we play." (*HM*, 1995)

Homme: "It was a pretty big shock . . . people at the label." (*Billboard*, January 1994)

Homme: "We're just excited to get something out . . . wait around either." (*Guitar For The Practicing Musician*, August 1994)

Ralbovsky: "By the time . . . where the fuck have I been?" (*Billboard*, January 1994)

Homme: "Is our curse and our blessing . . . can't we get it right?" (*Billboard*, January 1994)

CHAPTER 3

Garcia: "1993 was a fucked-up year . . . Kyuss never existed before this line-up!" (*RIP*, August 1994)

Reeder: "Everything that's happened . . . we waited this long . . ." (*RIP*, August 1994)

Garcia: "Black Sabbath was heavy . . . like it's outdoors." (*Billboard*, January 1994)

Homme: "I think stylistically everyone . . . we fill it in." (*Guitar For The Practicing Musician*, August 1994)

Homme: "It's a big area . . . ass end of our town." (*Hip Online*, October 1999)

Reeder: "Where we live is . . . out in the boonies." (*Thorazine*, 1994)

Reeder: "It still sounds fresh after a year . . . Pink Floyd, Jethro Tull." (*RIP*, August 1994)

Garcia: "There really isn't anything to say about it . . . what we do." (*RIP*, August 1994)

Reeder: "The Sabbath comparison . . . many other things." (*RIP*, August 1994)

Garcia: "I had heard Black Sabbath . . . I can see the similarities." (Keith Ingersoll, 1995)

Homme: "Like, the first seven albums with Ozzy . . . in my head." (Keith Ingersoll, 1995)

Garcia: "We were really stoned . . . Kyuss in a fuckin' nutshell." (*RIP*, August 1994)

Homme: "It's what the bands in this scene . . . it will remain low-key." (*Guitar For The Practicing Musician*, August 1994)

Garcia: "I could sit here and try to explain it all day . . . this is great!" (*RIP*, August 1994)

Reeder: "It's the clearest place in the world . . . must have been the animals." (*RIP*, August 1994)

Garcia: "These parties played a huge part . . . where we're from." (*RIP*, August 1994)

Hernandez: "Playing outside anywhere is very inspiring . . . dust in your face . . ." (*RIP*, August 1994)

Homme: "We just stay in our space . . . the only people that can throw us off track is us." (*HM*, 1995)

Homme: "The place was covered from floor to ceiling . . . power down the building." (*LA Weekly*, August 2002)

Bjork: "The kitchen is five feet . . . three days straight . . ." (*LA Weekly*, August 2002)

Homme: "It was just the right time . . . solid ending with a finishing point." (*Canoe*, 1999)

Homme: "We played for respect, mostly . . . for music's sake." (*Canoe*, 1999)

Homme: "I came from a scene . . . explain what we're doing to some jerk." (*Seattle Times*, October 2002)

Homme: "I didn't want to just play one type of music . . . see you at the barbecue on Sunday." (*FFWD*, 1999)

Homme: "Kyuss was very deliberate . . . who 'they' really are." (Guitar.com, 2000)

Homme: "Kyuss' first record was when I was 17 . . . So I did." (*LA Weekly*, August 2002)

CHAPTER 4

Homme: "I would say I was disillusioned . . . feeling like a snowflake." (Guitar.com, 2000)

Homme: "I quit for a year . . . I was only like 21 years old." (*Triple X*, January 2003)

Homme: "I lived in Seattle . . . I can't take it here any more!" (*Seattle Times*, October 2002)

Homme: "I went to the one place I knew music was dead . . . And it did." (*LA Weekly*, August 2002)

Lanegan: "I met Josh through Mike Johnson . . . my friend will do it." (*The Stranger*, 2002)

Homme: "It was great to be with the Trees . . . playing rhythm guitar and enjoying it." (*Canoe*, 1999)

Homme: "I was only gonna go for one tour . . . left that attitude behind." (*LA Weekly*, August 2002)

Homme: "It was a desert epiphany . . . down to molehills" (*LA Weekly*, August 2002)

Garcia: "After Kyuss broke up . . . they pay the consequences, whatever that may be." (author unknown, 1997)

Goss: "Josh and I became fast musical friends . . . he wanted to do." (*LA Weekly*, August 2002)

Homme: "I said to some friends . . . I'm calling in Nick right now!" (*Rolling Stone*, September 2000)

Oliveri: "I had two bands . . . vibing when I was younger." (*LA Weekly*, August 2002)

Goss: "Josh called me from Europe . . . Queens Of The Stone Age . . ." (*LA Weekly*, August 2002)

Homme: "We had this other name . . . make them giggle." (*Remix*, May 2001)

Goss: "I had called them that . . . limp wrist!" (*LA Weekly*, August 2002)

Homme: "If I had a choice, I would take that away . . . what we think is good." (*Canoe*, 1998)

Homme: "He (the Stonerrock.com founder) sent me a direct message . . . just said, I think it's fucked." (*AntiMTV*, 2000)

Homme: "We hate it . . . I just show up and play, you know." (*Canoe*, 1999)

Homme: "Desert Sessions is good . . . the sake of music." (*LA Weekly*, August 2002)

Homme: "Desert Sessions is just a musical experiment . . . I would like that." (Guitar.com, 2000)

Homme: "A vinegaroon is like a scorpion-like . . . vinegar flavour [in your mouth]" (ATN, 1995)

Homme: "After jamming so much . . . and not get fucked with." (*Magnet*, 2000)

CHAPTER 5

Homme: "I like nudity . . . it always fascinated me." (*Canoe*, 1999)

Homme: "I love to say clichés . . . I don't have a computer." (*Papermag*, September 2002)

Homme: "I think the rock world needs polka . . . people using instruments incorrectly." (*Papermag*, September 2002)

Homme: "The Stooges were the best band in the world . . . to straddle that line . . ." (*Papermag*, September 2002)

Homme: "I love old garage rock . . . favourite singers are." (*CD Now*, September 2002)

Hernandez: "We actually started . . . you get more able to absorb more." (*Virtual Cardiff*, November 1998)

Homme: "There's a lot of curiosity from Kyuss people . . . a larger percentage happy." (*Eye*, 1999)

Homme: "I'm sure some Kyuss fans . . . whatever you hear in your head." (*Canoe*, 1999)

Oliveri: "There's a lot going on in Europe . . . and a lot more like, robotic." (*Stonerama*, 11/98)

Oliveri: "We try to take a riff . . . We're having a lot of fun doing it." (*Stonerama*, 11/98)

Oliveri: "We all went out and did different bands . . . it's that good to me." (*Attitude*, October 1998)

Oliveri: "Mondo Generator went great . . . and broke it up!" (*Attitude*, October 1998)

Oliveri: "Me and Josh went over to Scott Reeder's . . . animals and fish, and shit!" (*Attitude*, October 1998)

Oliveri: "Unreleased Kyuss stuff . . . it got cut down." (*Attitude*, October 1998)

Homme: "What I love about Ween . . . For us, that's inspiring." (*Rolling Stone*, September 2001)

Homme: "In one way, 'stoner rock' elevated some . . . and I want to find where it is." (*Eye*, 1999)

Hernandez: "We're a little uncomfortable . . . Your thoughts tend to flow better." (*Canoe*, 1999)

Homme: "I saw some old Kyuss videos about a year ago . . . ZZ Top *Texas*-era production." (*Eye*, 1999)

Homme: "I think it's going to expand . . . and stuff we like." (*Caustic Truths*, May 1999)

Homme: "We're a little more stripped down . . . let someone else do that." (*Canoe*, 1999)

Homme: "I'm unable to scream . . . because we listen to a lot of different music." (*FFWD*, 1999)

Homme: "It's natural . . . it's great to be on the road." (*Canoe*, 1999)

Oliveri: "It's going really good . . . some pretty faces and some smiles." (*Caustic Truths*, May 1999)

Homme: "It's good to be the foreigner . . . in your face." (*Caustic Truths*, May 1999)

Oliveri: "We spun out . . . down this embankment." (*Zero*, June 1999)

Homme: "We grew up playing at parties . . . it almost nullifies it." (*Zero*, June 1999)

Oliveri: "When I go see other bands . . . I'll be honest." (*Zero*, June 1999)

Homme: "People that are into Ween . . . child actor, model and shit." (*Hip Online*, October 1999)

Homme: "They're all right . . . Limp Bizkit. Holy shit, man." (*Magnet*, 2002)

Homme: "We didn't really have any expectations . . . instead of doing shit." (*Hip Online*, October 1999)

Homme: "With Kyuss, we had a desire . . . just be different." (Guitar.com, 2000)

Oliveri: "The original soundtrack with Black Sabbath . . . all good, I guess." (KNAC, January 2002)

CHAPTER 6

Oliveri: "I think that a lot of bands . . . I was mad too." (*Spectator Online*, 2000)

Homme: "It's not a hit-type song . . . 13-year-olds." (*CD Now*, September 2002)

Homme: "We were in Studio B at Soundcity . . . sang backup on it." (*Hip Online*, August 2000)

Oliveri: "Josh wrote down . . . never bothered me." (KNAC, January 2002)

Homme: "My stance on drugs is that . . . social experiment has worked itself out!" (*The Fade*, August 2002)

Homme: "I feel like doing doughnuts . . . you could just bounce off everyone." (*Rolling Stone*, 2002)

Homme: "We really liked the song . . . because we really dig it." (*Hip Online*, August 2000)

Oliveri: "Working with Chris is really easy . . . we just tried them all." (Martin Popoff, 2000)

Homme: "The sound with Kyuss was identical . . . The inspiration is to keep searching." (*Guitarist*, 2002)

Homme: "It's still heavy-rock music . . . painted in a corner." (*Remix*, May 2001)

Homme: "There are no weird egos . . . something he knows nothing about." (Martin Popoff, 2000)

Homme: "Obviously we didn't want . . . song to song." (*Hip Online*, August 2000)

Homme: "I was at the meeting . . . the better it is for me." (*CD Now*, September 2002)

Oliveri: "Kyuss broke up in 1995 . . . I'm ready to, all right?" (Martin Popoff, 2000)

Oliveri: "I've been really busy . . . it's a really great record to listen to." (*Rough Edge*, September 2000)

Oliveri: "The first song on the Mondo disc . . . is on *Rated R*." (KNAC, January 2002)

Oliveri: "We change members a lot, add new life . . . I just don't know when." (*Rough Edge*, September 2000)

Oliveri: "We do Desert Sessions songs live . . . we do that." (KNAC, January 2002)

Homme: "Kyuss got noticed because it didn't give a shit . . . if I take drugs, I don't want people to know." (*Kerrang!*, 2000)

Homme: "Even though modern music . . . has to be good." (*LA Weekly*, August 2002)

Homme: "Inevitably a pit takes place . . . pissed off any more." (Guitar.com, 2000)

Oliveri: "It's going great, man . . . comes naturally instead of following the set-list." (*Hip Online*, August 2000)

Oliveri: "Every night, really, there's . . . a little out of myself, you know?" (Martin Popoff, 2000)

Homme: "Being the band . . . 'Terrifiedvision' tried to get us booked into a different hotel." (MTV News, 2000)

Homme: "What you don't realise . . . I can never tell until it's too late." (*Rolling Stone*, September 2000)

Oliveri: "The biggest kind of thing that I like . . . comfortable to see a band at." (KNAC, January 2002)

Oliveri: "We went into the studio . . . we just didn't want to put it out yet." (Martin Popoff, 2000)

Homme: "Ozzfest was gruelling . . . we're just a bunch of happy guys." (*AntiMTV*, 2000)

Homme: "We're almost trying to eliminate . . . bloody fuckin' nose?" (*Remix*, May 2001)

Homme: "Whatever scene or clique we're looking at . . . the negative one." (*CD Now*, September 2002)

Homme: "It's almost like the family has grown . . . hearing some new stuff from Unida." (*AntiMTV*, 2000)

Homme: "Yes, it was a lot of money . . . which is something that we are." (*AntiMTV*, 2000)

Homme: "This shop had just a banjo . . . messin' with my guitar would be it." (*Guitarist*, 2002)

Homme: "I think some of the young . . . heavy firearms." (*Rolling Stone*, 2000)

Oliveri: "We've been friends of Dave . . . to do with *Rated R.*" (*Play Louder*, October 2000)

Homme: "We're getting this feedback . . . if they don't know until it's too late." (*Rolling Stone*, 2000)

Oliveri: "You guys are so cool . . . 'that sounds like my average weekend'!" (*Metal Hammer*, September 2002)

Homme: "We were always a musician's band anyway . . . becoming successful." (*Music Week*, June 2002)

CHAPTER 7

Homme: "We're not setting any lofty goals . . . happy as well." (*Remix*, May 2001)

Homme: "We are really psyched . . . lots of drugs . . ." (*Play Louder*, October 2000)

Oliveri: "After we got done playing . . . wanted to make an example of me." (*Undercover*, 2001)

Oliveri: "I enter naked . . . I apologise to the public and the Brazilian people." (*Rolling Stone*, 2001)

Homme: "That was the worst show we've ever played . . . I didn't give a fuck at that point!" (*Rock Sound*, November 2002)

Homme: "Their album is amazing . . . I'm lucky!" (*Dare Devil*, 2001)

Homme: "[The Sessions were] kind of the reason . . . things that must be included." (*Magnet*, 2002)

Homme: "A lot of it has to do with guitar . . . and I'll transpose it a little." (*Guitarist*, 2002)

Homme: "Music is kind of like screwing . . . It's not intentional." (Nick Anderson, August 2002)

Homme: "Dave's a friend of ours . . . better than Dave Grohl." (*The Fade*, August 2002)

Homme: "We have an understanding . . . then we don't play it." (*The Fade*, August 2002)

Homme: "When you go see a band . . . you'll still need to see the fifth show." (*Hip Online*, 2000)

Homme: "We're kind of always writing . . . you need to, uh, smoke more!" (*Meanstreet*, September 2002)

Hawkins: "We all had our concerns, and maybe were questioning Dave's priorities." (*Rolling Stone*, 2002)

Grohl: "I wanted the Foo Fighters to take a break . . . the drugs are good." (*Rolling Stone*, 2002)

Homme: "For him to come back as . . . What the hell's wrong with Dave Grohl?" (*Chart Attack*, 2002)

Grohl: "I remember the first time I met Mark . . . Kurt really looked up to him." (*Blender*, September 2002)

Homme: "The collaboration came about . . . instead of a damn music teacher." (*Music Week*, June 2002)

Oliveri: "It's great . . . He's one of my favourite drummers of all time . . . He's a madman." (*Rolling Stone*, 2002)

CHAPTER 8

Homme: "This isn't work . . . I could fit it into my schedule." (*Guitarist*, 2002)

Homme: "There's a lot of darker material . . . there's got to be a way out." (Nick Anderson, August 2002)

Homme: "He worked on two albums . . . going in your pockets." (*Kinda Muzik*, October 2001)

Homme: "He just recorded it, actually . . . how do we do this?" (Nick Anderson, August 2002)

Homme: "We had . . . what are you doing to me?" (*Denver Rocky Mountain News*, September 2002)

Homme: "There was this one time . . . all ready to go." (*Music Week*, June 2002)

Homme: "I feel this was the toughest record . . . whether gracefully or violently." (Nick Anderson, August 2002)

Homme: "I've always stayed . . . it is a Rubik's cube." (*Denver Rocky Mountain News*, September 2002)

Oliveri: "I think it's gonna take . . . what the band has become." (*Kinda Muzik*, October 2001)

Oliveri: "We'd like to play the record from start to finish . . . helps make that happen." (*Guitarist*, 2002)

Homme: "I think we're a band that's trying to see what happens . . . but we are!" (*Guitarist*, 2002)

Homme: "QOTSA sound engineer Hutch . . . talk to them about it?" (*Papermag*, September 2002)

Homme: "I'm not light on my strings . . . I never search for the middle." (*Guitarist*, 2002)

Oliveri: "It has the radio flipping between songs . . . we should talk shit about them." (*Rolling Stone*, 2002)

Homme: "And we were trying to think . . . it sounds kind of silly, doesn't it?" (*CD Now*, September 2002)

Oliveri: "Commercial radio's not my thing . . . we're already gone." (*Cleveland Free Times*, September 2002)

Homme: "Our habit is to have no habit . . . make it possible for us to stick out." (*Papermag*, September 2002)

Homme: "It was really cool because . . . that I never would have thought of." (*Washington Post*, August 2002)

Homme: "Marilyn Manson . . . press it and sell it." (*Kinda Muzik*, October 2001)

Oliveri: "With a completely different line-up . . . records out for 2002." (*Kinda Muzik*, October 2001)

Homme: "It's funny, you know . . . secretive about it." (*Kinda Muzik*, October 2001)

Homme: "I don't smoke pot . . . Britney Spears and be like, whoo!" (*Rolling Stone*, January 2003)

Homme: "We don't act any different off the road . . . what's really going on . . ." (*The Fade*, August 2002)

Oliveri: "Queens are going to . . . one of us gets tired of it." (*Kinda Muzik*, October 2001)

Homme: "I think it's natural when something sounds great . . . to do it pretty maniacally." (*Chart Attack*, 2002)

Oliveri: "We set Queens up . . . The only rules are there are no rules." (*Blender*, September 2002)

Homme: "Don't ask about the DJs . . . groove-based song structure of the second." (*Music Week*, June 2002)

Lanegan: "This time around I'll be doing a lot of the dancing . . . Queens are a happy family." (*Boston Globe*, August 2002)

Homme: "I've learned a lot from Dave . . . going home to my mansion now . . ." (*Papermag*, September 2002)

Homme: "We've been jamming . . . it's like going to the side or going diagonal." (*Washington Post*, August 2002)

Oliveri: "I was pissed . . . play this shit out on the road?" (*Entertainment Weekly*, February 2003)

Castillo: "They threw me on the bus . . . they're serious about the band." (*The Age*, February 2004)

Homme: "I'm starting to get sick . . . good drummers really badly." (*CD Now*, September 2002)

Homme: "It would be a bad idea to take it that . . . while we're here." (*Washington Post*, August 2002)

Homme: "This one will be rated B for bizarre . . . much more universal." (*Magnet*, 2002)

Homme: "I think at first . . . negates any inspiration." (*The Fade*, August 2002)

Homme: "I feel like there's a lot of songs . . . that song sounds like." (Nick Anderson, August 2002)

Homme: "It's supposed to be tough . . . This is how I feel it and see it." (*CMJ*, September 2002)

Homme: "I think that's one of the reasons . . . My notes were wrong!" (*Meanstreet*, September 2002)

Homme: "It is darker . . . push it out as far as you can." (*Washington Post*, August 2002)

Homme: "That body groove . . . seems to be everywhere." (Nick Anderson, August 2002)

Homme: "We said to Dave in the beginning . . . played his ass off." (*Guitarist*, 2002)

Grohl: "I realise I was put . . . experience that again 10 years later." (*Blender*, September 2002)

Grohl: "This is the best album I've ever played on . . . be like the good cancer." (*Spin*, October 2002)

Homme: "He's one of the . . . this feel we never had before." (*Metal Hammer*, September 2002)

Oliveri: "Dave just instantly raised our game . . . you fear for his safety." (*Metal Hammer*, September 2002)

Homme: "I think our system works . . . best stuff now at this date." (*The Fade*, August 2002)

Homme: "My goal is to be a slippery fish . . . blame it on the cook and run away." (*Blender*, September 2002)

CHAPTER 9

Homme: "We have patience . . . sonic depth." (*The Fade*, August 2002)

Homme: "I've been thinking about this record . . . we'd lose people." (*CMJ*, September 2002)

Oliveri: "This record is how we are . . . stray too far away." (*CMJ*, September 2002)

Oliveri: "It's definitely a lot darker . . . so it's all cool." (*Stylus*, September 2002)

Oliveri: "I think what we've kind of done over the years . . . that's what we're doing." (*Triple X*, January 2003)

Homme: "Nick's style is more about not looking peripherally . . . it doesn't have a complaining aspect." (*Orange County Register*, October 2002)

Homme: "I don't own any houses . . . until I get sick of it." (*Meanstreet*, September 2002)

Oliveri: "We're really excited! . . . it just hangs right down to my knees." (*Record Collector*, September 2002)

Homme: "We know how . . . won't give us a good review!" (*Metal Hammer*, September 2002)

Oliveri: "We haven't been propelled to a false status . . . Get used to it." (*Metal Hammer*, September 2002)

Homme: "The heavier the mainstream . . . who we are right now." (*Metal Hammer*, September 2002)

Oliveri: "It's like the first . . . right place at the right time!" (*Metal Hammer*, September 2002)

Homme: "It's what's best about the two previous records . . . to never have a fucking plan." (*Metal Hammer*, September 2002)

Homme: "I think that people's ears are now ready . . . that I like." (*Alternative Press*, December 2002)

Homme: "I think we go through different cycles . . . the more it will just come out." (*Guitar For The Practicing Musician*, August 1994)

Homme: "There must be 50,000 bands . . . you're just showing up." (*Entertainment Weekly*, February 2003)

Homme: "I love Kylie Minogue . . . she's really tiny." (*Rolling Stone*, January 2003)

Homme: "I'm not too comfortable with that . . . take care of it myself." (*The Age*, February 2004)

Homme: "I had this one girl . . . Nerf balls off my head." (*Playboy*, 2004)

Homme: "In Melbourne somebody tried to take a swing . . . his mistake, you know." (*The Fade*, August 2002)

Homme: "It's strange . . . You never sit there and think about it." (*Triple X*, January 2003)

Oliveri: "I was at home when Josh called me . . . when we started out." (*The Post And Courier*, March 2003)

Homme: "Now we have our assistants . . . this other stuff is more new to me." (*Triple X*, January 2003)

Oliveri: "People have been saying . . . *Songs For The Deaf*." (*Metal Hammer*, September 2002)

Homme: "Will they say we sold out . . . I think we're onto a new phase . . ." (*Triple X*, January 2003)

Castillo: "It's one of the best times . . . hang-ups." (*The Age*, February 2004)

Homme: "It's animated . . . I've never seen anything like it." (*The Post And Courier*, March 2003)

Oliveri: "I appreciate my wife more . . . good to me." (*Dallas Music Guide*, 2003)

Oliveri: "It's not a thought-out thing . . . bring it back into style." (*X-Press*, January 2003)

Homme: "I'm a boisterous guy when I'm alone . . . more mysterious." (*Blender*, September 2002)

CHAPTER 10

Oliveri: "Josh has consistently hated me . . . There's no egos about it, man." (*Sydney Morning Herald*, January 2004)

Oliveri: "It's like I've known Josh . . . oh, that's cool. Whatever." (*IGN*, December 2002)

Oliveri: "He's really into it . . . to make music in the first place." (*X-Press*, January 2003)

Homme: "Queens Of The Stone Age is a family . . . to be brothers with Nick." (*NME*, 2004)

Oliveri: "I just wanted to tell you folks what's really goin' on . . . My favourite band is dead." (MondoGenerator.com, 2004)

Homme: "It feels almost like my kid went to jail . . . I like to party and fuck around, too." (MTV, 2004)

Oliveri: "He came over my house . . . It can't ever happen." (*Musictoday*, 2004)

Homme: "I like to keep my toes in the dirt . . . playing the drums." (*The Age*, 2004)

Homme: "The larger truth is that we're The Eagles Of Death Metal . . . death by sexy." (*Spin*, June 2004)

Manson: "It was so much fun . . . quite beyond me." (Garbage.com, 2004)

Oliveri: "I have never in 16 years . . . in the end it all worked out good!" (MondoGenerator.com, 2004)

Homme: "Honestly, I think it sounds . . . one song that's a bit twilight." (*Rolling Stone*, 2004)

Homme: "When asked about hitting Blag with a bottle . . . keep rappin' old whiteboy." (QOTSA.com, 2004)

Van Leeuwen: "I know March may seem far off . . . musical branding irons." (QOTSA.com, 2005)

Oliveri: "Josh came to my house . . . that is what we would be doing anyway!" (MondoGenerator.com, 2004)

Homme: "We've toured with everything . . . and we don't forget." (QOTSA.com, 2005)

Homme: "We're asked a lot where we fit in . . . the weight of hype." (*Metal Hammer*, September 2002)

Homme: "The Queens is an exercise . . . what to do." (*LA Weekly*, August 2002)

Oliveri: "I just wanted to make sure my old mates were doing good . . . I'm sure that we will at some point in our lives." (Author's interview, March 2005)

CHAPTER 11

Grohl: "The next project . . . suck bratwurst." (Mojo, 2005)

Homme: "That's not . . . keep our cool." (NME, 2006)

Homme: "Long ago . . . throat cutting motion]." (Ultimate Guitar Archive, 2007)

Van Leeuwen: "It was an opportunity . . . it's your art." (Suicide Girls, 2007)

Van Leeuwen: "We basically . . . sound and space." (Suicide Girls, 2007)

Van Leeuwen: "We all feel . . . in the moment." (Suicide Girls, 2007)

Van Leeuwen: "He's so great . . . going nuts." (Suicide Girls, 2007)

CHAPTER 12

Homme: "I woke up . . . going on." (Irish Independent, 2013)

Homme: "I didn't want . . . whole again." (Irish Independent, 2013)

Homme: "The wife . . . great place." (Irish Independent, 2013)

Garcia: "There is never . . . do some writing." (Rock-A-Rolla, 2011)

Homme: "Ha ha! . . . how you doing?" (Crack, 2011)

Bjork: "Josh filing . . . personal gain." (Rolling Stone, 2012)

Garcia: "I think a lot . . . another record." (About.com, 2013)

Homme: "Some people think . . . in the room." (Guardian, 2013)

Home: "To be honest . . . a year" (Jambase, 2013)

Homme: "I'm shaking hands . . . being inspected." (Guardian, 2013)

Homme: "There's a part . . . pass out." (The Skinny, 2013)

Homme: "Well, we're . . . cue from that." (The Skinny, 2013)

Homme: "He has his . . . fuck off." (CBC Radio 2, 2013)

Homme: "I thought for . . . the time." (Jambase, 2013)

Discography

All UK releases except where indicated

Kyuss Singles

1994	Warners EKR 192CD	Demon Cleaner
2/1995	Warners EKR 197CD	Gardenia
7/1995	Warners 7559643982	One Inch Man (Germany only)

Kyuss Albums

1990	Black Highway no cat. no.	Sons Of Kyuss (US only, as Sons Of Kyuss, 500 LPs only)
1991	Warners 7559612562	Wretch
2/1993	Warners 3705613402	Blues For The Red Sun
6/1994	Warners 7559615712	Sky Valley
7/1995	Warners 7559618112	. . . And The Circus Leaves Town
12/2000	Warners 7559625712	Muchas Gracias: The Best Of Kyuss

Queens Of The Stone Age Singles

8/2000	Polydor 4973922	The Lost Art Of Keeping A Secret
11/2000	Polydor 4974552	Feelgood Hit Of The Summer
11/2002	Polydor 4978082	No One Knows
4/2003	Polydor 4978700	Go With The Flow
8/2003	Universal, various cat. no's	First It Giveth (overseas only)
3/2005	Polydor 9880672	Little Sister
6/2005	Interscope	In My Head
1/2006	Interscope	Burn The Witch
5/2007	Interscope	Sick, Sick, Sick
6/2007	Interscope	3's & 7's
10/2007	Interscope	Make It Wit Chu
4/2013	Matador	My God Is The Sun
8/2013	Matador	I Sat By The Ocean
4/2014	Matador	Smooth Sailing

Queens Of The Stone Age Albums

9/1998	Roadrunner RR 86742	Queens Of The Stone Age
11/2000	Interscope 4908632	Rated R (later versions with bonus disc)
9/2002	Interscope 4934352	Songs For The Deaf
3/2005	Polydor 9880297	Lullabies To Paralyze (some versions with bonus DVD)
6/2007	Interscope	Era Vulgaris
6/2013	Matador	...Like Clockwork

Mondo Generator Albums

7/2000	Southern Lord SUNN 7CD	Cocaine Rodeo
11/2003	Ipecac IPC 41	A Drug Habit That Never Existed
1/2005	Tornado TORNADO 2	Tour (EP)
tbc	Cargo cat. no. tba	III (EP)
tbc	tbc	Demolition Day

Desert Sessions Single

11/2003	Island 9812964	Crawl Home (Josh Homme and Polly Harvey)

Desert Sessions Albums

2/98	Man's Ruin MR 93CD	Desert Sessions, Volumes 1 & 2
10/1998	Man's Ruin MR 111CD	Desert Sessions, Volumes 3 & 4
9/1999	Man's Ruin MR 123CD	Desert Sessions, Volumes 5 & 6
9/2001	Rekords Rekords REK 01	Desert Sessions, Volumes 7 & 8
11/2003	Island 9865704	Desert Sessions, Volumes 9 & 10
tba	tba	Desert Sessions, Volumes 11 & 12

Eagles Of Death Metal Albums

5/2004	Ant Acid Audio I 498416	Peace, Love And Death Metal
4/2006	Downtown	Death By Sexy
tba	tba	Death By Sexy

Selected QOTSA Compilation Appearances

1998	Roadrunner RR 8838-2	Burn One Up (Europe)
4/2000	Restless 737332	Heavy Metal 2000

10/2000	Milan 74321803722	Blair Witch II: Book Of Shadows
3/2001	Priority CDPTY 210	Ozzfest Second Stage Live
3/2002	Universal 5848582	Supercharged
4/2002	Rykodisc 38406212	This Is Where I Belong: The Songs Of Ray Davies & The Kinks
6/2002	Milan I 367396	Dangerous Lives Of Altar Boys
7/2002	Universal AA694933142	WWF Tough Enough II
10/2002	Universal 0645332	xXx
5/2003	Warners 0927499709	Later . . . Louder With Jools Holland (DVD)
11/2004	Ascension I 388460	Alpha Motherfuckers: A Tribute To Turbonegro

Them Crooked Vultures Singles

| 10/2009 | Interscope/Sony BMG | New Fang |
| 11/2009 | Interscope/Sony BMG | Mind Eraser, No Chaser |

Them Crooked Vultures Album

| 11/2009 | Interscope/Sony BMG | Them Crooked Vultures |

Index

All song and album titles by Queens Of The Stone Age except where indicated.

THE KILLERS
DAYS & AGES
by Mark Beaumont

Few bands have done for their home-town what The Killers did for Las Vegas. They took Sin City's heady mix of neon glitz and dangerous undercurrent and turned it into vibrant music that made them one of the biggest bands in the world.

Days & Ages traces their rise through a decade of driving ambition and unbeatable synth-rock melodies to today's global fame and acclaim from their own heroes including Bono, Elton John, Neil Tennant, Bruce Springsteen and legions of fans.

Through first-hand interviews with close associates, famous tour-mates and the band themselves, biographer Mark Beaumont tells the incredible, in-depth story of The Killers, the band that slayed the world.

Mark Beaumont is a music journalist whose work has appeared in numerous publications including NME, The Guardian, Shortlist, Classic Rock, The Times, The Mail On Sunday, Uncut, Melody Maker, Loaded *and* The Modern Review. *He is the author of* Out Of This World: The Story Of Muse, Jay-Z: King Of America *(2012) and* Bon Iver: Good Winter *(2013). His debut novel [6666666666] is available on Kindle.*

Available from all good book shops & **www.omnibuspress.com**

ISBN: 978.1.78305.045.1
Order No: OP55352

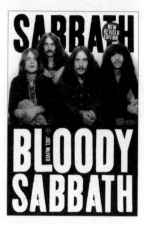

SABBATH BLOODY SABBATH

by Joel McIver

The gloriously chaotic career of Black Sabbath stands as testament to the inde-structibility of British Rock at its most extreme. Ozzy, Tony, Geezer and Bill have survived against almost impossible odds, always making one more comeback than whatever the latest tally of disbandments might be - and always celebrating it with yet another thunderous album.

Joel McIver unravels the frenzied story of the reprobate Birmingham band - in-cluding those members who came and went over the years - as well as Ozzy's uneasy relations with more or less everybody involved in the group. The resulting book is surely the ultimate guide to the Black Sabbath legend, full of first-hand facts drawn directly from those who were there at every stage as the Sabbath travelled from distant 1970 through a series of crises, conflicts and triumphs to the present day.

Since the original edition of *Sabbath Bloody Sabbath* appeared in 2005, an entirely new version of Sabbath – formed under the name Heaven And Hell – has been and gone. In response to the huge fanbase for the Ronnie James Dio-era albums of the 1980s and 90s, Tony Iommi recruited Dio plus Geezer Butler and drum-mer Vinnie Appice for three years of tours. Heaven And Hell might well have continued into the foreseeable future, had the band not been struck down by the illness and death of Dio in 2010. The new edition of Joel McIver's book covers this late-career incarnation of Sabbath in detail, with new interviews, analyses of the music and speculation about the band members' futures.

Joel McIver contributes to several music magazines including Classic Rock, Metal Hammer *and* Total Guitar *and has written 10 books to date: his 2004 bestseller* Justice For All: The Truth About Metallica *(Omnibus Press) was hailed as the ultimate book about the band. He appears regularly on radio and TV and can be contacted via www.joelmciver.co.uk.*

Available from all good book shops & **www.omnibuspress.com**

ISBN: 978.1.78305.517.3
Order No: OP55781